The Autobiography of a Journalist

Stillman, William James

Contents

PREFACE 7
CHAPTER I A NEW ENGLAND MOTHER AND HER FAMILY 10
CHAPTER II NATURE WORSHIP--EARLY RELIGIOUS EXPERIENCE 24
CHAPTER III AN AMERICAN EDUCATION 40
CHAPTER IV COLLEGE LIFE 58
CHAPTER V ART STUDY IN AMERICA 75
CHAPTER VI ART STUDY IN ENGLAND 83
CHAPTER VII ON A MISSION FOR KOSSUTH 95
CHAPTER VIII AN ART STUDENT IN PARIS 108
CHAPTER IX SPIRITISM 118
CHAPTER X LIFE IN THE WILDERNESS 130
CHAPTER XI JOURNALISM 142
CHAPTER XII CAMBRIDGE 151
CHAPTER XIII THE ADIRONDACK CLUB--EMERSON AND AGASSIZ 161
CHAPTER XIV LOWELL 173
CHAPTER XV THE ADIRONDACK AND FLORIDA 181
CHAPTER XVI ENGLAND AGAIN 189
CHAPTER XVII SWITZERLAND 198
CHAPTER XVIII PARIS AGAIN THE CIVIL WAR IN AMERICA 209
CHAPTER XIX MY ROMAN CONSULATE 217

THE AUTOBIOGRAPHY OF A JOURNALIST

BY

Stillman, William James

PREFACE

That a man should assume that his life is worth the venture of a record in the form of an autobiography suggests a degree of self-conceit of which I am not guilty. From my own initiative this would never have been written, and the first suggestion that I should write it, coming from a man of such experience in books and judgment of men as the late Mr. Houghton, then head of the firm of Houghton, Mifflin & Co., was as much a surprise to me as the publication will be to any one. The impression it made on me was so vivid that I have never forgotten the details of the occasion which called it out. I had gone with Mr. Houghton and his daughters to the ruins of the Villa of Hadrian, at Tivoli, and, wandering idly amongst them on a beautiful autumn morning, not in the spirit of crude sightseeing, I was led to talk of my experiences more than is my wont to do. "You should write your life," he said to me with a manner of authority which at once convinced me, and I decided that if there should come in my life a pause in which the past could be considered rather than the needs of the present and the cares of the future, I would set about it. Had I at some earlier date entertained such a project, I should have preserved many documents and data now lost, and have been able to write more precisely of some things of greater interest than my personal adventures. But in that part of my life which may be considered relatively of a public character, or in which events of a public interest occurred, I have ample record made at the time. In what is peculiar to myself, and so of relatively trivial moment, dates and the order of events are of little importance. It occurred to me in the connection, that to give a human document of Puritan family life, and the development of a mind from the archaic severity of New England Puritanism to a complete freedom of thought, by a purely evolutionary process, without revolt or revulsion, might be worth doing. For what it is worth I have done it without much consideration of my own dignity, and, candidly, not as to my blunders and peccadilloes, which are of no importance to the story, but as to the earlier mental conditions which were a part of the process. So much for the personality.

Orthodox journalists may object to my assumption of their title. In my multifarious occupation and random life I have, as I see when I look back found my highest activity, and rendered my most serious services to others, in my occupation as a journalist--all the rest was fringe or failure. If I have been good for anything it was in connection with, or through my position on, the press. And it would be ungrateful and dishonest if I should omit to bear my testimony to the noble character and large sincerity of the great journal to which the most of my strength for more than twenty years has been given. If ever I had a noble impulse, aroused by wrongs that came to my knowledge during those years, a good cause to defend, or a public abuse to attack, "The Times" has never refused to give me room to tell my story, nor have I ever been expected to conform my views to those of the office, or shape my correspondence to any ulterior purpose; nor have I ever done so. And I consider it the greatest honor that has ever come to me to have been so many years in its service, and to have maintained the confidence of its direction.

To my critics much that I have told may seem trivial. I cannot judge of what may interest others. I should hardly have believed that my life as a whole could interest a public that does not know me, and I am equally unable to judge of the value which its details may have to others. In default of any criterion beyond my own judgment, I have selected the items which had to me most importance, or had a marked influence on my life or an interest beyond myself. I have told things that will seem trite to Americans, and others that will be commonplace to Englishmen, but I have two publics to think of, differing in slight matters in their knowledge of things.

In affixing to the book the portraits of myself, I have yielded my own opinion, which was opposed to it, to that of the publishers and my friends, who urged it. To me it seemed a vanity for one almost unknown to assume that a public would care what manner of man he might be, and that such an assumption should follow an expressed general desire; but the views of the publishers are imperative, and those of my friends weightier than my own.

The drawing by Rowse was done about 1856, so that the interval between its doing and that by my daughter in 1900 included all the active period of my life, unless I except the Hungarian expedition. When the Rowse drawing was executed, Lowell said of it, "You have nothing to do for the rest of your life but to try to look like it." Since that time every friend I then had, except Rowse and Norton, is gone where I must soon follow.

DEEPDENE, FRIMLEY GREEN, Surrey, England.

CHAPTER I
A NEW ENGLAND MOTHER AND HER FAMILY

A theory is advanced by some students of character that in what concerns the formation of the individual nature, the shaping and determination of it in the plastic stage, and especially in respect to the moral elements on which the stability and purpose of a man's life depend, a man is indebted to his mother, for good or for ill. The question is too abstruse for argument, but, so far as my own observation goes, it tends to a confirmation of the theory. I have often noticed in children of friends that in childhood the likeness to the mother was so vivid that one found no trace of the father, but that in maturity this likeness disappeared to give place to that of the father. In my own case, taking it for what it is worth, I can only wish that the mother's part had been more enduring, not that I regret the effect of my father's influence, but because I think my mother had some qualities from which my best are derived, and which I should like to see completely carried out in the life of a man, while I recognize in a certain vagarious tendency in my father the probable hereditary basis of the inconstancy of purpose and pursuit, which may not have deprived my life of interest to others, but which has made it comparatively barren of practical result. As a study of a characteristic phase of New England life which has now entirely disappeared, I believe that a picture of her and her family will be of interest to some readers.

In my oldest brother, Thomas B. Stillman, known in the last generation as the chief of the steam engineering of his day in the United States, the mentor of that profession, I can see more of my mother than in any other of the six brothers. He inherited, like all of us, his father's mechanical tendency and inventiveness, and added to it a persistency and constancy of purpose peculiarly hers, which none of the other children inherited to the same extent; and he had in its fullness the devotional sentiment, the absorption in religious duties, as the chief motive in life, which was her ruling passion,--for passion it was in her,--the hanging on the Cross of everything she most valued in life.

My mother, Eliza Ward Maxson, was born in Newport, Rhode Island, on September 11, 1783, my father being seven years her senior. The childhood of both was, therefore, surrounded by the facts and associations of the war of American independence. He, in fact, as I have heard him say, was born under the rule of the King of England, and his father considered the Revolution so little justified that to the day of his death he refused to recognize the government of the United States; but, living a quiet life on his farm, he was never disturbed by the pressure which exiled the noted and active Tories.

My mother's earliest recorded ancestor was a John Maxson, one of the band of Roger Williams, driven by the Puritans out of Massachusetts into the wilder parts of "Rhode Island and Providence Plantations," where--in the absence of all established law, as well as government--they might worship God in the way their consciences dictated, free from the restrictions on the liberty of conscience imposed by the Pilgrim Fathers. There, at last, complete freedom of dissent was found, and one of the consequences was that the colony became a sort of field for Christian dialectics, where the most extreme doctrines on all points of Christian belief were discussed without other or more serious results of the ***odium theologicum*** than the building of many meeting-houses and the multiplication of sects. Among these sects was one which played an important part in the local theology of that day and for many years afterward, that known as the "Seventh-Day Baptist," to which, it seems, John Maxson belonged. It was not a new invention of the colonists, but had existed in England since the days of early dissent, and it is possible that John Maxson had brought the doctrine with him from England. Adhering to the practice of baptism by immersion, the sect also maintained the immutable obligation of the Seventh-Day Sabbath of the Ten Commandments, the Jewish day of rest.

The grave disabilities imposed on them in Massachusetts by the obligatory abstention from labor on two days, on one day by conscience and the other by the rigorous laws of the Puritans, made Roger Williams's little state the paradise of the Sabbatarians, and the sect flourished greatly in it, while the social isolation consequent on the practice of contracting marriages only in their church membership--

made imperative if family dissensions were to be avoided on a question of primary importance to that community, which had sacrificed all worldly advantages to what it believed to be obedience to the Word of God--at once knit together their church in closer relations, and drew to it others from the outside, attracted by the magnetism of a more ascetic faith.

Amongst the emigrants from England on the Restoration were a family by the name of Stillman, who, having had relations with the regicides, went into what was then the most obscure and remote part of New England and settled at Wethersfield, in Connecticut. One of the brothers,--George,--hearing of this strange doctrine denying the sanctity of the "Lord's Day," came to Newport to convert the erring brothers; but, convinced by them, remained in the colony, where he became a shining light. Thus it happened that both lines of my ancestry became involved in the mystic bonds of a faith which was shut off in a peculiar manner from all around them. The consequent isolation, I fear, made much for self-righteousness. In their eyes it was this observance which maintained continuity between the Christian church and the institutions imposed in Paradise, and therefore made them peculiarly the people of God. This amiable fanaticism, fervent without being uncharitable, interfered in no wise with the widest exercise of Christian sympathy with other sects, the observance of the Seventh-Day Sabbath not being held as an essential to godliness or to Christian fellowship, the non-observance being possibly only due to ignorance, so that the relations of the historic First Seventh-Day Baptist Church at Newport with the churches observing the "Lord's-Day Sabbath" were always most kindly. The meeting-house occupied by the Sabbatarians on the seventh day was occupied by one of the Sunday-observing sects on the first, and the preachers of one often officiated for the other. But the worldly advantage enjoyed by the Sunday keeper was so considerable that all who did not hold to the finest scruple of conscience in their conduct passed over to the majority, and were excluded from the communion as a precaution against the Sunday keepers becoming a majority in the church and taking it away from the Sabbath keepers, as did actually occur with one of their congregations in Vermont. In our community generally there was a most scrupulous avoidance of any occupation on Sunday which might annoy those who held it as Sabbath, and though in the State of New York the laws were extremely liberal in this respect, my father in my boyhood always made it a point not to allow in his workshop any work which would be heard by the neighbors.

The absolute freedom of religious belief and practice, for the first time found in this colony, had, as its first effect, the banishment of all forms of sectarian persecution, so that the maxim of the Broad Church--"Freedom in non-essentials"--was here put in practical activity to an extent probably never before known in the Christian world.

It can be readily understood that this continual selection of the most scrupulous consciences, the closest thinkers, and the least worldly characters in the church of my ancestors must have developed a singularly fine and cutting-edge temper in its adherents, and the succession of generations of men and women who had graduated in the school of Scripture dialectics, and knew every text and its various interpretations, made a community of Bible disputants such as even Massachusetts could not show.

Amongst the refugees for religious liberty who found their billet at Newport were many Jews, between whom and the Sabbatarians the community of the Sabbath was a strong tie, and amongst the formulas of prayer in use even down to my own boyhood I remember a common petition for the restoration of Israel; and the Sabbatarian eye of prophecy looked forward to the day when, in the peace of the millennium, the Jews in Jerusalem should be the witnesses of the faith of the Seventh-Day Baptist Church in the keeping alive the observance of the Eden repose initiated by the Creator. Amongst my own earliest personal recollections concerning Newport is that of a visit of some Jewish friends of my mother's girlhood, who lived there, to my father's house in Schenectady.

My mother's grandfather, on her mother's side, was a clergyman, Elder Bliss, who, though a non-combatant, was a fiery patriot, two of whose sons were in the Revolutionary army. His house was in a valley under the fort held by the British force in occupation, between whose guns and those of a battery held by the rebels there was occasional firing, during which the balls sometimes went through the house, so that when the first shot was heard he used to order all the family down into the cellar, which afforded a valid protection. The girls of the household were patriots, in whom zeal often overran discretion, and the pranks they played on the British officers must sometimes have tasked the gentlemen in the latter to a point on the limits of endurance. I remember one incident recounted by my grandmother to my mother, and by her to me, in which two of the girls stole past the sentry in the British fort, or battery, for I could never learn exactly what was the nature of these two outposts of authority and rebellion, and, running the flag down, tore it into thirteen stripes and ran it up again and escaped unseen. This insult brought the whole force about their ears, and the commandant came, with his staff, to question the household if any clue to it could be found. Fortunately, when the girls had come back from their expedition and went giggling in their glee to their mother, she suspected some dangerous venture and peremptorily ordered them to hold their tongues and not come to her with any of their mischief. She was thus able to reply to the officer charged with the inquisition that she knew nothing of the matter, and such was the rigid obligation of the truth in that Puritan community that even the danger of a court-martial would not have induced her to tell a falsehood, however the truth might compromise the family. The officers, who well knew their sometime hosts, were so well assured of this that the seniors were at once acquitted, and, regarding the girls, they were too gentlemanly to push an inquiry which might have punished a childish freak with the gravest military consequences, for, as the officer on the quest said, "Even it's being a woman would not protect the author of such a grave insult to the flag." Irrepressible as they were, in spite of the danger they had so narrowly escaped, they, not much later, stole the sword of one of the officers when they were all temporarily quartered on the preacher, and, when the island was evacuated by the British forces, brought it out and gave it to the brother, an officer in the American army.

A feat of practical housewifery, which my mother used to tell of, shows another side of the Rhode-Islander, which is not less illustrative of the stock. One of the boys of the pastor's family volunteered, or was drawn, in the militia for active service; but, as he had no clothes fit for the camp, the sisters had a black and white sheep brought from the pasture and clipped, and within twenty-four hours had spun, woven, and made up a suit of mixed gray clothes for the brother to go to the war in. No doubt such things have been done in many another home, even in later times, but this is the home I have to deal with, and in this my mother grew up. She was the eldest of a family of five, left motherless when she was sixteen. Her father was the director of the smallpox hospital in Newport, then an institution of grave importance to the community, as the practice of obligatory inoculation prevailed, and all the young people of the colony had to go up in classes to the hospital and pass the ordeal. Her mother's death left her the matron of the hospital and caretaker of her sister and brothers, and the stories of her life at that time, which she told me now and then, showed that, with the position, she assumed the effective authority, and ruled her brothers with a severity which my own experience of her maturer years enables me to understand. "Spare the rod and spoil the child" was the maxim which flamed in the air before every father and mother of that New England, and my mother's physical vigor at sixty, when her conception of authority began to relax,--I being then a lad six feet high and indisposed to physical persuasion,--satisfied me that when her duty had required her to assume the responsibility bequeathed her by her mother, she was fully competent to meet it.

Accustomed to the hardest life, the most rigid economy in the household, and without servants, for, except rare and lately emancipated negro slaves, there was then no servile class in that colony, the children had to perform all the duties pertaining to the daily life, official or private, and my mother was able to pull an oar or manage the sail-boat with her brothers, and catch the horses and ride them bareback from pasture, when necessary for the daily work, which was not insignificant, for Newport was really the seaport of that section of the State, and as it was on an island of importance, the intercourse with the mainland called for sea and land service. The boys were all fishermen, for a large part of the subsistence of the family came from the fishing-grounds outside the harbor, and, as the oldest brother took early to the sailor's life, my mother had to assume a larger share of all the harder services. The hospital was also the quarantine station, and received all the cases of smallpox which came to the port, and they must have been many and fatal, for I have heard her say that she had to go the rounds of the hospital at night, and that there would sometimes be five or six dead in the dead-room at once.

The first acquaintance of my parents with each other was made in the inoculating class, my father being resident in Westerly, a town of Rhode Island on the borders of Connecticut. The marriage must have taken place about two years later, on the second marriage of my grandfather Maxson to the daughter of Samuel Ward, one of the leading delegates from Rhode Island to the convention which drew up and promulgated the Declaration of Independence[1]. Their early days of married

---
1 Mr. Ward died just before the signing of the Declaration, so that his name does not figure in the list of signers.

life must have been passed in an extreme frugality, for my father was one of a large number of children, and, brought up on a farm, learned the trade of ship-carpenter, which he alternated, as was generally the habit of the young men of the New England coast, with fishing on the banks of Newfoundland in the cod-fishing season. Having, in addition, a share of the Yankee inventiveness, he became interested in the perfecting of a fulling-machine, to introduce which into what was then the West, he made a temporary residence in New York State, at the old Dutch town of Schenectady, at that time the entrepot of commerce between the Eastern cities and New York, and the Northwest. Utica was then a frontier settlement, Buffalo an outpost in the wilderness, and, the country having barely recovered from the war of 1812-15 between the United States and England, enterprise and exploration had just begun to push through the thin lines of settlements along the valleys of the Mohawk and upper Hudson, westward by Buffalo and the great lakes to Ohio (then the Far West), and northward to the valley of the St. Lawrence. Schenectady was the distributing point of this wagon-borne commerce and movement until the completion of the Erie Canal, which, down to my own period of recollection, was the quickest channel of communication westward, with its horse "packets," traveling at the creditable speed of four miles an hour, the traffic barges making scarcely more than two.

Hardly established in what was intended for a temporary visit, the residence of the family became fixed at Schenectady, owing to the partner of my father, left to manage the business at Westerly, becoming involved in personal embarrassments which brought on the bankruptcy of the firm and the seizure of all my father's little property, and, what was worse, the certainty of imprisonment for debt in the case of his returning home. Owing to the judgments hanging over him, which a succession of misfortunes prevented him from ever satisfying, it was late in my own remembrance, I think about 1848 or 1850, before he was enabled to visit his early home. Hard times came on the whole people of that section, and the practical destruction of his business by the loss of all his capital drove him into seeking any employment which would give a momentary relief.

Of this period of their existence my mother rarely spoke, and it must have been one of severe privations. She has told me that she often went to bed hungry, that the children might have enough to eat. She had no assistance in her household duties, except that of her daughter, a girl of tender years, and, having her husband's five journeymen as members of the household, with five children, of whom my sister was the second, she not only did the daily household duties, including washing and baking, but spun and wove the cloth for the clothes of her husband and children, cut and made them up. Her cheerful faith in an overruling Providence must have been, in those days, a supreme consolation, for, even in recalling them in the days of my boyhood, the light of it still illumined her, and she never questioned that He who had led them into the wilderness would maintain them in it. She seemed to have but one care in her life while I knew her--to know and do her duty. She found a special providence in every instance of relief from their pressing wants, and I recall the religious serenity with which she told me of the greatest strait of the hardest winter of that period, when resources seemed to have been exhausted to the last crumb, and they unexpectedly received from one of her half brothers, who had gone farther west, and lived in what was practically the wilderness, a barrel of salted pigeons' breasts. There had been one of those almost fabulous flights of the now nearly extinct passenger pigeons, which used to come north to breed in such numbers that the forests where they colonized were so filled with their nests that the settlers went into them and beat the young down with poles, and the branches became so overloaded with the broods in their nests that their weight often broke them down and threw the young on the ground. They had that year chosen the forests in my uncle's neighborhood for their nesting ground, and had been killed by thousands and salted down for winter provision, only the breast being used, owing to the superabundance of the birds. The gift came like the answer to a prayer, for there was hunger in the house and the snow was heavy on the ground, all the community being more or less in the same straits.

    Being the youngest of nine children, I can remember my mother only in the days of comparative freedom from anxiety, when, the day's work over and the house quiet, she used, as she sat by the fire with her knitting, which occupied all the moments when her hands were not required for other duties,--she knit all the stockings required for the family,--to tell me incidents of her past life, mostly to show how kind God had been to her and hers, and how faith in his providence was justified in the event. Of herself she spoke only incidentally. Dominating every act and thought of her existence was the profoundest religious veneration I have ever met with, an openness of her mind upward, as if she felt that the eternal eye was on her and reading her thoughts. The sense of her responsibility was so serious that I think that only the absorbing activity of her daily life, and the way in which every moment was occupied with positive duties, prevented her from falling into religious insanity. Her life was a constant prayer, a wrestling with God for the salvation of her children. No image of her remains in my mind so clear as that in which I see her sitting by the fireside in the dim light of our single home-made candle, her knitting-needles flying and her lips moving in prayer, while the tears stole down her cheeks in the fervency of her devotion, until she felt that she was being noticed, when the windows of her soul were suddenly shut, and she turned to some subject of common interest, as if ashamed to be discovered praying, for she permitted herself no ostentation of devotion, but reserved it for her nights and solitary moments. Of her own salvation she had only a faltering hope, harassed always by a fear that she had at some time in her life committed the unpardonable sin, as to the nature of which she knew nothing, and which was, therefore, all the more feared, as the nature of it was to her the terrible mystery of life and death.

What I inherit from her, and doubtless the indelible impression of her fervent faith overshadowing my young life, produced a moulding of my character which has never changed. I lived in an atmosphere of prayer and trust in God which impressed me so that to this day the habit of thought and conduct so formed is invincible, and in all the subsequent modifications of the primitive and Hebraic conception of the spiritual life which she inoculated me with, an unconscious aspiration in prayer and an absolute and organic trust in the protection of the divine Providence persist in my character, though reason has long assured me that this is but a crude and personal conception of the divine law. Truly from the environment of our early religious education we can never escape. This the Jesuits know and profit by.

My mother was also haunted by the dread of God's wrath at her loving her children more than she did Him, for, with all the fervency of her gentle devotion, she never escaped the ghastly Hebrew conception of God, always in wrath at every omission or transgression of the Law, who, at the last great day, would demand of her an account of every neglect of duty, every idle word and thought, and especially of the manner in which she had taught her children to obey his commandments. She seemed to scan her life continually to find some sin in the past, for which she had not specifically repented, and, at times, as I knew by the confidences of my later years, when she would appeal to me for my opinion, the problem of the unpardonable sin became one of absorbing study, which she finally laid aside in the supreme trust in his goodness, who alone knew her intentions and desire to be obedient to the Law.

Every one of her sons, as they were born, she dedicated to the service of the Lord, in the ardent hope that one of them would become a minister, and over me, the last, she let her hopes linger longest, for, as I was considered a delicate child, unable to support the life of hard work to which my older brothers had taken, she hoped that I might be spared for study. Only the eldest son ever responded to her desire by the wish to enter the service of the church, and he was far too important to my father's little workshop to be spared for the necessary schooling. He struggled through night schools, and in the intervals of day leisure, to qualify himself to enter the college in our city. Before doing so he fell under the notice of old Dr. Nott, president of the college, who was, beside being a teacher of wonderful ability, a clever inventor, and, perceiving my brother's mechanical capacity, persuaded him to abandon the plan of entering the ministry, and made him foreman of his establishment, the "Novelty Iron Works," at New York, for many years known as the leading establishment of its kind in America. The next two brothers, having more or less the same gifts, followed the eldest to New York; the next, an incurable stammerer, was disqualified for the pulpit, and studied medicine, being moreover of a fragile constitution; and the next, having the least possible sympathy for the calling, also took to medicine.

With the migration of the three older brothers to New York, the diminution of the family, and the aid the brothers in New York were able to give the younger children at home, my mother's life took on a new activity, in her resolute determination that the younger boys should have such an education as the college (Union) afforded them. This determination was opposed by my father, whose idea of the education needed by boys did not go beyond the elements, and who wanted them in the workshop. But it had become to my mother a conception of her duty, that, as the relations between my eldest brother and the president of the college led to an offer of what was practically a free education, the younger boys should be permitted to profit by the offer, and when duty entered her head there was no force capable of driving it out. Charles, the first of us to graduate, became the college bell-ringer, to pay his fees, but Jacob and myself were in turn excused, even from this service. My father's practical opposition, the refusal to pay the incidental expenses for what he always persisted in regarding as a useless education, was met, in Charles's case, by my mother's taking in the students' washing, to provide them. In the cases of Jacob and myself, this drudgery was exchanged for that of a students' boarding-house.

In all the housework involved in this complication of her duties, she never had a servant until shortly before my birth, when she took into the house a liberated African slave, the only other assistance in the house, in my childhood, being a sister six years older than myself and the daughter of one of our neighbors, who came as a "help" at the time of my birth, and subsequently married my second brother. My mother was also the family doctor, for, except in very grave cases, we never had any other physician. She pulled our teeth and prescribed all our medicines. I was well grown before I wore a suit which was not of her cutting and making, though sometimes she was obliged to have in a sewing-woman for the light work. She made all the bread we ate, cured the hams, and made great batches of sausages and mince-meat for pies, sufficient for the winter's consumption, as well as huge pig's-head cheeses. How she accomplished all she did I never understood.

But with all her passionate desire to see one of her boys in what she considered the service of God, there was never, on my mother's part, the least pressure in that direction, no suggestion that the sacrifices she was making demanded any measure of deviation from our views as to the future. It was her hope that one of us would feel as she did, but she cheerfully resigned the hope, as son after son turned the other way. A boy who was born three years before me, and whose death occurred before my birth, was, perhaps, in her mind, the fulfillment of her dedication, for he was, according to the accounts of friends of the family, a child of extraordinary intelligence, and she felt that God had taken him from her. In one of those moments of confidence, in the years when I had become a counselor to her, I remember her telling me of this boy (known in the family as "little William," to distinguish him from me), and the sufferings she endured through her doubts, lest he should have lived long enough to sin, and had not repented, for, though her dreary creed taught that the rigors of eternal damnation rested on every one who had not repented of each individual sin, and that adult baptism was the only assurance of redemption, it did not teach, nor did she believe, that the innocence of childhood required the certificate of the church. All the rest of her children had professed religion and received baptism according to the rites of the Baptist Church, but little William left in the mother's heart the sting of uncertainty. Had he lived long enough to transgress the Law and not repented? was to her an ever-present question of terrible import. Years rolled by without weakening this torture of apprehension that this little lamb of all her flock might be expiating the sin of Adam in the flames of Eternity, a perpetual babyhood of woe. The depth of the misery this haunting fear inflicted on her can only be imagined by one who knew the passionate intensity of her love for her children,--a love which she feared to be sinful, but could not abate. Finally, one night, as she lay perplexing her soul with this and other problems of sin and righteousness, she saw, standing near her bed, her lost child, not as she supposed him to be, a baby for eternity, but apparently a youth of sixteen, regarding her silently, but with an expression of such radiant happiness in his face that the shadow passed from her soul forever. She needed no longer to be told that he was amongst the blessed. She told me this one day, timidly, as something she had never dared tell the older children, lest they should think her superstitious, or, perhaps, dissipate her consolation by the assurance that she had dreamed. Dream she was convinced it was not; but only to me, in her old age, had she ever dared to confide this assurance, which had been so precious to her.

In charity, comfort for the afflicted, help,--not in money, for of that there was little to spare,--but in food; in watching with the sick and consoling the bereaved in her own loving, sympathetic mother's way, she abounded. There was always something for the really needy, and I remember that one of her most painful experiences came from having refused food to a begging woman, to whose deathbed she was called the next day, a deathbed of literal starvation. She recognized the woman, who had come to our house with a story of a family of starving children, but as my mother's experienced eye assured her she had never been a mother, she refused her as a deceiver what the poor always got. "Why did you tell me you had children," mother asked her, "when you came to me yesterday?" "It was not true," said the dying woman, "but I was starving, and I thought you would be more willing to help me if you thought I had children." But from that day no beggar was turned from our door without food. Silently and in secret she did what good works came to her to be done, letting not her right hand know what her left hand was doing, but all the poor knew her and her works.

Silent too and undemonstrative in all her domestic relations she always was, and I question if to any other of her family than myself she ever confided her secret hopes or fears. And to me even she was so undemonstrative that I never remember her kissing me from a passing warmth; only when I went away on a journey or returned from one did she offer to kiss me, and this was the manner of the family. And her maintenance of family discipline was on the same rigorous level, dispassionate as the law. If I transgressed the commands of herself or of my father the punishment was inevitable, never in wrath, generally on the day after the offense, but inexorable; she never meant to spoil the child by sparing the rod, but flogged with tears in her eyes and an aching heart, often giving the punishment herself, to prevent my father from giving it, as he always flogged mercilessly and in anger, though if I could keep out of his sight till the next day he forgot all about it; she never forgot, and though the flogging might not come for a week, it was never omitted when promised. And her worst severity never raised a feeling of resentment in me, for I recognized it as deserved, while my father's floggings, inflicted in the unreasoning severity of anger, always made me rebellious. I remember only one occasion on which I was punished unjustly by my mother.

A neighboring farmer had asked me to go to his field and shake down the fruit from two apple-trees. It was in the hour before dinner, and the regulations of the family were very severe about being at meals, and unfortunately I had, in my glee at having a job of paying work to do, infringed on the dinnertime. In payment for my services I received from the farmer two huge pumpkins, charged with which I hastened home, looking forward to my mother's praise and pleasure, but was met by her in the hall, strap in hand, with which she administered a solid flogging, explaining that my father was so angry at my being out at dinner that she gave me the punishment to forestall his, which would be, as I well knew, much severer. It is more than sixty years since that punishment fell on my shoulders, but the astonishment with which I received the flogging instead of the thanks I anticipated for the wages I was bringing her, the haste with which my mother administered it lest my father should anticipate her and beat me after his fashion, are as vivid in my recollection as if it had taken place last year. This was a sample of the family discipline. I was forbidden to walk with other boys when I drove the cow to pasture; forbidden to bathe in the mill-pond near by except at stated times, to play with certain children, to amuse myself on the Sabbath, and other similar doings, all to my childish apprehension harmless in themselves, and the punishment never failed to follow the discovery of the transgression. Naturally I learned to lie, a thing contrary to my inclination and nature, and a torture to my conscience, but I had not the courage to meet the flogging, or the firmness to resist temptation and the persuasion of my young companions who rejoiced in a domestic freedom of which I knew nothing. My father's severity finally brought emancipation by its excess. He used to follow me to see if I obeyed his orders, and one day when I had been persuaded by some boys of our neighborhood to go and bathe in the forbidden hours, he found me in the pond, led me home, and, cutting two tough peartree switches about the thickness, at the butt, of his forefinger, he took me down into the cellar, and making me strip off my jacket, broke them up to the stumps over my back, protected only by a cotton shirt. This was the deciding event which determined me to run away from home, which I did the next week, and though my escapade did not last beyond ten days, on my return the rod was buried.

CHAPTER II
NATURE WORSHIP--EARLY RELIGIOUS EXPERIENCES

Looking back at my mother, after a lapse of nearly forty years since I saw her last, I am surprised at the largeness of character developed in the narrow and illiberal mould of the exclusive Puritanism of the church of her inheritance, her freedom from bigotry, and the breadth of her knowledge of human nature, as well as at the justice of her instincts of religious essentials, which always kept her cheerful and hopeful in spite of the gloomy doctrine imposed on her by her education and surroundings. Believing firmly in the eternity of hell-fire, with the logical and terrible day of judgment casting its gloomy shadow over her life, she maintained an unbounded charity for all humanity except herself, admitting the extenuation of ignorance for all others, keeping for herself even to the tithes of mint and cummin, but condoning, in her judgment of those who differed from her, the offenses which for herself she would have thought mortal sins. In her own household all latitude in religious observance was resisted with all her strength.

In my paternal grandfather's house the Seventh Day was a day of feasting, and after the church services all the connection went to the ancestral home to eat the most sumptuous dinner of the week. Against this infraction of the law which forbade on the Sabbath all work not of mercy or necessity, my mother set her face, and when this was done there was no long resistance possible and my father had to give way, so that on that day we had a cold dinner, cooked on Friday. At sunset on Friday, all work and all secular reading or amusements ceased, and only a Sabbath day's journey was permitted so far as she could control. But my father was a rover from his youth, and Saturday being his only leisure day he used to take me with him on long walks in the woods and fields, according to the season; and the weather and the length of the day were his only limitations. In the house she ruled, but out of it he made his own conscience, and so it happened that the only pleasures that I owe him, except the bringing me a few books when he came back from his business trips to New York to sell his machines, were those long walks in the face of nature. He was, in his family, apparently a cold, hard man, but out of it, kindly and benevolent, melting always to distress which came in his way; with a passionate love of animals and of nature. He was a poor business man, for he could never press for the payment of debts due to him, but his honesty was so rigid that it became a proverb in our town that a man should be "as honest as old Joe Stillman," and that good name was all he gave or left his children.

My father died in one of my occasional absences in Europe, and when I saw my old mother in the black she never again laid off, she told me, tranquilly and with a firm voice, but with the tears running down her cheeks, how he died, and said, "He was so handsome that I wanted to keep him another day." The warmth of expression struck me strangely, for in all my home experience I had never heard before a word which could be taken as a token of conjugal tenderness, but when I reflected, I could see that it was and always had been the same with the children. Of the nine children she bore, five died before she did, including her second and, during my life, her only daughter, but in all the bereavements she retained her calm, self-contained manner, weeping silently, and tranquilly going about the house, comforting those who shared the bereavement, uncomplaining, reconciled in advance; she had consigned her beloved to the God who gave them to her, and would have thought it rebellion to repine at any dispensation which He sent her. In the most sudden and crushing grief I remember her to have experienced, that which came with the news that my brother Alfred had been killed by the explosion of a steamboat boiler at New Orleans, there was one brief break-down of her fortitude, an hour's yielding, and then all her thought was for the widow and the children. No detail of the household duties was neglected, and nothing was forgotten that concerned the comfort of others. She avoided all external signs of grief, and, until my father died, she never wore mourning. Her bereavements and her prayers were matters that concerned only God and herself.

What I have said might give her the character of an ascetic, but nothing could be further from her. She was always optimistic as to earthly troubles, always cheerful and fond of mild festivities. At times no one was more merry than she, and I have seen her laughing at a good joke or story till the tears ran down her cheeks. Cheerfulness was to her a duty which was never violated except when she was laying her case before God.

Her ardent desire that her children should have a liberal education came to a climax on me, the last, born at the end of the period of child-bearing. She taught me my letters before I could articulate them, when I was two I could read, and at three I was put on a high stool to read the Bible for visitors, so that I cannot remember when I could not read, and when not more than five or six I used to be at the head of the spelling classes and spelling matches, in which all the boys and girls were divided into equal companies, and the school-teacher gave out the hardest words in the spelling-book to each side in turn, all who failed to spell their word sitting down, until the solitary survivor on one side or the other decided the victory, and even before I was seven I was generally that survivor. I read insatiably all the good story-books they would let me have, and I cannot recall the time at which there was anything even in the Bible new to me. With an incipient passion for nature and animal life, I read with delight all the books of natural history I could get, and I have heard in later years that in all the community of Sabbatarianism I was known as a prodigy. Fortunately I was saved from a probable idiocy in my later life by a severe attack of typhoid fever at seven, out of which attack I came a model of stupidity, and so remained until I was fourteen, my thinking powers being so completely suspended that at the dame's school to which I was sent I was repeatedly flogged for not comprehending the simplest things. I got through simple arithmetic as far as "Long Division," and there had to turn back to the beginning three times before I could be made to understand the principle of division by more than one figure.

In the humiliation of this period of my life, in which I came to consider myself as little better than a fool, my only consolation was the large liberty I enjoyed in the woods and fields with my father on Saturdays, or with my brothers Charles and Jacob on their long botanizing excursions, or in the moments of leisure when I was not wanted to turn the grindstone or blow the bellows in the workshop. Those long walks, in which I was indefatigable, and the days or nights when I went fishing with my brother Jacob, who was ten years older than myself, and who inherited the wandering and adventurous longings of my father, are the only things I can remember of this period which gave me any pleasure. I can see vividly the banks of the Mohawk, where we used to fish for perch, bream, and pike-perch; recall where, with my brother Charles, we found the rarer flowers of the valley, the cypripediums, the most rare wild-ginger, only to be found in one locality, the walking fern, equally rare, and the long walks in the pine forests, whose murmuring branches in the west wind fascinated me more than any other thing in nature.

Perhaps I mingle in recollection the nature-worship of the two septennates, for of the former was my first rapturous vision of the open sea, which comes back to me with the memory of the pines. I had gone with my father and mother to New York on a visit to my eldest brother, who had just then finished the engines of the steamer Diamond, which was the first that by her build was enabled to run through from New York to Albany, past the "overslough" or bar formed in the Hudson, which prevented the steamers of greater draught from getting up to the wharf at Albany; and he had profited by her first trip to visit home again and take us back with him. My brother pointed out to me the Clermont, Fulton's trial steamer, then disused and lying at Hoboken, but a cockboat to the Diamond, which was one of the greatest successes of the day. Machinery fascinated me, being of the mechanical breed, and I can recall the engines of the boat, which were of a new type, working horizontally, and so permitting larger engines in proportion to the draught of the steamer than had been before used. We all went one day to Coney Island, on the southern shore of Long Island, since a fashionable bathing place for New York, but then a solitary stretch of seashore, with a temporary structure where bathers might get refreshments, and a few bathing boxes. We drove out in my brother's buggy, and as, at a turn in the road, I caught a glimpse of the distant sea horizon, I rose in the buggy, shouting, "The sea! the sea!" and, in an uncontrollable frenzy, caught the whip from my brother's hand and slashed the horse in wild delirium, unconscious of what I was doing. The emotion remains uneffaceable after more than threescore years, one of the most vivid of my life. It was a rapture and an interesting case of heredity, for I had not before been within a hundred and fifty miles of the sea.

And how ecstatic was the sensation of the plunge into the breakers, holding fast to my mother's hand, and then the race up the beach before the next comber, trembling lest it should catch me, as if it were a living thing ready to devour me. They never come back, these first emotions of childhood; and though I have loved the sea all my life, I have never again felt the sight of it as then.

Of this first period, I remember very well the grand occasion of the opening of the Hudson and Mohawk Railroad, the first link in that line which is now the New York Central, and see vividly the curious old coaches,--three coach bodies together on one truck. This was in 1832, when I was four years old. The road was, I believe, the first successful passenger railway in America, and was sixteen miles long, with two inclined planes up which the trains were drawn, and down which they were lowered by cables. There was an opposition line of stagecoaches between Albany and Schenectady, running at the same price and making the same time.

Of the second period, that of nature worship, was my first trout, another delirium. My mother had taken me to visit one of her brothers, a farmer in the western section of New York, soon after made famous by the anti-rent war, in which my uncle was one of the "Indian Chiefs[2]," and there I went fishing in the brook that ran through his farm. I caught a small trout and did not know what fish it might be, till I saw the crimson spots on his side and remembered that the trout in books bore them, and then I threw him on the grass and danced a wild dance around him, a powwow as furious as a red Indian's scalp-dance, while he, poor little fingerling, jumped in the unkindly herb. Then I caught him up and raced to the house nearly half a mile, to show him, and put him in the trough under the pump, where he arrived still gasping but alive, and where he remained for all my recollection of his fate thereafter. But I remember that the beauty of the little creature gave me more pleasure than the capture.

About this time I began to try to draw, and especially birds and beautiful forms, though years before I had begun to color the wood-cuts in my books. And my mother, who had an utterly uncultivated but most tender love of art, gave up finally the oft-renewed ambition to see one of her boys in the pulpit, and made every opportunity for me to learn drawing,--I never quite understood why, for my abilities in that line were little more than nine boys out of ten show.

It was a fortunate thing for my after-life that I lived so near the forests that <u>all my odd time was spent in them and in the surrounding fields</u>, and I knew ev-

---

2   The bands which carried on what became an actual insurrection against the civic authorities were led by men disguised as red Indians and called chiefs.

ery apple-tree of early fruiting for miles, and every hickory-tree whose nuts were choice; and one of the joyous experiences of the time was running down a young gray squirrel in the woods, and catching him with my bare hands, and badly bitten they were. I took him home and tamed him perfectly, and was very happy with him, my first pet. He used to come and sleep in my pocket, and was never kept in a cage. My father one morning left the window of our room open, and "Bob" went out to explore, but, when he tried to find his way back again, a dog of the neighborhood, as a neighbor told us, chased him away, and to my intense grief he was shot by a hunter a few days after in the adjoining forest. I cannot to this day see a squirrel without emotion and affectionate remembrance of "Bob." The love of animals, which I inherited from my father, was one of the passions of my childhood, and I had an insatiate longing for pets.

Naturally my religious education during these early years was of the severest orthodox character, and my mother's sincere, fervent, and practical piety brought home to me, with the conviction of certainty, the persuasion of its divine authority. Hell and its terrors were always present to me, and she taught me that the wandering suggestions of childish imagination, the recurrence of profane expressions heard from others, and all forms of irreverent fantasies were the very whisperings of the devil, to her, as to me, consequently, an ever-present spirit, perpetually tempting me to repeat, and so make myself responsible for the wickedness in them. I remember with great vividness a caricature of Mrs. Trollope in a satirical illustrated edition of her travels in America, representing her sitting in a large armchair surrounded by negroes on their knees, one of whom was represented as saying, "De Lord lub Missee Trollope," an expression which my mother stigmatized as impious and not to be repeated, but which perhaps for that very reason would recur to me in thought, and which I set myself to pray against as the very whisper of the devil in my ears. And naturally, the more I tried to put it out of my head, the more it got fixed there, and it was long a source of great misery to me that I could not keep the devil away from my ears. I was never allowed a candle to go to bed with, and as I slept in the huge garret, covering the whole house, I used to shut my eyes when I left the kitchen, where we all sat in the evening, and groped my way to bed without ever again opening my eyes until the next morning, for fear of seeing the devil on my way. Awful spiritual presences haunted me always in the dark, when I passed a churchyard or an empty and solitary house. Such a house stood in the pasture where I used to drive the cow, and when it happened that she had not come home at nightfall, and I had to go to find her, the panic I endured from the necessity of searching around this old house no one can imagine but a boy naturally timid and accustomed to see ghosts and evil spirits in the dusk. But I kept my fears to myself and always made a conscientious search.

The peculiar ideas concerning conversion and regeneration, held in common by all the branches of the adult-Baptist churches, were in my mother's mind an obsession. Conviction of sin, repentance, the public confession, profession of faith, and baptism were the necessary degrees to regeneration, and, looking back on the tortures to which my mother was subjected by those theological problems and the daily anxiety she endured until each of us had passed through the gates of salvation into the narrow way, I must wonder at that divine maternal instinct which made her rejoice at my birth, as I know she did.

The whole community in which we lived, with the exception of a small Episcopal church, had the same ideas of conversion and regeneration, and a prominent feature in our social existence was the frequent recurrence of the great revival meetings in which all the rude eloquence of celebrated and powerful preachers, Baptist, Methodist, and of other sects, was poured out on excited congregations. There were "protracted meetings," or campaigns of prayer and exhortation, lasting often a fortnight, at which all the resources of popular theology were employed to awaken and maintain their audiences in a state of frenzy and religious delirium, during which conviction of sin was supposed to enter the heart more effectually. The tortures of hell alternated with the delights of heaven, in imagery calculated to drive the timid and conscientious young folks to insanity, at these meetings, to which, once awakened, the subject of conviction went three times a day, until the hysteria, the prolonged excitement so produced, came as a sign of acceptance. As each new convert rose on the "anxious seat[3]," where he or she went when the first feeling of conviction came, and afterwards made the declaration of salvation found, the shouts and cries of "Glory to God," the sobbing and groans of the congregation were redoubled, and the exhortations of the preacher renewed, to the still unconvicted to come forward to the anxious seat where they would become subject to the

---

3   The front line of seats next the pulpit, set apart for those who had "found conviction."

concentrated and personal prayers of the whole assembly. These meetings were the substitutes for all other social diversions or emotions. There was a revival preacher by the name of Knapp, whose lurid eloquence in this vein made him famous, and whose imagery was equal in ghastliness to anything that the Catholic Church could produce. I remember one of his most dramatic bits, borrowed from a much earlier preacher, a passage in his description of hell. In hell, he said, there was a clock, which, instead of "tick," "tick," said, "Eternity," "Eternity," and when the damned, weary of their tortures down in the depths, came up to see what time it was, they heard the sentence of the clock, and turned in despair to go down into the depths again as far as they could.

 To these meetings my mother used to send me, giving me a holiday from school for all the time the protracted meeting lasted. But conviction never came. I was honest with myself, and though the frenzied and ghastly exhortations harried my soul with dread, and I longed for the coming of the ecstasy which was the recognizable sign of the grace of God, I could not rise to the participation in it which the most material and hysterical of the congregation enjoyed, and day after day I went home saddened by the conviction that I was still one of the unregenerate. The sign never came, but several years later I went to make a visit to my brother Charles, who had then removed to Plainfield, N.J., where he practiced medicine, and was one of the main supports of the church in a community where the sect was large enough to have a constant worship, which it never had in Schenectady. Here I came under the influence of a beloved brother of my mother, one of the most earnest and humble Christians I have ever known, and here were gathered others of the denomination at a protracted meeting, at which some of my friends of my own age became seriously inclined, and we drifted together into the profession of Christian faith. But here there was nothing of the ghastly terrors of the great revival agitations. My uncle was a man of the world, had been all his early life a sailor, and had taken late to what, in his experiences of men and the vicissitudes of life, he considered the only reality, the duty of making known to his fellows the importance of the spiritual life. To fit himself for the ministry, he taught himself Hebrew and Greek as well as Latin, and many years later was chosen as one of the New Testament revisers for the American revision committee. But to him the profession of religion was an act of the reason, not of revival excitement, and in his ministrations he shunned carefully all the frenzied exhortation of the revivalists. Associated with him in the ministry and leading the meetings was another of the Sabbatarian pastors, Elder Estee, a grave and earnest man like my uncle, who inspired me with great confidence.

As I look back from the standpoint of one who reposes in the evolutionary philosophy, in which the accidental and ecstatic disappear, upon this phase of psychology, in which hysteria becomes an element of moral reform, it seems to me worth while to record the experience of one subjected to the forces which were counted as such powerful aids to the spread of Christianity,--of one either under the influences of the pomp of ceremony, the stimulus of music, the purely sensuous stimulants to devotion,--or in the crude form of that ecstatic exaltation in which the individual is carried into a supersensuous state, in which perception, reason, and even responsibility to a great extent are, if not suspended, so far made abnormal that analysis becomes impossible. The term for this latter condition amongst revivalists was "the power," and it was distinctly a phenomenon sought for as the evidence of divine grace. The uncle of whom I have spoken had once during his prior religious experience felt the "power," and described it as an emotion which for the time lifted him above the consideration of his surroundings, and left him subsequently indifferent to that very curious shame which generally accompanies the early yielding to the revivalist urgency of acknowledging the necessity of change of heart,--a sense of having made one's self ridiculous, which was, in my own and many other cases in my knowledge, a powerful influence adverse to the "going forward" at the meetings, or being understood to be "religious," as those were considered who became serious in their attention at the meetings. This was recognized by the preachers as the "fear of the world," and was the object of attack of the most eloquent adjurations. Once carried away by this hysteria, one had no longer any of this shame or fear of the taunts of his irreligious companions, which was very heavy with a nervous and sensitive boy like myself. But though I had all through my attendance on the revival meetings earnestly desired to attain to that exaltation, and considered it an indication of my graceless state, that I was so insensible to the "spirit," which was another term for the frenzy, I found it impossible to provoke it. It is a curious subject, this usurpation of the reasoning faculties by the irrational, which is permitted when religion becomes emotional, either in the revolutionary condition of the revivalist or that of the conservative and decorous ecclesiastical forms.

The movement at Plainfield, finding me in different surroundings from those in my native place, and under the influence of deliberate and sober-minded people, put the religious question under another light, but, still under the persuasion, the natural result of my life's training, that some special emotion or spiritual change, recognizable as such, was an indispensable sign of the "change of heart" which was desired, I was unhappy that no such sign appeared. I can distinctly remember that the desire to satisfy my mother's passionate longing for what she considered my regeneration was a large part of my desire to meet the change, and, if I might, provoke it. I did not in spite of my efforts really understand the view which my mother, in common with most evangelical Christians, took of the work of regeneration. The calm, rational conviction that all men are sinners, was clear enough to me even in my youth, and the necessity of turning from what we call "the world," to the cultivation of the higher and spiritual development of character was equally clear, though not so in all points was the distinction between the things condemned as worldly and those approved as religious, the theatre, games of chance, dancing, and frivolous amusements in general being all in the index of those severe theologians.

As I remember my extreme youth I was, in spite of occasional falsehoods,--mainly the consequence of the severity of the parental discipline and the desire to escape the punishments I had to endure when transgressing the sometimes whimsical injunctions laid on me,--morbidly conscientious. I was absent-minded and often forgot my duties, feeling, however, always the sting of remorse for any omission, but, beyond taking apples or nuts for my own eating, I do not think that I ever transgressed a commandment deliberately or knowingly; I was, in fact, regarded by the boys of the neighborhood as hopelessly "goody." I could not understand why the desire to go to a dancing-school and dance should be a moral transgression, though when I asked permission of my father to accept the offer of an ex-dancing-master for whom I had been able to do some work in the workshop, to give me preparatory lessons so that I might appear less clumsy on entering the class, I was sternly brought to a sense of the enormity of the matter by my father's replying, "William! I would rather see you in your grave than in a dancing-school." I could only understand that I had not been lifted by the divine grace from the condition of total depravity in which I had been born, and I knew that the preternatural indication of my redemption, which would be recognized in the descent of the spirit in the form of the revival frenzy, was wanting. I longed for it, prayed for it, and considered myself forsaken of God because it would not come, but come it never did, and it seemed to me that I was attempting to deceive both my mother and the church when I finally yielded to the current which carried along my young friends, and took the grace for granted, since, as I thought, having asked the special prayers of the elders, men of God, and powerful in influence with Him, I had a right to assume the desired descent of the redeeming light on me, though I had never had that peculiar manifestation of it which my companions seemed to have experienced. I felt not a little twinge of conscience in assuming so much, but I could not consent to prolong my mother's suspense and grave concern at the exclusion of one of her children from the fold of grace. I put down the doubts, accepted the conversion as logical and real, and went forward with the others. I remember that at the relation of our "experience" which followed as a rite on the presentation of the convert for membership of the church, I was the only one who told it calmly and audibly, all the others being inaudible from their excitement and timidity, so that the presiding elder was obliged to repeat to the audience what they said in his ear, trembling, weeping with the emotion of the event. I felt as if I were a hypocrite, and only the thought of my mother's satisfaction gave me the courage to go through the ceremony. We were baptized, my companions and I, in the little river in midwinter, after a partial thaw, the blocks of ice floating by us in the water.

I must have been about ten or eleven when I went through this experience, and I never got rid of the feeling of a certain unreality in the whole transaction, but on the other hand I had the same feeling of unreality in the system of theology which led to it. I tried to do my best to carry out the line of spiritual duties imposed upon me. I made no question that I was a bad boy, but the conception of total depravity in the theological sense never gained a hold on me, and once inside the church there seemed to be a certain safeguard thrown over me. The sense of ***ecstasy*** (which my Uncle William had experienced in his religious relation, the "power" of the revivalists) I have since known in conditions of extraordinary mental exaltation, and understand it as a mental phenomenon, as the momentary extension of the consciousness of the individual beyond the limitations of the bodily sense--a being snatched away from the body and made to see and feel things not describable in terms of ordinary experience, but in my religious evolution it had no place, then or since.

The intellectual slowness of which I have spoken continued through all these years. I had left the dame's school, where the rule of long division proved my ***pons asinorum***, and went to a man's school, where I earned my schooling by making the fires and sweeping the schoolroom, and here I learned some Latin and the higher rules in arithmetic by rote, always with the reputation of a stupid boy, good in the snowball fights of the intermission, when we had two snow forts to capture and defend; in running foot-races, the speediest, and in backhand wrestling, the strongest, but mentally hopeless. All this period of my life seems dreary and void, except when I got to nature, and the delight of my hours in the fields and woods is all that remains to me of a childhood tormented by burdens of conscience laid on me prematurely, and by a domestic discipline the severity of which, with all the reverence and gratitude I bear my parents, I can hardly consider otherwise than gravely mistaken and disastrous to me, though my mother's discipline has never made me an enemy of the rod for children. My own experience as child and parent convinces me that an inexorable, though mild, physical punishment is the only remedy for the obstinacy of certain fractious child natures, in the years before reason operates, and for the assurance of necessary discipline in families.

The incessant Bible lessons, filling my mind with indigestible conceptions of life present and to come, mysteries for the contemplation of a philosopher, not for a boy of ten; the recognition of my total depravity, as manifested in the trivial transgressions of a thoughtless child, to whom life had hardly yet offered a duty to fulfill or transgress; the terrible gloom of this Puritan horizon, on which no light showed me promise of better things, only to be hoped for through a process of repentance and atonement for the sins of Adam, the fitness and method of which process were far beyond my capacity to comprehend, as beyond that of any child,--all these things made my intellectual life so sombre that I can but regard the long interval of intellectual apathy as a fortunate provision against some form of mental malady consequent on the morbid development of my early childhood.

Our winters were long and hard, and I remember the snow falling on Thanksgiving Day (the last Thursday in November) and not thawing again until the beginning of March, and that, in the house where I was born, we had the fall of snow so heavy that we could tunnel the path to the barn, the drift covering the door of the house. The coming of spring was my constant preoccupation through the winter, and my joy was intense at the first swelling of the buds, the coming color in the willow twigs, which ushered in the changes of spring; then the catkins, the willow leaves, and the long rains which carried off the snow, all welcome as daylight after a weary night, because they restored me to the forests and the wildflowers, the fields and the streams; and for miles around I knew every sunny spot where came the first anemones, hepaticas, and, above all, the trailing arbutus, joy of my childhood, the little white violets, their yellow sisters, then the "dog-tooth violet," and a long list of flowers whose names I have forgotten long ago.

The perennial delight of this return of springtime was the great feature of my life, and then began the excursions into the forests around us, and the succession of sights and sounds, the order of the unfolding of the leaves, from the willow to the oak, the singing of the frogs in the marshes, and the birds in the copses and fields (for in the great woods there are few singing birds). I knew them all, and when and where to hear them. The bluebird, or blue robin, as it was called in our neighborhood, was the first, and he assured us that spring had really come with a plaintive song, the sweetest to memory of all nature's voices; then the American robin (the migratory thrush), a bold, cheery note, full of summer life; and after those the chief was the bobolink, singing up into the sky like the skylark, and with which we connected the ripening of the strawberry, the merriest and most rollicking of all bird songs, as that of the bluebird was the tenderest. Then came the hermit thrush, heard only in the depth of the forest, shy and remote in his life and nesting, and the whip-poor-will, in the evening. Each was a new leaf turned over in my book of life, the reading of which was my only happiness. What else, or more, could be expected of an existence hedged in by the terrors of eternity, the hauntings of an inevitable condemnation, unless I could obtain some mysterious renovation, only attainable through an act of divine grace which no human merit could entitle me to, and which I tried in vain to win the benediction of? And how dreary seemed the heaven I was set to win--no birds, no flowers, no fields or forests, only the eternal continuation of the hymn-singing and protracted meetings, in which, in our system, consisted the glorification of God, which was the end and aim of our existences! I wonder how many religious parents remember the misery of child life under such influences.

The struggles of conscience through which I went in those days can be imagined by no one, and I can hardly realize them myself, except by recalling little incidents which show what the pressure must have been. I have mentioned an escapade of this period, connected with the last flogging my father gave me, but of which that was only the secondary cause, determining the moment but not the movement. It was a matter of conscience at bottom. My mother had, when I was about six years old, taken a little octoroon girl of three, the illegitimate daughter of a quadroon in our neighborhood, with the intention of bringing her up as a servant. The child was quick-witted and irrepressible, and disputes began between us as soon as she felt at home. I suppose she must have been inclined to impertinence, for she had to be whipped, and as at her age no difference of condition was evident to her, she became a severe trial to my equanimity. Every outbreak of temper induced by her conduct toward me became occasion of a period of penitence, for I was taught that such outbreaks were sinful, and as neither had I the amount of self-control that I needed to overlook the provocations she gave, nor had she the power of understanding the position, the transgressions that my conscience had to bear up under became an intolerable load.

At this juncture came the brutal and as I felt most unmerited flogging of which I have told the story earlier: this precipitated a decision which had been slowly forming from my conscientious worries. I determined to go away from home, and seek a state of life in which I could maintain my spiritual tranquillity. I discussed the subject with a playmate of my age, the son of a gardener living near us, and, as his father had even a stronger propensity to the rod than mine, we sympathized on that ground and agreed to run away and work our passages on some ship to a land where we could live in a modified Robinson Crusoe manner,--not an uninhabited land, but one where we could earn, by fishing and similar devices, enough to live. I had been employed for a few months before in carrying to and fro the students' clothes for a washerwoman, one of the neighbors, and had earned three or four dollars which my mother had, as usual with any trifle I earned, put into the fund for the daily expenses. I do not know how it was with the older boys, but for me the rule was rigid--what I could earn was a part of the household income. I inwardly rebelled against this, but to no effect, so I never had any pocket-money. I submitted, as any son of my mother would have done at my age or have given a solid reason why not; but on this occasion, when money was indispensable to that expedition on which so much depended, I quietly reasserted my right to my earnings, and took the wages I had received, from the drawer where they were kept. My companion had no money at all, and thus my trifle had to pay for both as far as it would go,--fortunately, perhaps, as it shortened the duration of the expedition.

We went by train to Albany, where we took deck passage on a towing steamer for New York. The run was longer than that of a passenger steamer, so that the New York police who were warned to look out for us by the post, had given us up when we arrived and search was diverted in another direction. We arrived at New York with my funds already nearly exhausted by the food expenses *en route*, and my companion's courage had already given out--he was homesick and discouraged, and announced his determination to return home. My own courage, I can honestly say, had not failed me,--I was ready for hardship, but to go alone into a strange world damped my ascetic ardor and confounded all the plans I had made. I yielded, and with the last few "York shillings"[4] in my pocket bargained for a deck passage without board on a barge back to Albany. It was midsummer, and the sleeping on some bags of wool which formed the better part of the deck-load gave me no inconvenience, and the want of provisions of any sort was remedied as well as might be by a pile of salt codfish which was the other part of the deck-load, and which was the only food we had until our arrival at Albany, which we reached at night after a voyage of twenty-four hours. We slept under a boat overturned by the shore that night until the rising tide drove us out, when we decided to take the road back to Schenectady on foot, through a wide pine forest which occupied the intervening country, a distance of about sixteen miles. Passing on the way a stable in which there was nobody, not even a beast, we turned in to sleep away the darkness, and I remember very well what a yielding bed a manger filled with salt gave me. With the dawn we resumed the journey, and by the way ate our fill of whortleberries, with which the forest abounded.

The joy of my mother at our unhoped-for arrival--for she had received no news of us since our departure--is easily imagined, but for me the failure of all my plans for an ascetic and more spiritual life was made more bitter by the fact that the little octoroon, who had heard read the letter which I left for my mother, giving the motives for my self-exile, had repeated it to all the neighborhood, so that I not

---

4   12 1/2 cents each.

only had failed, but became the butt of the jokes of the boys of the neighborhood, who already held a pique against me for my serious ways and my habit of rebuking certain vices amongst them. I was jeered at as the boy "who left his mother to seek religion," and this made life for a time almost intolerable. But it was in part compensated for by the change in the situation in the household. It was clear that I had ceased to be the boy I used to be, and that I was to be taken seriously, and reasoned with rather than flogged. I had escaped from the pupa state of existence. But what I still look back to with surprise was my unflinching confidence in the future to which I committed myself in this escapade. I thought I was right, and that the aspiration for spiritual freedom, which was the chief motive of my leaving home, was certain to be supported by Providence, to whom I looked with serene complacence. If my companion had not deserted me I should not have turned back, but his defection destroyed all my plans. In several of my maturer ventures, I can recognize the same mental condition of serene indifference to danger while doing what I thought my duty, owing, perhaps, in a great measure to ignorance or incapacity to realize the danger, but also largely to ingrained confidence in an overruling Providence which took account of my steps and would carry me through.

CHAPTER III
AN AMERICAN EDUCATION

Whether on account of the escapade related in the preceding chapter or from influences of which I knew, and still know, nothing, it was decided not long after that I should go to New York to attend a public school there and live with my eldest brother, who, being twenty-five years older than myself, and childless, had always treated me with an indulgence which was perhaps due in part to the rigor of my father's rule, and in part to his fondness for me, of which I retain some early recollections in his annual visits home. My brother's wife, a fellow townswoman of ours, and a marriage-convert to the Seventh Day Baptist Church, was one of the most disagreeable persons I have ever had to deal with, and hysterical to a degree of occasional insanity. She had adopted the severities of our Puritanic system with aggravations. The Sabbath under her rule became a day of preatonement for the sins I was foreordained to commit. Dinner, as was the general custom in those days, was at noon, but on Saturday I had none till I had committed to heart and recited a portion of Scripture, and as the mental apathy of the period still weighed on me, the task of the Seventh Day was a sarcastic comment on the divine rest, in commemoration of which it was supposed to be instituted, and it made me grateful for the Sunday, which I generally passed in mechanical occupations in the workshop of my third brother, Paul, the foreman of the department in which the minor articles of the works were made, steam-gauges, models of inventions, etc., and as I had my share of the family manual dexterity, I found interest enough in the workshop. As my brothers always observed the Sabbath rigidly, they attracted around them a few of the New England mechanics who were "Sabbath-keepers" and mostly related to us, and so we had a small congregation and a church of our way of thinking.

The school to which I was sent was one of those founded by the Public School Society, a voluntary association of well-to-do citizens, who, in the absence of any municipal initiative, had organized themselves for the encouragement and support of primary education. As they were originally excluded from the management of the schools, the politicians, finding this a new field of operations and partisan activity, presently established the rival system of the municipal schools called "ward schools." At that time the political intrigues of the Catholic Church for the control of the public school system had just begun. The Public School Society had been organized for the free and non-sectarian education of all children unable to meet the expense of education in the private schools, and received subsidies from the municipality. Not only were all children under sixteen admitted to these schools without any fees, but the books, stationery, and all other material necessary were furnished gratuitously, and those who were shoeless were even provided with shoes, the only requisites being cleanliness and regular attendance. The direction was rigidly non-sectarian. The trustees were unpaid, and they comprised many of the leading citizens interested in popular education. They had built for their service sixteen schoolhouses in New York, and in each of these there were on an average a thousand children. The schoolhouses, of three stories, had a primary department for such children as were too young to be taught their letters or were not yet able to read and write, and to them the basement was given, the second story to the older girls, and the upper to the boys. The teaching for the boys' department was limited to the elements of arithmetic, elementary algebra, astronomy, and geometry, but within these limits the education was thorough, and all who went through it were qualified for places in offices or counting-rooms. The day was always opened by the reading of Scripture and prayer by the principal or one of the assistants, and this practice was made the ground of attack by the Catholic politicians, who objected to the Protestant Bible, all the school-books being already expurgated of every passage to which the bishops objected.

As our assistant principal was a Catholic, and often had to read the chapter, there could have been little harm done even to a Catholic pupil, but the political pressure was sufficient to induce the corporation of the city to adopt the political or "ward school" system, controlled by the politicians, and the new schools, one of which was or was to be established in each ward of the city, began to run an active opposition to the society schools, which they eventually drove out of existence.

At the time I was in the school, the interference of politics had just begun to make itself felt in the schools, but the corporation had not the courage to introduce its system on a large scale by supplanting *en bloc* the society schools, which might have made a political revolt; the Irish Catholic influence was still a feeble one, and the population at large was hardly aware of its tendency, but as the ward schools were gradually brought into active competition with the society schools the children were drawn off from the latter by various inducements and pressure on the parents. Each of our schools had four paid teachers--the principal, an assistant, and a junior and a senior monitor; and the elder pupils were employed in the instruction of the younger and in the preservation of order in school and in the school yard during the intermissions in which the gymnastics were enforced. My mental apathy must have been still very profound, for I remember that it often happened that when a question which had passed other pupils came to me in the class, the senior monitor used to address me, "Well, stupid, what do you say?" I evidently was the most stupid boy in the class--nothing seemed to penetrate my mental dullness, but, having grown tall and strong for my age, I was often made "yard monitor," to keep order during the physical training.

There was a gang of young ruffians, street boys, who used to hang around the school gates and maltreat the stragglers and even the boys in the yard, if the gate was left open, and I remember one day three or four of them invading the schoolyard after I had dismissed the boys to go upstairs at the end of the intermission, thinking that they would have a fine game with the monitor. One made a pretext to quarrel with me, and, gripping me round the body, called to his companions to go and get some stones to pound me on the head with, this being the approved manner of the young roughs of New York. Finding that I could not extricate myself from his grip, I dragged him to the wall, and, catching him by the ears, beat his head against the rough stones until he dropped insensible, when, to the astonishment of his comrades, instead of stamping on him and finishing him at once, I ran upstairs as fast as my legs could carry me, so that when they came with their stones they had only their champion to carry out.

On the holidays there were generally stone-fights between the boys of our quarter and one of the adjoining quarters, and I shall carry to my grave the scars on my head of cuts received in one of these field combats, in which I refused to follow my party in flight, and took the onslaught of the whole vanguard of the enemy, armed with stones, and had my head pounded yellow, being only saved from worse by the intervention of the men of the vicinity. This fight gave me the unmerited reputation of courage and fighting power, and I was thereafter unmolested by the young roughs, though, in fact, I was timid to a degree and only stood my ground from nervous obstinacy; I never provoked a quarrel, and only revolted against a bully when the position became intolerable. I can remember the amazement of a companion older than myself, who had been in the habit of bullying me freely, until one day he went too far and I took him by the collar and shook and swung him till he was dizzy and begged for mercy, for of downright pugilistics I knew nothing, and a deliberate blow in the face with my fist in cold blood was a measure too brutal to enter into my mind.

The dreariness of this portion of my life was beyond description. The oppression of my sister-in-law at home, the severities of the teachers at school, and the exclusion from the influences of nature, in which I had so long lived without restraint, resulted in an attack of nostalgia which, when the coming of the first wildflowers brought it to a crisis, induced my brother to send me home.

My brother was attached to me, but the jealousy of his wife towards anybody who seemed to have any influence over him made it impossible for him to show any feeling even to me, for it brought on furious attacks of hysteria, to appease which he had sometimes to resort to humiliating devices. One day she became so excited that she fell into an extreme prostration and declared that she was dying. She had every indication, indeed, of approaching dissolution, and made her last dispositions, when my brother Charles, who was the family physician, seeing that the danger was real, assured her husband that unless some diversion of her humor was effected she would die. He advised exciting her jealousy, and her husband, accordingly, as if taking her dispositions for his conduct after her death, asked her what she thought of his marrying, in that contingency, a certain lady, whose name he mentioned, whereupon she rose in her bed in such a rage at the suggestion (the woman being her especial detestation) that she threw off all the symptoms of illness, and the next day went about the house as usual. This cure proved a grave misfortune to the whole family.

In spite of my aversion I was sent back to New York the next autumn for another winter's schooling. I landed from the steamer at the foot of Cortlandt Street two or three days after a great fire in New York, and I saw the ruins still smoking and the firemen playing on them. My baggage--a biscuit box, with my scanty wardrobe and a bag of hickory-nuts for my city cousins--I carried on my shoulders and walked the length of the city, my brother living in what was then farther New York, in Seventh Street, near the East River. At that time Fourteenth Street was the extreme limit of the city's growth, except for a few scattering residences. Beyond, and, on the East River side, even most of what lay beyond Seventh Street, was unreclaimed land. I sailed my toy boats on the salt marshes where Tompkins Square now is, and I used to shoot, botanize, and hunt for crystals all over the island beyond Thirty-Second Street, the land being sparsely inhabited. I discovered a little wild cactus growing freely amongst the rocks, and carried a handkerchief full of it home, getting myself well pricked by the spines, but to my botanical enthusiasm this was nothing in view of the discovery. Only here and there patches of arable land maintained small farm-houses, but the greater part of the surface of Manhattan Island was composed of a poor grazing land, interspersed with rolling ledges of bare granite, on which were visible what were then known as "diluvial scratches," which my brother Charles, who was an ardent naturalist, explained to me as the grooves made by the irruption of the deluge, which carried masses of stone across the broad ledges and left these scratches, then held widely as testimony to the actuality of the great deluge of Genesis. I think that we had to wait for Agassiz to show us that the "diluvial scratches" were really glacial abrasions, caused by the great glacier which came down the valley of the Hudson and went to sea off Sandy Hook. At this time my brother was making conchology his special study, and many holidays we spent on the harbor, dredging for shells, and great was our joy when he discovered a new species, which was named after him by the Lyceum of Natural History of New York.

The following year my fifth brother, Jacob, on leaving college, took charge of a school in the centre of New York State, built by the Sabbatarian community at large, in De Ruyter, a village of which many of the inhabitants were Sabbatarians, and it was decided that I should go there to follow my studies in preparation for college. I was to "board out" a debt which an uncle owed to my eldest brother, and which was uncollectible in any other way, and there I made my first acquaintance with semi-independent life, exchanging a home for a dormitory and a boarding-house. My uncle was to supply also my bedding, the academy being provided with bedsteads; but he was a heedless man, and I remember that I had to sleep six weeks on the bed-cords, with my wearing apparel as my only covering, before he awoke to the fact that I had a prepaid claim on him for mattress and bedding. But we were on the edge of a great forest, and in the almost primeval woodland I found compensation for many discomforts, and what time my tasks spared me was spent wandering there. The persistent apathy which had oppressed me for so many years still refused to lift, and my stupidity in learning was such that my brother threatened to send me home as a disgrace to the family. I had taken up Latin again, algebra, and geometry, and, though I was up by candlelight in the morning, and rarely put my books away till after ten at night except for meals, it was impossible for me to construe half of the lesson in Virgil, and the geometry was learned by rote. I at length gave up exercise to gain time for study, and my despairing struggles were misery. I was then fourteen, and in the seventh year of this darkness, and it seemed to me hopeless.

What happened I know not, but about the middle of the first term the mental fog broke away suddenly, and before the term ended I could construe the Latin in less time than it took to recite it, and the demonstrations of Euclid were as plain and clear as a fairy story. My memory came back so completely that I could recite long poems after a single reading, and no member of the class passed a more brilliant examination at the end of the term than I. At the end of the second term I could recite the whole of Legendre's geometry, plane and spherical, from beginning to end, without a question, and the class examination was recorded as the most remarkable which the academy had witnessed for many years. I have never been able to conceive an explanation of this curious phenomenon, which I record only as of possible interest to some one interested in psychology. Unfortunately, the academy failed to meet the expenses, and at the end of my second term the students dispersed to their homes, I going with great regret, for I enjoyed intensely this life on the edge of a large natural forest, through which ran a trout brook, and in which such wild woodland creatures as still survived our civilization were tolerably abundant. Amongst my fellow-students at De Ruyter was Charles Dudley Warner, with whom I contracted a friendship which survives in activity, though our paths in life have been since widely separated. I recall him as a sensitive, poetical boy,--

almost girlish in his delicacy of temperament,--and showing the fine *esprit* which has made him one of the first of our humorists. His "Being a Boy" is a delightful and faithful record of the existence of a genuine New England boy, which will remain to future generations as a paleontological record when the race of them is extinct, if indeed it be not so already.

Returning to Schenectady, I found that the family had begun to discuss the future of my career, which had arrived at the point of divergences. My father, who had no opinion of the utility of advanced education for boys in our station, was tenacious in his intention to have me in his workshop, where he needed more apprentices, but my mother was still more obstinate in hers that I should have the education; and in the decision the voices of my brothers were too potent not to hold the casting vote. In the stern, Puritanical manner of the family, I had been more or less the *enfant gate* of all its members, except my brother Paul, the third of my brothers, who, coming into the knowledge of domestic affairs at the time when the family was at its greatest straits, had expressed himself bitterly at my birth, over the imprudence of our parents' increasing their obligations when they were unable to provide for the education of the children they had already, and had always retained for me a little of the bitterness of those days. On the whole, the vote of the family council was for the education. My own wishes were hardly consulted, for I differed from both opinions, having an intense enthusiasm for art, to which I wished to devote myself.

The collective decision, in which my father and myself were alike overruled, was that I should go to Union College, in Schenectady, as the collegiate education was supposed to be a facilitation for whatever occupation I might afterwards decide on. This was, so far as I was concerned, a fatal error, and one of a kind far too common in New England communities, where education is estimated by the extent of the ground it covers, without relation to the superstructure to be raised on it. I had always been a greedy reader of books, and especially of histories and the natural sciences,--everything in the vegetable or animal world fascinated me,--and I had no ambition for academic honors, nor did I ever acquire any, but I passionately desired a technical education in the arts, and the decision of the family deferred the first steps in that direction for years, and precisely those years when facility of hand is most completely acquired and enthusiasm against difficulties is strongest--the years when, if ever, the artist is made.

That one of the gravest difficulties in our modern civilized life is the excessive number of liberally educated young men whose professional ambitions are, and can be, given no outlet, is now well recognized, and of these, many no doubt, like myself, are diverted from a natural bent to follow one which has no natural leading or sequence. It was very possible for a clever man three hundred years ago to learn all that science could show him without interference with the acquisition of the special knowledge required to fit him for the attainment of eminence in a technical study, or the technical mastery in the working it out, but now the range of a liberal education is so great that those who are required to take respectable rank in a specialty must devote themselves exclusively to it, during the years in which alone technical mastery is possible of acquirement. There will always be many to whom the devotion to study for study's sake is invincible, but the ranks of the brain-workers are so overcrowded that it is a great pity to force into them a man or woman who would be content to be a worker in another and humbler line, especially in those of the manual occupations which bring their happiness in the following of them. In my case the result of the imposed career was a disaster; I was diverted from the only occupation to which I ever had a recognizable calling, and ultimately I drifted into journalism, as the consequence of a certain literary facility developed by the exercises of the college course. The consequences were the graver that I was naturally too much disposed to a vagrant life; and the want of a dominant interest in my occupation led to indulgence, on every occasion that offered in later life, of the tendency to wander. I came out of the experience with a divided allegiance, enough devotion to letters to make it a satisfaction to occupy myself with them, but too much interest in art to be able to abandon it entirely. Before entering college, art was a passion, but when, at the age of twenty, the release gave me the liberty to throw myself into painting, the finer roots of enthusiasm were dead, and I became only a dilettante, for the years when one acquires the mastery of hand and will which make the successful artist were past.

It was decided that I should continue my preparation for college in the Lyceum of my native town, a quaint octagonal building in which the students were seated in two tiers of stalls, the partitions between which were on radii drawn from a centre on the master's desk, so that nothing the pupil did escaped his supervision.

The larger boys, some of whom were over sixteen, were in a basement similarly arranged with a single tier of desks, and I earned my instruction by supervising this room. I had here full authority so far as the maintenance of order was concerned and kept it, though some of the pupils were older than myself. I remember that one of them, about my own age and presumed strength, but himself convinced of his superiority, repeated some act which I had reprimanded him for, and as I knew that to allow it to pass unpunished was to put an end to my authority and position, yet did not feel competent or authorized to give him a regular flogging, I caught him by the collar and jerked him into the middle of the room, setting him down on the floor with force enough to bewilder him a little, and ordered him to sit there till I released him, and his surprise was such that he actually did not move till I told him to. I met no attempt to put my authority at defiance after that. A schoolfellow here and classmate in college was Chester A. Arthur, afterward President of the United States, a brilliant Hellenist, and one of the best scholars and thinkers in the class.

There were two associate principals at the head of the school, one for the classics, and the other for mathematics. Of the former I became a favorite on account of the facility with which I got on in his branches, and when the year was up I passed easily the examinations for entrance into college, and by his advice entered in the freshman year, though fairly well prepared to enter the sophomore with slight conditions. He was anxious that I should do him credit in college. But long before the term was out I found that the routine gave me hardly an occupation. I had already done all the mathematics of the year at De Ruyter, and the Latin and Greek came so easy that I found myself idle most of my time. I decided to try a fresh examination in order to gain a year by reentering as a sophomore. The faculty declared such a thing unprecedented and inadmissible, to which I replied that I would then go to another college and enter, quite oblivious of the fact that I had neither the means nor the consent of my family to leave its protection and go to another city. The classical principal of the Lyceum, who was also a tutor in the college, did what he could to dissuade me, but I persisted and offered myself for examination, and found him on the examining committee. He was really fond of me, and in my own interest wanted me to go through college with honors, but this was to me of trivial importance, compared with the abbreviation by a year of the captivity of college life. He punished me by putting me to read for examination a passage of Juvenal, which I had never opened, as it did not come in the course even of the sophomores, but I passed fairly well on it, and he, with a little irritation, gave me the certificate, saying that it was not for what I did, but for what he knew me to be capable of. So, conditioned by some trivial supplementary examinations on subjects which I do not remember, I went up a class.

The constitution of Union College, like most of the American schools of the highest grade at that time, differed from that of the English model in some respects very widely. The "University" of Union was completed by collegated schools for medicine, divinity, law, and technical education. The medical and law schools of Union were at Albany, the capital of New York State. Our college buildings were three--one, West College, in the town, for the freshman and sophomore classes, and two on the hill above the town, North and South colleges, for the juniors and seniors. As a large proportion of the students were young men to whom the expenses of the education were a serious matter, many prepared themselves at home to enter the junior class, so that a class which only numbered a score as freshmen, often graduated a hundred. Others, again, used to spend the winter term and vacations in teaching in the rural or "district" schools to pay the expenses of the other terms, and the majority of the graduates were of these classes of men, often adults on entering, so that the class gathered seriousness as it went on.

The freshmen and sophomores, delegated to the care of the junior professors and tutors, indulged in many of the escapades of juvenility for which university life in most countries is distinguished, and were continually brought under the inflictions of college discipline, and now and then some one was expelled. The favorite tricks of getting a horse or cow into the recitation rooms, fastening the tutors in their rooms just before the class hours, tying up, or stealing, the bell which used to wake the students and call them to prayers or recitations, with rare and perilous excursions into the civic domain, or a fire alarm caused by setting fire to the outhouses, which always brought down on us the wrath of the firemen, varied the monotony of the student life, as everywhere else; but as I roomed at home for the first year I never had part in these escapades, and in my sophomore winter I took a district school in one of the valleys tributary to that of the Mohawk, in which the town lies.

The community in which the school was situated was almost exclusively composed of Scotch Cameronians, of whom several families were the descendants of a then still vigorous patriarch of the sternest type of that creed. It was necessary to pass a special examination to get the State certificate necessary to teach a district school, and this I had passed, but had still to undergo the questioning of the trustees of the district, canny and cautious beyond the common. The wages for such a school were twelve dollars a month and "board around," i.e. staying at the houses of the parents a week for each pupil in turn, beginning with those in best estate, so that, as the school had never less than twenty or thirty pupils, the poorer families were never called on. One of the boys intended to go to college, and his father was willing to pay a special contribution to secure a teacher of Latin, and this brought my wages up to sixteen dollars a month. But the cautious Scots urged a conditional engagement,--a trial of one month,--a condition which, as I might have anticipated, would end the engagement with the month, considering the composition of the district and the usual difference of views among the people. The two most advanced and oldest of the pupils belonged to families bound together by the most cordial jealousy which a petty community could inspire, and one of these was my Latin pupil. His rival was a lazy student and a turbulent scholar, with whom I had difficulties from insubordination from the beginning. As, however, I had adopted the rule of depending entirely on moral suasion in the government of the school and refused to flog, but instead offered prizes for good behavior and studiousness at my own expense for each week, my confidence in the better qualities of human nature betrayed me from the beginning. The prizes went to stimulate the jealousies between the two leaders, and the only punishment I would inflict, that of sending the pupil home for disobedience, made domestic difficulties.

 The first week of the month I was boarded in the family of our patriarch, whose grandsons furnished a number of the pupils, and the life they led me was not one to make me regret the termination of the engagement. I was awaked while it was still night to join in family prayers, which were of a severity of which I had never dreamed. First a long selection of Psalms was read, then another long one sung, and then a prayer which, as I noticed by the clock, varied from ten to twelve minutes, through which, being still drowsy, I slept, being awakened by the family rising from their knees. This was the invariable routine gone through twice a day. As in our own family, with the exception of the Saturday morning family service, the devotions were always those of the closet, this tedium of godliness was a serious infliction. I was waked out of sound sleep, and bored through, before breakfast, by vain repetitions lasting on an average half an hour, after having endured the same for another half-hour before being allowed to go to bed. No escape was permitted even to the ill-willing, and it may easily be imagined that this addendum to the annoyances of my school hours made the position of the district schoolmaster one for which sixteen dollars a month was no compensation.

The conflicts in the school, if they gave me less tedium, were all the more acute. My Latin scholar was a lad who meant to profit by his opportunities and devoted himself to his studies, and, naturally, had a most cordial collaboration on my part, while the son of the rival citizen was both lazy and refractory, so that, with my system of inflicting no corporal punishments, he got none of the weekly prizes, and got such milder punishments as could be inflicted. To tell the truth, the pupils who were refractory to my system were few in proportion, and the school was a pleasanter place than if the rod had been always in hand, as in the days of my boyhood. But the month of trial did not elapse without signs of a storm brewing in the valley. My novel system of sparing the rod and spoiling the children could not fail to provoke the disapproval of the orthodox, and the head of the conspiracy was the father of my lazy schoolboy.

I left the valley for a visit home, on the last week of the month on Friday night, and started back on foot, a walk of fifteen or twenty miles, on Sunday afternoon, too late for convenience as I discovered in the event. That portion of the valley of the Mohawk, a broad and level plain, is bounded on the west by a range or ranges of hills divided by deep valleys running north and south, perpendicular to the course of the river, and in one of these valleys lay the township of Princeton, in the middle of which was the schoolhouse, the farms of the community being scattered over the hills around, and some of them at distances of a mile or two. It was the head of the glen, and the lay of the land was almost that of an amphitheatre, cannily chosen by the father of the colony, the old Cameronian whose prayers and long services grated so on my New England Puritanism. Before I turned out of the Mohawk valley into that of Princeton, the sun had set, with all the signs of a coming snowstorm, which broke on me suddenly in the glen with a furious north wind tearing down the gorge and drifting the snow as it fell, so that before I had gone a mile with the snow in my face, it was almost impossible to force my way against snow and wind. I wore a long Spanish cloak, such as was much in vogue then and there; wrapping my face in it so that only my eyes were free, I fought on, sometimes only able to walk backward from the cutting cold against my face and eyes, making very slow progress; but it was Sunday night, and the school must be opened at 9 A.M. on Monday. The snow gathered in drifts often up to my middle, with bare, wind-swept spaces between, and these drifts at times were crusted with wind-packed snow too hard to be waded through, and I was obliged to break the snow crust by throwing myself at full length on it. In this way I struggled on till ten at night, when I came to a solitary house by the roadside, at which I stopped to ask a night's lodging, for I could fight the weather no longer. The house was dark and the family asleep, but I was admitted. The bed given me was as cold as the snow outside, but it was luxury compared to some of the quarters I had in my school district. At one of the houses at which I had to take my turn, I remember that there had been, as an afterthought of the house architect, a door cut between the room I slept in and the farmyard, but, whether from indifference or inability, the door had never been put in, and a curtain which supplied its place and was intended to keep the snow out, did it so incompletely that I found in the morning--after a snowy night--that a heavy drift had formed between the opening and the bed. In this room, too, I shared the bed of the hired man, who was paid the same wages as mine, and in the eyes of the community was therefore in every way my equal.

On reaching the schoolhouse the next morning, I found gathered there not only a part of the scholars, but some of their parents,--including the trustees of the school,--and was not long in learning that my absence had been made use of by the disaffected of the district to depose me. We had a brief debate, not on the question whether I should go or not, but on the grounds of disaffection. The father of my lazy boy was, of course, the spokesman, and it seemed as if he resented his son's not being flogged, for want of discipline and partiality were the burden of his complaint. This gave me ample opportunity for a statement of my principles in instruction, and to say that his son was the laziest and most stupid boy in the school, and that instruction was wasted on him, and to contrast his progress and qualities with those of my Latin boy. It was malicious, I admit, but it was successful in infuriating the debate, and as I saw by the gathering that the majority had decided to avail themselves of the month's conditional engagement to dismiss me, I was quite indifferent to the discord I left behind me.

"It's all very fine for you," said my antagonist, whose Scotch I will not attempt to reproduce, "to sit up there on your desk and get your sixteen dollars a month, as if you were a hard-working man,"--to which I replied, "Perhaps you think you can come up here and earn it." As I was quite indifferent to the dismissal, and only did not avail myself of the privilege of going because I always had an obstinate way of sticking to a thing I had begun till it was finished, I made no attempt to conciliate, and it was with neither surprise nor serious annoyance that I received my notice of dismissal. The only things I had enjoyed, indeed, during the month, had been the walks through the dense forest from the farmhouses to the schoolhouse in the quiet sunshine of the winter mornings. The woods were more natural and older than those around my home, and there was a freshness in the early day which I never had realized so fully as in these morning walks to school, and I shall always remember the snowy silence of that forest, the first, on that scale, I had become familiar with.

But the poverty of the lives of these prosperous farmers was a revelation even to me, accustomed as I was to a domestic simplicity which would surprise modern Americans of any degree. New books were a luxury none of them indulged in; beyond the Bible and two or three volumes of general information, there was no reading except a weekly newspaper, and the diet was such as I had never been used to, even at De Ruyter. But for the vegetables of the farm, sailors at sea would fare better than these landsmen. In later years I boarded with one of the farmers in an adjoining valley, where I was engaged in painting a cascade of great beauty, and for the six weeks I lived in the family I saw only two articles of animal food--salt mackerel for breakfast and salt pork for dinner. The narrowness of intellectual range and the bigotry--political and religious--prevailing amongst them was such as I had in no experience ever encountered, even in the "straitest sect of the Pharisees," the Seventh Day Baptist Church of my youth. In the community in which I had grown, there was always the early influence of the sea to widen the range of thought and sympathy, but here, in the narrow valley to which the farmer was confined, neither nature nor religion seemed to have any liberating or liberalizing power. A sturdy independence was the dominant trait of character, but this independence was converted into a self-enslavement by the narrow range of thought which everywhere prevailed. The old Cameronian patriarch, in his sectarian exaltation, seemed almost a luminary in the intellectual twilight of that secluded community, and it was possible there to understand how even a narrow religious fanaticism could become an ennobling element in the character of a community living in such a restricted and materializing atmosphere. A few weeks in such a state of society enables one to understand better the irresistible attraction of cities and the life in the midst of multitudes to the rustic, born and raised in the back-water stagnation of a rural life like that of the farmers of my school district.

The remaining two months of the broken term of the college course and the better part of the vacation were spent in my father's workshop, where the work was rather pressing and the shop short-handed. My father's business was mainly the manufacture of certain mechanical implements for which he and his brother held the patents, and in the spring and autumn he was accustomed to carry the consignments of them to his customers in New York. His workshop was resorted to by several ingenious fellow New Englanders who had inventions to work out, and in the execution of these I was found useful. Among these was one Daniel Ball, whose specialty was locks, of which he invented, patented, and sold the patents of a new one every year, all worked out in my father's shop. Ball was a man of remarkable mechanical ingenuity and extraordinary profanity--of a savage temper, and very exclusive in his human sympathies; but he had a profound reverence for my father, of whom he used to say that "Old Joe Stillman was the only honest man God ever made," and I am inclined to think, looking back on a long life and wide experience in men of all classes and many nations, that Ball was justified in the esteem he held my father in, though admissibly wrong in his exclusiveness,--for I cannot recall, in all my memories of the old man, a single instance of his hesitating over the most trivial transaction in which a question of honesty was involved, and I have known him to relinquish his clear rights rather than to provoke a disagreement with a neighbor. He had a profound aversion to any ostentation of religious fervor, as had my mother. If he had lived to-day he would certainly have been an advanced evolutionist; even then his liberality in matters of doctrine and his unbounded charity towards all differences of opinion in religious questions used to cause my mother great anxiety as to his orthodoxy. He thought the fields and woods better places to pass the Sabbath in than a meeting-house, and this was a subject of great pain to her, the more that he developed the same feeling in me; but he never deferred in these matters to anybody, and never held a shade of that reverence for the clergy which was almost a passion in my mother's nature. While of an extreme tenderness of heart to all suffering or hardship outside the family, even towards animals, his domestic discipline was brutal and narrow. In the latter respect he was a survival of the old New England system; in the former, himself.

I had a parrot given me by one of my brothers returning from the Southern States, and the bird took an extravagant fondness for my father rather than for me. He was allowed to go free about the house and garden, and would go and sit on the fence when my father should be coming back from the workshop to dinner and supper, and run to meet his footstep long before he was in sight, chuckling and chattering with delight. Early one morning the parrot got shut, by chance, in the cupboard, and, attempting to gnaw his way out, was mistaken for a rat, and father took the shovel to kill him, while mother carefully opened the door so that the rat might squeeze his way out to be killed, but poor Poll got the blow instead, and had his neck broken. All that day my father stayed at home weeping for Polly, and no business misfortune in my recollection ever affected him as the death of the parrot did. He could flog me without mercy, but he could not see the suffering of a domestic or wild animal without tears, nor would he tolerate in us children the slightest tendency to cruelty to the least living thing.

I have alluded to the differences between him and my mother on the subject of education, the inutility of which, beyond a common-school standard, he made an article of faith, and the return to the workshop for the balance of the vacation, after my school-teaching failure, was the occasion of the final battle. As the vacation drew to an end, and the time which was still available for studying up the subjects of the last term, for the examination on reentering, approached its imperative limit, I notified him that I must stop work. He said nothing until I had actually given it up and gone back to my study, about two weeks before the examination day. Coming home from the shop that day to dinner, in a very bad humor, he asked me why I had not been at work. I replied that I had barely the time absolutely necessary to make up my arrears of study to enter college for the next term. Then he broke out on me with a torrent of abuse as an idle, shirking boy, who only cared to avoid work, ending with the accusation that all I wanted was to "eat the bread of idleness," a phrase he was very fond of. I suppose I inherited some of his inequality of temper, and I replied by leaving the table, throwing my chair across the room as I did so; and, assuring him that when I ate another morsel of bread in his house he would know the reason why, I left the house in a towering rage. Having forewarned him days before that I must go, without his making the least objection, and having postponed the step to the latest possible moment, out of consideration for the work in hand, I considered this treatment as ungenerous, and was indignant.

I do not think that, weighing all the circumstances of the case, one could say that my father was entitled to impose his authority in a purely arbitrary interference with a matter in which the family council had decided on my course, and which involved all my future, or that my refusal to obey an irrational command implies any disrespect to him. At all events, I decided at once that I would not yield in this matter, and I made my preparations to seek another home, even with a modification in my career. If I must abandon the liberal education, I would not waste my life in a little workshop with three workmen, and no opportunity to widen the sphere of activity, or opening into a larger occupation. If I should be obliged to leave the college, it should be for something in the direction of art, and in this light I did not much regret the change. I had not, however, calculated on my mother's tenacity, or the imperceptible domination she exercised over my father.

When I returned to the house to get my clothes and make my preparations for leaving home for good, I had a most painful scene with my mother, and it was the only serious misunderstanding I ever had with her. She went through, in a rapid resume, the history of my life, from the day when I was given her in consolation for the little brother before me, who died, with a word for each of the crises through which her care had carried me,--accidents, grave maladies, for I was apparently not a strong child, and at several conjunctures my life had been despaired of; all the story being told as she walked up and down rapidly in the chamber, with the tears running down her cheeks, and with a passionate vehemence I had never suspected her to be capable of, since she had the most complete self-restraint I ever knew in a woman. But it was an *impasse*--I neither could nor would go back from the career decided upon, nor would the family have consented, and to return to the workshop at my father's insistence was to lose everything. It seemed brutal to refuse mother's entreaties to ignore the collision of wills, and to go on as if nothing had happened, but to do this and remain in the house with my father, in the perpetual danger of another conflict, was impossible. The question had to be settled, and all I could do was to insist on father's making a distinct disavowal of any right or intention to demand my services in the shop at any future time, and leaving me free to follow the programme agreed on in the family council. It was in effect a frank apology that I wanted, but I knew him too well to suppose he would ever consent to make an apology in words, or to admit to me that he had made a mistake; and I left the solution in my mother's hands, with the understanding that the definite promise should be made to her, and I knew too that this would hold him as completely as if made to a public authority. Nothing could bring her to contradict him openly, and in all my life I never saw her make a sign of disrespect for his mastery in domestic things, but I knew that once this promise was made to her I could count on his being held to it sternly.

That evening the matter was settled, but of what had passed, or what was said, I never knew anything, for my mother never wasted words; and, while no apology was made, or any retraction expressed, neither my father nor myself ever alluded to the subject of my working in the shop again, nor did I ever, as before, go into it during the vacations, or offer to assist when affairs were hurried. The habit of asserting the paternal authority and the sense of it, in my father, were so strong that I never risked again reviving it.

CHAPTER IV
COLLEGE LIFE

I passed my examination and resumed my place in the class, but I never tried district school-teaching again. Entering upon my junior year I had a room in the north college. Each of the upper buildings--which properly should have been called halls--was divided into five sections, in effect separate residences, each being under the custody of one of the professors or tutors, who was responsible for order in the same, the two end sections of each of the colleges being an official residence for one of the senior professors with families. The rule required the students to be in their rooms after supper, but it was almost as much honored in the breach as in the observance, and, though the skylarking which resulted from the former often brought the section officer up, those who had any tact avoided too close an insistence on the regulations, so that the students in the same sections commonly visited each other in the evenings, and not infrequently those from the other sections came in.

Our quarters were of the simplest,--one room for two students, with one wide bed,--and there we lived and studied. At half-past five the bell rang to wake us, and half an hour later for prayers, the sleepy ones returning to sleep after the waking bell, and thrusting themselves into their clothes as they ran when the prayer-bell rang, to get to prayers before the roll-call was over. From prayers again we dispersed to the recitation rooms for the morning recitations, and then to breakfast, mostly in town. There were two boarding-houses, one at each end of the college walk, known as "North" and "South" halls and forming part of the architectural scheme of the institution, and here board was provided at somewhat lower terms than at the private boarding-houses in town, and of very much inferior quality. The price at the halls was, if I remember correctly, $1.25 a week for three meals a day, that in the town ranging from $1.50 to $1.75. Furnished rooms in the town cost 75 cents per week more, and a few favored or wealthier students had permission to room in them, but as a rule the undergraduates of Union were men of very limited means, on which account the president and founder of the college, Dr. Nott, had planned its regulations to facilitate the attendance of that class of students, and the rules were such as closely to restrict the students from any participation in the social life of the towns-people. The visits of the section officers to the rooms of the students were irregular, and the inquisition into the causes of absence so thorough, that few, not of the most reckless, cared to risk a visit to the town, half a mile from the upper buildings; and the old doctor's police was too good for men to escape detection in any serious indulgence in irregular hours.

Union was, at this epoch, and during the active life of the doctor, the third university of the United States, coming, in the general estimation and the number of its graduates, immediately after Yale, Harvard being then, as always, the first; and it owed its character and peculiar reputation to the strong and singular personality of its first president. I have, in the course of my life, become more or less acquainted with many able men, and Dr. Nott was the most remarkable of all the teachers I have ever known, considering the limitation of his position and profession,--that of a Presbyterian clergyman in a time when sectarian differences ran high, and his sect had no lead in public opinion. He had attained his position by the force of his character assisted by his extraordinary tact and eloquence, but unaided by patronage, and this at the beginning of the nineteenth century, a time when institutions were forming and nothing was settled in the character of society. The manual of public speakers which we used to draw on for the speeches in class recitations included, as one of the most brilliant examples, the doctor's oration on the death of Alexander Hamilton, killed in a duel with Aaron Burr, one of the earliest and the most prominent of the demagogues of America. I have not read the oration for fifty years; but, as I remember it, it was, in the fashion of the day, one of the most eloquent of all our readings.

As I was a favorite of the doctor in the last year of my course and for years after, and as no one has ever in my estimation done him justice, it is to me a debt of gratitude, as well as a matter of justice, to repair as best I may this neglect. No one but a pupil could ever have fairly estimated his force of character, and no pupil whose intercourse with him was not carried into the post-graduate years could measure the ability with which he advised, especially in political matters, with his old pupils. In the days of his activity, no institution in the country furnished so large an element to the practical statesmanship of the United States as did Union. Seward was one of his favorite pupils, and it is well known that, up to the period of the American Civil War, he never took a step in politics without the advice of the doctor. Having had a struggle with poverty in his own early life, Dr. Nott sympathized heartily with the poorer students, and a practical education was more easily gained at Union than was then possible at Yale or Harvard. Men were allowed to defer payment of the fees till later life when their means had increased; and, though there were no scholarships, there were many students whose burdens were so far alleviated by the regulations that an earnest man who was determined to take his degree and work his way if he must, needed never leave college unsatisfied.

The doctor's reading of character and detective powers were barely short of the miraculous, and his management of refractory students became so well known that many who had been expelled from the other universities were sent to Union and graduated with credit, so that the college acquired the nickname of "Botany Bay." There came to him once for admission a student expelled from Yale for persistent violation of the regulations, and naturally without the letter which by general usage was required from the president of one university to another, certifying the good standing of the student. The president of Yale wrote to the doctor to ask "if he meant to take that scoundrel into his college." The doctor, who had made a rapid examination of the man, replied, "Yes, and make a man of him." In one of my post-graduate years, when I was staying with the doctor, he told me the story of this man. He had estimated his character at a glance correctly, and saw in him a mismanaged student. He was admitted unconditionally, as if he had come with the best of characters, and for a time he justified the confidence reposed in him. But the uneasy nature one day broke out, and he committed a gross violation of the rules. The discipline of the doctor began always with a friendly conversation, and with some men ended with it, for he knew so well how to paint the consequences of expulsion that it sufficed; but on the entry of this student into his library, he saw on looking at him that he "had the devil in his eye." He had, in fact, said to his roommate on getting the summons to the interview, "If the doctor thinks he is going to break me in he'll find himself mistaken." The doctor had a curious kind of vision which made it impossible to say which of the persons in the room he was looking at, and when, while seeming to be engaged on his book, he had looked into the eyes of the student, and saw that the light of battle was kindled in them, he waited for a little, and then, as if preoccupied, said to him in his most kindly tone, "I am very much occupied at this moment, my son; won't you come in to-morrow evening?" The young man went back to his room already half conquered by the affectionate manner, but the important point gained in the doctor's tactics was that the psychological moment of combat in the student had been reached and could not be kept up for a day, and when on the next evening the interview took place, his combativeness had given place to perplexity and complete demoralization. In this state the doctor gave him a paternal lesson on the consequences to his future life of the rebellion against necessary discipline and of persistent disorderly conduct, but without any actual reproof or mention of his offense, and all in his invariably kindly tone as if it were a talk on generalities, and then dismissed him to think it over. He had established cordial relations with the rebel, and from that day had no trouble with him, and he graduated at the head of his class.

And the doctor understood men so well that he never wasted his trouble on those who had nothing in them, but let them drift through the course unnoted. Expulsions were very rare, and the secret police of the university was so competent that the almost absolute certainty of detection generally deterred the men from serious infractions of the rules. The government seemed to be based on the policy of giving an earnest man all the advantages to be got out of the institution, and getting the indifferent through the course with the least discredit. In a state of society in which the collegiate standing was of importance to a man's career, this condition of things would have been a grave objection to the college, but in our western world the degree had very little importance, and the honors no effect on the future position. Most of the prominent men of our past had not even been through any university, and in politics it was often rather an obstacle than a recommendation that a man was a "college man." What the doctor tried to do, then, was to make a man when he found the material for one, and to ignore the futile intellects. This was the scheme of the education at Union when I was there, and it rarely failed to find the best men in the class and bring them forward.

Our college life may have been to the men of sufficient means more largely supplied with the elements of excitement, but for the poorer students there was little romance in it. Now and then a demonstration against an unpopular professor, a "bolt," i.e. abstention *en masse* from a recitation; or a rarer invasion of the town and hostile demonstration gave us a fillip, but the doctor had so well policed the college and so completely brought under his moral influence the town, that no serious row ever took place in my time. Later he told me how he managed one of the worst early conflicts, in which the students on one side of the college road, and the town boys on the other, were arrayed in battle order, determined to fight out the question who were the better men. The doctor had early notice of the imminent row, and, fetching a circuit behind the "town," encouraged the boys on that side with assurances of his impartiality and even his satisfaction with a little punishment of the students, if they were aggressive. "But," said he, "don't begin the fight and put yourselves in the wrong. If my boys come over, thrash them well, but let them strike the first blow." Having put them in the strongest defensive attitude, believing that they had the doctor with them, he went round to the students and applied the same inducements to the defensive, leaving them under the persuasion that he entirely approved their fighting, and then he went home and left them to their conclusions. As time passed and neither took the offensive, they all cooled off and went home.

The tact with which he dealt with the occasional outbreaks in the college was very interesting. If it was a case of wanton defiance of the habitual order, there was a very slight probability of its being overlooked. A favorite prank of the stealing of the college bell was invariably punished, first by having a hand-bell rung a little earlier than regulation hours all through the sections; and, when his secret police had discovered the offenders, they were punished according to custom, never very severely, but sufficiently so to make them feel humiliated. But the mystery of his police was never explained, and we were always at a loss to conjecture how he discovered the most elaborately concealed combinations, so that suddenly, even weeks after, when the culprits thought they had finally escaped detection, he would announce at prayers that they were to come to his study to explain. If the outbreak, however, had been in any way justified by an arbitrary or unwise act of discipline by any of the professors, he used to ignore it altogether.

The professor of mensuration, a fussy and consequential little fellow, a volunteer on the staff, and a man of singularly slight knowledge of young men, very fond of showing his authority, especially at the public examinations at the end of the term, had incurred the wrath of the class and become the butt of all its practical jokes. Having boasted one evening in society of the town that the students dared not rebel against him, and the boast coming to their knowledge, not a single student presented himself at the recitation next morning. The next day he was greeted with such disorder that it was necessary to suspend the exercises, and one of the most violent demonstrators finished by throwing a huge wooden spoon at him, which, hitting him on the head, ended the row. His public examinations were the most severe we had to go through, and often quite needlessly so, in order to impress the visitors with his own knowledge rather than with ours, and as the end of a term drew near, I think in my last junior term, a conspiracy was got up to put him ***hors de combat*** for that examination. It was decided to take him out of his room in the section (he was section officer in my own section) and bring him into the pine woods in the rear of the college, and there, unless he solemnly promised to stay away from his class examination, to cut off his hair and tar his head first, then crop his beard, and, if he was still refractory, to strip him (it was midsummer) and tie him to a tree and leave him all night, under the conviction that he would not show himself at examination after that experience.

In the small hours, the conspirators, provided with a duplicate key to the professor's door, made a stealthy attempt to open it, but found his key on the inside and were unable to open the door, but woke the victim, who, however, dared not raise an alarm. One of the smaller students tried to climb in through the ventilator, but this was nailed down, and then as a last resort the "smoking machine" was brought into action. This was an "infernal machine," employed in hazing students who had in any way offended the opinion of the class, especially by indecorous subservience to the authorities or informing against their fellow students. The latter was a rare offense and never pardoned. The smoking machine consisted of a short length of stove-pipe with a nozzle at each end, into one of which was introduced a bellows, and the other was put through the keyhole of the door of the offender. In the body of the pipe was a bed of lighted charcoal, and on this was sprinkled tobacco and assafoetida, and the smoke was driven into the room in such quantities that no human being could resist it more than a few minutes. The smoking was continued for ten minutes, when, as the professor did not surrender, it began to be feared that the joke had gone too far, and two of the conspirators went out to see if there were any external signs of vitality, and found that the victim had opened his window and was lying with his head below the window-sill so as to be out of the smoke which poured out over him. I suppose that the delegates were drunk, for one of them threw a block of wood at the professor's head which, missing him, drove in the window pane and finished the experiment.

It was the gravest outrage of my time, and had there not been so large a part of the senior class implicated in the conspiracy, directly or indirectly, there is no doubt that the doctor would have taken the most severe measures for the punishment of those concerned. No partial punishment would have been possible, and the general irritation against that particular professor was so great in the class, and his course had been so little in conformity with the usages of the college, that the doctor thought best to ignore the affair completely. The professor was completely cowed, and we had no more browbeating from him. But the practical jokes played on him were never attempted with any other member of the faculty, all of them having been trained in the doctor's own school. Except possibly the oldest of them, all were graduates at Union under him; and his system of elastic, unceasing pressure, constant and unobtrusive surveillance, and simple appeals to the students' higher interests and manly feeling were so generally potent in the government of the college that the petty tyranny of the mensuration professor, nicknamed "Geodesy," found no support in the faculty, though the same elastic system which threw the responsibility of final results on the individual left him the same freedom of action which it gave us, and he had to learn his lesson while he taught us ours.

The students mostly joined one or other of a large number of secret societies, mainly social and never scholastic, which had, almost without exception, originated at Union, spreading to other universities by migration or initiation of their members. The distinction most sought for by ambitious students, the marshalship of the "commencement" ceremonies,--i.e. the conferring of degrees, speech-making, etc., of the graduating class,--was an elective office and voted for by all the members of the class, so that, for this position of a day, scholarship was only of secondary importance, the personal popularity of the candidates determining the election. The societies grouped themselves in two parties, the most popular man in each party was its candidate, and the canvassing ran more or less actively through the senior year, occupying largely the attention of the students. These societies were in general boyish imitations of the Freemasons, though the most eminent, the Phi Beta Kappa, was an old and dignified institution, having been founded in 1776, at William and Mary College, whence it soon spread to Harvard and Yale, eventually establishing itself in most of the principal colleges of the country; at Union, under the control of the faculty, it became the high literary distinction of the class, only the third of the class with the highest collective record being admitted at graduation. Each of the societies had its secrets, its secret meetings, its grip and passwords, and it always seemed to me, though I was early initiated into one which had a distinguished record and literary reputation, that it was a folly and a waste of the energies of the students. Opposed to them all was an anti-secret society, and this, like the others, was known by the initials of the secret name, which was supposed to be Greek and to indicate, mysteriously, the character of the society. Students at the earliest date, generally in the first weeks of attendance, were thoroughly canvassed by the members of these societies, and invited, in accordance with their characters, to enter one or the other, those of a studious tendency finding most favor with that to which I was invited, and which consisted mostly of poor and studious men, others according to their social standing or wealth, or even their tendency to a wild life.

Besides this we had a house of representatives for the juniors and a senate for the seniors, over which two of the senior professors presided, knowing the rules of the respective branches of Congress, and requiring their observance in the debates, which echoed the grave political questions of the day. There was no lecturing system, and there was no such thing known as coaching; and the recitations consisted, like those in the juvenile schools, in answering questions taken from the lesson in standard textbooks, and called out no special abilities in the students which could distinguish the men of mark from the merest bookworms. There were men who never read the lesson and depended on being prompted by a friend. One of these derelicts, the son of a famous brewer, gave us a laugh which no member of the class can have forgotten. He was known for drinking enormous quantities of his father's beer and sleeping even in class; and when the question put him was, "Who was the reputed inventor of poetry amongst the Greeks?" he had no answer till the man behind him whispered, "Orpheus." He caught it badly, and roared, "Morpheus." The laugh that followed stopped recitation for ten minutes. A laugh in a large class had a curious way of going on indefinitely.

Until we reached the senior year, and came under the direct care of the old doctor, there was nothing in the course to awaken special ambitions. The honors, determined chiefly by the marks given at the end of the term, being mainly the reward of a diligence rather stupid than otherwise, as a rule were regarded with great indifference, and, for the most part, fell to the men who "poled" most assiduously, and got the best marks for attention, diligence, and correct recitation of the set tasks. As I look back on the life and work of that period, it seems to me that it was most unintelligently spent, and when I reached my senior year, and came under the direct stimulus of Dr. Nott, I recognized that, so far as the true education was concerned, I had wasted two years, and had I been master of my future I should have been inclined to go back to the beginning and repeat the three years' course of study under the new light, and with a recognition of the purpose of higher study, for I saw that all that I had gained was little more than parrot learning. The doctor indeed tried to make us think, and he used to say that the textbook was a matter of entire indifference, and that he would as soon have a book of riddles as Kames's "Elements of Criticism," so long as he could make us think out our conclusions. With him our recitations were a perpetual contest of our wits against his; he showed us the shallowness of our acquisitions, and dissected mercilessly both textbook and the responses to the questions which he had drawn from it, admitting nothing and pushing the pupil perpetually into the deeper water as soon as he began to think his foot had touched firm land. The first term under the doctor brought up every intellectual faculty I possessed, and I suppose it was to this intense appreciation of his leading that I owed his friendship and partiality in the following years. So far as the influence of school can go, I owe to him the best of my education, and especially the perception of the meaning of the word itself. In the senior year I turned back in my life and sought not to hasten, but to linger in the precincts of study, and the imperious necessity of getting to the only occupation which would give me the independence I desired, alone deterred me from a post-graduate course of study to compensate for the inadequacy of the past years.

In entering the church, Dr. Nott had deprived the world of a statesman of no ordinary calibre, but in the eyes of the Protestant, as of the Catholic Church, in the country which had its precedents to make, as in that which had precedents a thousand years old, the maxim, "once a priest always a priest," kept him in the pulpit, to which he had no irresistible call, and to which the accident of his career only had led him. Had the church to which he belonged been organized with an episcopal government, he had certainly been its primate; but in the vague and incoherent condition of the Congregational churches, to one of which he belonged, there was no career beyond that of the isolated pastorate of a single congregation. In this insufficiency of interest for an active and influential life there was only the educational calling left to satisfy his enormous mental activity, and in this he found his place. The future, which may look for his record in libraries, or in the results of research, scientific or literary, will not find him to occupy a position. He had, however, great mechanical inventive powers, as well as a marvelous knowledge of human nature; the former solved the problem, amongst others, of anthracite coal combustion for American steamers. In the latter lay his qualifications as the greatest teacher of young men of his generation.

Nobody could know him except the pupils to whom he disclosed himself, and to whom his kindly and magnanimous nature was unreservedly open, and they were few, and the list is fast being canceled; when we are gone, no one will ever comprehend how he could have been what he was. But the power he always exercised over his favorite boys was extraordinary; any of us would have done anything permitted to human nature to satisfy his wish. An instance of his influence, occurring later in my life, will illustrate his power over his old pupils. When, several years subsequent to my graduation, and on the election of Lincoln as President, I had used what influence I could enlist with the government (my brother being a prominent Republican) to get the appointment as consul to Venice, which was generally given to an artist, the principal petition in my favor went from Cambridge. It was written by Judge Gray (now on the Supreme Court bench), headed by Agassiz and signed by nearly every eminent literary or scientific man in Cambridge, but it lay at the Department of State more than six months, unnoticed. In the interim the war broke out and I had gone home from Paris, where I was then living, to volunteer in the army; but, being excluded by the medical requirements, and the ranks being full,--800,000 volunteers being then enrolled,--I turned to my project for Venice, and wrote a word to Dr. Nott, recalling his promise of years before to use his influence in my favor, if ever it were needed. He inclosed my letter, with one containing an indorsement of it, and sent it to Seward, the Secretary of State, and the appointment--not to Venice, which had just been given to Howells, but to Rome--came by return of post.

Union was then the only university of importance not under some form of denominational control, and for this reason had, perhaps, more than the usual share of extreme liberalism, or atheism, as it was at that time considered amongst the students; and one of my classmates, a man a couple of years older than myself, and of far more than the average intellectual power, made an active propaganda of the most advanced opinions. He also introduced Philip James Bailey's "Festus" to our attention, and for a time I was carried away by both. The great revulsion from my previous straitened theological convictions was the cause of infinite perplexity and distress. Up to that time nothing had ever shaken me in my orthodox persuasions, and the necessity of concealing from my mother and family my doubts and halting faith in the old ideas made it all the more perplexing. I had to fight out the question all alone. It was impossible to follow my classmate so completely as to accept his conclusions and become the materialist that he was, and so find a relative repose; and the conflict became very grave. The entire scheme of Christianity disappeared from my firmament; but, in the immediately previous years, I had been a reader of Swedenborg, and I held immovably an intuition of immortality,--or, if the term intuition be denied me, the conviction that immortality was the foundation of human existence, grounded in my earliest thoughts, and as clear as the sense of light,--and this never failed me. In this respect Swedenborg helped my reason in its struggle, though I could never see my way to the entire acceptance of his doctrine.

My dogmatic theological education had been entirely incidental, for my mother never discussed dogmas or doctrines, but the simple duties and promises of religion, and my intelligence had never been, therefore, so kept captive as to make release grateful. Christianity had never been a doctrinal burden to me, or any form of belief inconsistent in my mind with true Christianity. In my mother's thought there was only one thing utterly profane, and that was self-righteousness. And there happened to me in this conjuncture, what has in my later life been often seen, that the modification of religious views imposed on us by the superior force of another mind--a persuasion of what seems to be truth as it is only seen by others' vision--could not hold its own against the early convictions, and that a revulsion to the old faith was sooner or later inevitable and generally healthy. The epidemic passed, and, though it gave me great distress for the time, it made my essential religious convictions stronger in the end. It is, I think, Max Mueller who says that no man can escape from the environment of his early religious education. I have seen, in my experience of life and men, many curious proofs of that law, men who have lived for many years in the most absolute rejection of all religions, returning in their old age to the simple faith of childhood, ending as they began. The change of religious convictions which holds its own against all influences is that which comes from the healthy evolution of our own thought. At any rate, in my own case, the rationalistic revolution completed its circle and brought me back to that simple faith to remain in which is a reproach to no man, and the departure from which, to be healthy, must be made on lines conformed to our better natures. I felt the better for my excursion into new regions, and the freedom of movement I acquired I never lost.

As I am telling the story of a phase of human life in which the study of the religious character will be to some readers, perhaps, one of the chief subjects of interest, and as to me the whole subject is now purely objective, as a mental phenomenon in the life of another man would be, I am tempted to tell a romantic incident of this period of my evolution, because it illustrates clearly the state of mind and sentiment developed by the peculiar education and surroundings of my youth. In one of the winter vacations of my course, my brother Paul, who was an ardent and sanguine proselyter in the Seventh-Day doctrine, charged me with an expedition up the Mohawk valley as a colporteur, to distribute Sabbath tracts, and, occasion arising, to discuss, with those who offered, the doctrine involved. The snow was deep, and, wading in it from house to house in all the towns as far as Utica, I finished with a visit to the home at Whitestown, near by, of my old friend the former preceptress of the De Ruyter Academy, with whom I had always been a favorite, and who had taught me French (very little) and drawing (very little more), but who was a charming and poetical creature. I had not heard of her for years, and the latest news was that she had become insane through a cruel disappointment in love,--her lover having wantonly, and without offering a pretext, broken off the engagement just before the wedding day,--and had been sent to a lunatic asylum. I found her at home, a wretched shadow of her old self, listless, and in a settled melancholy, which the doctors said was incurable. She had in fact been discharged from the asylum as a hopeless lunatic, though the violent phase of the insanity had passed. It occurred to me that a diversion to old times would awaken her again to a sense of the present, and I tried to draw her back to the academy life by talking of it as if nothing had happened. That something unwonted was passing in her mind soon became evident, and finally she burst out with, "Why, Willie" (she had always so called me in the old times), "didn't you know I had been crazy?" The manner, the suddenness of the conflict between old associations and her present state, the mingling of our old affection, for I had in my boyhood held her very dear, as she had me, so overpowered me that I burst into tears, and she threw her arms around me and kissed me again and again. What the feeling which sprang up on her part was I could never quite understand,--doubtless it was partly the delight of a sudden relief from the old, monotonous pain, the unexpected unbending of a tense and overborne mind and momentary obliteration of the dreary immediate past, and partly the outburst of a passionate temperament which I had never suspected; but on my part there arose an attachment as chivalric as ever a knight of Arthur's time felt, yet perfectly platonic. That she was nearly old enough to have been my mother did not in the least matter--it was no question of love as young folks feel it; but in my heart I offered myself a bearer of her sorrows. I had only recently recovered from my wandering into the wilderness of doubt, and my religious faith was as vivid as when I had been at my mother's knee--Providence ruled, and God answered prayer. This phase of my life, juvenile as I now perceive it to be, I respect as the most honest in it. I honor the weakness as I cannot always what seems the later strength. Those who read my life may put the estimate on it which suits their creed; I only speak of it as a phenomenon of my Puritan youth. I prayed earnestly that I might take on myself her afflictions, if so she might be healed and come back to her right mind. That was Friday night, for her family were "Seventh-Day keepers," and I had gone to pass the Sabbath with them, so I stayed two days, continuing my devotions earnestly. On Monday I went back to my colportage, but that night I was taken with a sharp attack of bronchitis, with high fever, and obliged to keep my room at the hotel. The next day, finding the matter serious, I sallied out and returned to the house of her parents, and remained there while the attack lasted. A naturally strong constitution was my safety, and made light of what was really a sharp attack of acute trouble, which kept me in the house a considerable time, the care and happy charge of my friend.

What any physician of minds would have foreseen took place. She found in the attention to her patient the diversion from all the train of past preoccupations, and forgot in this absolutely novel situation the old trouble. To the delight of the family she began to take an interest in the affairs of the house, and, though for years she had utterly neglected the most trivial attention to her dress and personal appearance, and had shown such a determinedly suicidal disposition that her mother had been obliged to sleep in the same bed with her to be able to watch her effectively, she now became bright and cheerful and seemed her old self again. From that time forward she rapidly recovered, and when I went back to college we began a close correspondence which was the beginning of my real literary education, for her taste in literature was excellent, if a little sentimental, and her criticisms were so sound that in some respects they have never lost their effect on my way of thinking and expressing thought. She was persuaded to come to Schenectady and pass the period of my next vacation in our family. Her insanity absolutely disappeared, she returned to healthy activity in her old vocation as teacher, and the year after, to my great annoyance, married her former fiance. I was angry with her, not for marrying, but for marrying him after his shameful treatment of her. She seemed to me, and to her family also, to have thrown herself away on a man who had proved himself utterly unworthy any woman's devotion. All my chivalry, too, seemed wasted, and the only result of the experiment was the dissipation of an ideal, the naive expectation of the vicarious penalty to which I had in my sincerity offered myself having passed away. Convinced, that I had cured her, I was indignant at having cured her for him, but I suffered no visitation of contempt for women, and my indignation was the deepest feeling that remained from the experience, except the literary impulse born of the persistent effort to interest her in my correspondence and the consequent search for material for letters in the details of college life and the nature around us; and the habit of noticing and memorizing what might be of interest to others in the most trivial incidents of life never quite left me. I became a profuse letter-writer from inclination, and, though all the letters of that part of my life and for years after were recalled and burnt scrupulously, I am convinced that what literary ability I possess is in a great degree owing to the impulse I received in that romantic attachment.

What was, perhaps, more important, was that the vicarious offering of myself, made in my morbid enthusiasm, and the commonplace result of it, hastened the end of that phase of my religious experience. It was only because my boyhood had been frozen up in those seven years of apathy and began to thaw out in later years, when manhood should have been taking the reins, that all that passage of childhood and unsophisticated devotion intruded in the wrong place, to fill up the void in the formation. My religious status, as well as my conception of life, were only advanced to where they should have been at an earlier period.

Atheism was at that time beginning to work strongly among the students, and in opposition to it there began an antagonistic evangelical movement, with prayer-meetings amongst those religiously inclined. In my class, at this time, were several who became in after life eminent in clerical activity, and amongst them were the brothers Nevius, distinguished in the missionary service in the far East. I had no liking for the prayer-meetings of the students, but I joined the movement for holding religious services in the city almshouse, a primitive institution which had no chaplain, and where were sent not only the incurably poor and the incurably sick, but the idiots and half-witted, as well as the temporarily incapacitated poor, who would have been, in a better and more complete social organization, sent to a hospital, which did not exist in Schenectady. With several other students and two or three young ladies of the city we held services at the "poorhouse" every Sunday. Short exhortations with prayers and the singing of hymns composed the service, and I remember that one day, in giving out a hymn in long metre, I started it to a short metre tune, and had to go through it alone, the ladies whose business was the musical part of the service not being able to accommodate their measure to my leading. I made my solo as short as possible, and finished with the ill-suppressed giggling of the girls, but my audience of poor cripples and weak-minded were equally impressed.

No doubt the struggles with Festus and my atheistic friend, and the partial influence of the ambient, the sincere piety of the old doctor, which dominated the life of the college, helped to strengthen the reaffirmation of my orthodox Christianity, and, for several years after, I had no more question of the divine authority of the tenets of our church, including the Seventh Day Sabbath, than I had of the laws of nature; but the truly spiritual character of my mother's religion saved me from becoming a bigot. If I had been trained in the dogmas of Christianity, I have no doubt I should have then become an atheist. Nor was I a prig. I must confess that I enjoyed the occasional larks in which my classmates sometimes led and sometimes followed me, as well as any of them. Our Greek professor, Doctor R., was a bit of a snob, and the plebeians of the class, much the largest part, always held him in ill will; and as his garden bordered on our section, and his fowls roosted in the trees overhanging the green, we one day decided to mulct him in a supper. That night a party of the students of the section scaled the fence (I well remember tearing my trousers in climbing it) and wrung the necks of four of his fowls, which we sent into town next morning to be roasted, and which, accompanied by sundry mince-pies and a huge bowl of eggnog, made us a luxurious supper next midnight, the fragments being carefully--bones and bits of pie-crusts included--deposited at the professor's front door before daylight of next day, which happened to be Sunday. The package, carefully made up and directed like an express parcel, was addressed to him in all the fullness of formality, but it had rained in the interval, and when in the morning the servant took it up, on opening the door, the wet paper broke and the remnants of the feast bestrewed the doorway. The boy afterwards told me that the profanity of the professor was terrible to hear, and as he cut me two in my report of the Greek that term, I always suspected that he comprised me in the execration. As it happened the cut was undeserved, for there were few men in the class who did their Greek better than I, and the cut cost me the Phi Beta Kappa, which went to all the class whose aggregate marks made an average per term of 98 1/2, mine being 98 1/4. But as he always held me in disrespect on account of my father's occupation, and as assiduously paid court and gave good reports to the sons of wealthy men, there was a mutual aversion. He gave *max*. that term to the son of a famous quack doctor, who always came to me to be crammed for the recitation, while I got 98. Naturally we had little respect for the marking.

Of my college course, I retained only what held my sympathies. I never went in for honors, or occupied myself beyond the required measure with studies which did not *per se* interest me. Greek and Latin, but especially physics, the humanities, and literature enlisted all my ambitions, and the little weekly paper which was read at the meetings of our secret society occupied me more than was in due measure perhaps. I took my degree of course, but not with distinction. The majority of the family having, prior to my graduation, gathered at or near New York city, my father and mother, having attained their object in remaining in Schenectady, moved to New York, and I, finally liberated for the study of art, gave myself seriously to that end.

CHAPTER V
ART STUDY IN AMERICA

During the time of my preparation for entry to college, a wandering artist had happened to find his way to Schenectady, one of the restless victims of his temperament, to whose unrest fate had given other motives for change than his occupation. He was an Englishman by the name of John Wilson, a pupil of the brothers Alfred and Edward Chalons, fashionable London miniature painters of the early part of the century. In years long gone by he had established himself at St. Petersburg as a portrait painter, but, losing his wife and two children by a flood of the Neva, which occurred during his momentary absence in England, he abandoned Russia and went to one of the Western States of America and gave himself up to agriculture. Here fate found him again, and, after losing another wife and other children, he became a wanderer, interested in everything new and strange. He had been taken by Pitman's then new phonography, and his chief occupation at that time was teaching it wherever at any school he could form a class. He came to Union College, to this end, and had been recommended to my mother for board and lodging, and she gladly availed herself of the opportunity to get for me lessons in drawing in return for his board. He was a constitutional reformer, a radical as radicalism was then possible, had become an atheist with Robert Dale Owen, indignant at the treatment accorded him by destiny, and was *au fond* an honest and philanthropic man. He taught me the simplest rudiments of portrait and landscape in water-color, and of perspective, of which he was master, and, as he failed to find a field for his phonographic mission, I got up a small class in drawing for him, and after our dozen lessons he went his way to new regions and I never heard from him again. What he taught me I soon lost, except the perspective.

A little later, and while at work in my father's shop, there came in for a piece of ironwork our local artist, a man of curious artistic faculties, a shoemaker by trade, who had taught himself painting and had made himself a certain position as the portrait painter of the region. He desired to make for himself a lay-figure, and for the articulations had conceived a new form of universal joint, which he desired my father to put into shape. My father refused the job, as out of the line of his work, and I volunteered to take it, stipulating for some instruction in painting in return. The joint did not answer when worked out, but the friendship between Sexton and myself lasted through his life, and a truer example of the artistic nature never came under my study. All that he knew of painting he got from books, save for an annual visit to the exhibition of the American Academy at New York, but his conception of the nature of art was very lofty and correct, and had his education been in keeping with his natural gifts, he would have taken a high position as a painter. His was one of the most pathetic lives I can recall--a fine sensitive nature, full of the enthusiasms of the outer world, with rare gifts in the embryonic state and mental powers far above the average, limited in every direction, in facilities, in education in art and in letters, and having his lot cast in a community where, except the wife of President Nott, there was not a single person who was capable of giving him sympathy or artistic appreciation. Not least in the pathos of his situation was the simplicity and humility with which he accepted himself, with his whole nature yearning towards an ideal which he knew to be as unattainable as the stars, without impatience or bitterness towards men or fate. If he was not content with what was given him, no one could see it, and he was so filled with the happiness that nature and his limited art gave him that he had no room for discontent at the limitations.

Happy days were those in which my leisure gave me the opportunity to share this man's walks and make my crude sketches of his favorite nooks and bends of our beautiful river Mohawk, and listen to his experiences while he worked. I can see now that it was more nature than art that evoked my enthusiasms, and that in art I felt mainly the expression of the love of the beauty of nature. Sexton gave me some idea of the use of oils, and from that time most of my leisure hours and my vacant days were given to painting in an otherwise untaught manner, copying such pictures as I could borrow, or translating engravings into color--wretched things most certainly, but to me then, with my crude enthusiasm, productive of greater pleasure than the better productions of later years.

The three years of my college course had left me little room or leisure for such studies, and at the end of them I realized that so far as the object I had set before me was concerned, I had wasted the years and blunted the edge of my enthusiasms. In preparation for the career which I proposed to myself I had, however, been in correspondence with Thomas Cole, then the leading painter of landscape in America, and an artist to this day unrivaled in certain poetic and imaginative gifts by any American painter. He was a curious result of the influence of the old masters on a strongly individual English mind, inclined to nature worship, born in England in the epoch of the poetic English school to which Girtin, Turner, and their colleagues belonged, and migrating to America in boyhood, early enough to become impressed by the influence of primitive nature as a subject of art. Self-taught in technique and isolated in his development, he became inevitably devoted to the element of subject rather than to technical attainment, and in the purely literary quality of art he has perhaps been surpassed by no landscape painter of any time. His indifference to technical qualities has left him in neglect at present, but in the influence he had on American art, and for his part in the history of it, he remains an important individuality now much underrated. It was settled that I should become his pupil in the winter following my graduation, but a few months before that he died.

At that moment there was not in the United States a single school of art, and except Cole, who had one or two pupils when he died, there was no competent landscape painter who accepted pupils, nor perhaps one who was capable of teaching. Drawing masters there were here and there, mostly in the conventional style adapted to the seminaries for young ladies. Inman, the leading portrait painter of the day, had taken pupils, but his powers did not extend to the treatment of landscape, and my sympathies did not go beyond it. I applied to A.B. Durand, then the president of our Academy, the only rival of Cole, though in a purely naturalistic vein, and a painter of real power in a manner quite his own, which borrowed, however, more from the Dutch than from the Italian feeling, to which Cole inclined. Durand was originally an engraver of the first order, and afterwards a portrait painter, but his careful painting from nature and a sunny serenity in his rendering of her marked him, even in the absence of imaginative feeling, as a specialist in landscape, to which he later gave himself entirely. His was a serene and beautiful nature, perfectly reflected in his art, and he first showed American artists what could be done by faithful and unaffected direct study of nature in large studies carefully finished on the spot, though never carried to the elaboration of later and younger painters. But he was so restrained by an excess of humility as to his own work, and so justly diffident of his knowledge of technique, that he could not bring himself to accept a pupil, and I finally applied to F.E. Church, a young painter, pupil of Cole, and for many years after the leading landscape painter of the country. He was then in his first success, and I was his first pupil.

    Church in many respects was the most remarkable painter of the phenomena of nature I have ever known, and had he been trained in a school of wider scope, he might have taken a place amongst the great individualities of his art. But he had little imagination, and his technical training had not emancipated him from an exaggerated insistence on detail, which so completely controlled his treatment of his subject that breadth and repose were entirely lost sight of. A graceful composition, and most happy command of all the actual effects of the landscape which he had seen, were his highest qualities; his retention of the minutest details of the generic or specific characteristics of tree, rock, or cloud was unsurpassed by the work of any landscape painter whose work I know, and everything he knew he rendered with a rapidity and precision which were simply inconceivable by one who had not seen him at work. I think that his vision and retention of even the most transitory facts of nature passing before him must have been at the maximum of which the human mind is capable, but he had no comprehension of the higher and broader qualities of art. His mind seemed a camera obscura in which everything that passed before it was recorded permanently, but he added in the rendering of its record nothing which sprang from human emotion, or which involved that remoulding of the perception that makes it conception, and individual. The primrose on the river's brim he saw with a vision as clear as that of a photographic lens, but it remained to him a primrose and nothing more to the end. All that he did or could do was the recording, form and color, of what had flitted past his eyes, with unsurpassed fidelity of memory; but it left one as cold as the painting of an iceberg. His recognition of art as distinguished from nature was far too rudimentary to fit him for a teacher, for his love of facts and detail blinded him to every other aspect of our relations with nature, in the recognition of which consist the highest gifts of the artist.

    My study with Church lasted one winter, and showed me that nothing was to be hoped for from him, and that the most intimate superficial acquaintance with nature did not involve the perception of her more intimate relation with art. I learned from him nothing that was worth remembering, but I made acquaintance with a young portrait painter, who had a studio in the same building, an Irishman named Boyle, a pupil of Inman, whose ideas of art were of a far higher order, and to my intercourse with him during that winter and the following summer, which we spent together sketching in the valley of the Mohawk, I owe the first clear ideas of what lay before me in artist life. At Church's studio I met Edgar A. Poe, a slender, nervous, vivacious, and extremely refined personage. But at that juncture I came across "Modern Painters," and, like many others, wiser or otherwise, I received from it a stimulus to nature worship, to which I was already too much inclined, which made ineffaceable the confusion in my mind between nature and art. Another acquaintance I made that winter was of great importance in developing my technical abilities--that of a well-known amateur of New York, afterwards a professional artist, Dr. Edward Ruggles, a physician whose love of painting finally drove him out of medicine. He had the most catholic and correct taste I had then met, and he introduced me to William Page, the most remarkable portrait painter in many respects America has ever produced, whose talks on art used to make me sleepless with enthusiasm. Page was the most brilliant talker I ever met, and a dear friend of Lowell.

Returning to Schenectady the following summer, I made my first direct and thorough studies from nature, and amongst these was one, a view from my window across gardens and a churchyard with the church spire in the distance; a small study which incidentally had a most potent effect on all my later life. It was bought in the autumn by the Art Union of New York, and on the proceeds, thirty dollars, the first considerable sum of money I had ever earned, I decided to go to Europe and see what the English painters were doing. Of English art I then knew only directly the pictures of Doughty, an early artistic immigrant from England, and, as afterwards appeared to me, a fair example of the school which had its lead from Constable, to whom he had, however, no resemblance except in choice of motive. He had a comprehension of technique possessed by none of our home painters--a rapid and masterly execution with a scale of color limited to cool grays, but, within this gamut, of exquisite refinement. Constant repetitions of the same motive wore out his welcome on the part of the American public, but his pictures had a charm which was long in losing its power over me, and had an influence in determining me to go to England at the first opportunity. But to see Turner's pictures was always the chief motive, and was the one which decided me to go.

    I was, in knowledge of worldly life, scarcely less a child then than I had been when, at the age of ten, I determined to go out into the world and make my own career, free from the obstacles I imagined to be preventing me from following my ideals. The ever-present feeling developed in me by the religious training of my mother, that an overruling Providence had my life in keeping, made me quite oblivious of or indifferent to the chances of disaster, for the assurance of protection and leading to the best end left no place for anxieties. It was a mental phenomenon which I now look back on with a wonder which I think most sane people will share, that, at the age when most boys have become men, for I graduated at twenty, I should have been capable of going out into a strange world like one of the children of the Children's Crusade, with an unfaltering faith that I should be led and cared for by Providence as I had been by my parents. I had no apprehension, from the moment that one of the ship-owners who was in business relations with my elder brother offered me a free passage on one of his sailing ships to Liverpool, that I should not find a similar bridge back again; and with my thirty dollars changed into six sovereigns, and a little valise with only a change of clothes, I went on board the Garrick, a packet of the Black Ball line, sailing in the last days of December, 1849. There had been a thaw and the Hudson River was full of floating ice, which in the ebbing of the tide endangered the shipping lying out in the stream, and the captain made such haste to get out of the danger (the extent of which was shown by the topmasts of an Austrian brig, showing above water where she had been sunk by the floating ice) that the ship had her anchor apeak before the boat which carried my brother and myself out could reach it. We barely arrived in time for me to get aboard, the difficulty of threading our way amongst the masses of ice making our boating difficult. That my childish faith in Providence was a family trait might be deduced from the fact that my brother, who had from boyhood stood to me *in loco parentis*, had not asked me, until I was on the point of going aboard, what my means of subsistence were, and, when he found that I had only my six sovereigns, he told me to wait at Liverpool for a letter of credit he would send me by the steamer which followed.

That voyage is one of the most delightful memories of my life. I loved the sea; and every phase of it, storm or calm, was a new joy. I had one fellow-passenger, a German doctor of philosophy, Dr. Seemann, who had been an ardent radical in Germany, and had been studying in the United States the development of political intelligence under democratic conditions, returning to his native land with the profound conviction that democratic government was destined to be a failure. We had hot debates on the subject, in which the doctor adduced his conversations with the intelligent farmers of New England, whom he had especially studied, to show that their political education was such as to endanger the best interests of the community from its extreme superficiality; I, with an unfaltering faith in the processes of universal suffrage, disputed his conclusions, so hotly in fact that we quarreled and he took one side of the quarter-deck for his promenades and I the other. But the conditions of sea life, with a companionship limited to two persons, are such that no quarrel that was not mortal, or from rivalry in the affections of a woman, could endure many days, and after a few such days we drew to the same side of the deck and were better friends than before, but we dropped politics.

This was in January of 1850, and I am driven to curiosity as to the subsequent career of the young German savant, who in that state of American political evolution was capable of drawing the horoscope of a nation, as it has been in recent times fulfilled; who saw in the crude notions of political economy of that prosperous yesterday the germs of the political blunders and errors of to-day. I drew his portrait, I made a few studies of sea and sky, but for the most part the sensation of simple existence under the conditions of illimitable freedom in space, with no reminder of anything beyond, was sufficient for me. I used to lie on my back on the roof of the wheel-house and look into the sky, and try to make friends with the sea-gulls which sailed around over me, curiously peering down with their dove-like eyes as if to see what this thing might be. Then the nights, so luminous with the "breeming" of the sea as we got into the Gulf Stream, and the flitting and sudden population of the ocean, always bringing us surprises; the more exciting and delightful storms which came on us in the region in which they were always to be expected, and which, though we had some that made lying in one's berth difficult, were never enough to satisfy my desire for rough weather,--all these things filled my life so full of the pure delight in nature that when, at the end of nearly three weeks at sea, we came in sight of the Irish coast, I hated the land. Life was enough under the sea conditions, and the prospect of the return to the limitations of living amongst men was absolute pain.

We made Liverpool in twenty-one days from New York, and the steamer which had left that port the next week did not arrive till three or four days after, so that my waiting for the letter of credit involved a hotel bill which nearly exhausted my money in hand. The kindly captain, knowing my circumstances, made the hotel keeper throw off fifty per cent. of his bill (for I went to the "captain's hotel"), and thus I succeeded in getting to London with the money which was to have paid my expenses for six weeks (according to the careful calculations I had made, at the rate of a pound a week) reduced to provision for three, after which Providence was expected to provide me with a passage home. In these weeks I had planned to see Turner's pictures, Copley Fielding's, with Creswick's, and all the others Ruskin had mentioned. But the railways and hotels had never come into my arithmetic, and that was always, and remains, my weak point. However, the letter of credit was for fifty pounds, and so I felt justified in my faith in Providence, my brother going to the general credit of that account.

CHAPTER VI
ART STUDY IN ENGLAND

Arrived at Euston Station in the small hours of the morning, I bought a penny loaf and walked the streets eating it and carrying my valise until the day was sufficiently advanced for me to go to present a letter of introduction given me by G.P. Putnam, the publisher, to his agent in England, Mr. Delf, who at once took me to a lodging-house in Bouverie Street, in which I got a room for six shillings a week, service included, and an honest, kindly landlady to whom I still feel indebted for the affectionate interest she took in me. I had letters to Mr. S.C. Hall, editor of the "Art Journal," and the Rev. William Black, pastor of the little Seventh Day Baptist Church at Millyard in Goodmansfields, Leman Street, a very ancient and well-endowed foundation, made by some Sabbatarian of centuries ago, with a parsonage and provision for two sermons every Saturday; and under Mr. Black's preaching I sat all the time I was in London. He was a man of archaeological tastes whose researches had led him to the conviction that the Seventh Day was the true Christian Sabbath, and to fellowship with the congregation of Millyard. I was admitted to honorary membership in the church, and the listening to the two dry-as-dust sermons was compensated for by the cordial friendship of the pastor, an invitation to dinner every Saturday, and the motherly interest of his wife and daughters. My childhood's faith and my mother's creed still hung so closely to me that the observances of our ancient church were to me sacred, and the Sabbath day at Millyard still held me to the simple ways of home. In that secluded nook, out of all the rush and noise of London, we lived as we might have lived in an English village; it was an *impasse*, and one who entered from the narrow and squalid alleys which led to it was surprised to find the little square of the old and disused graveyard, with its huge hawthorn trees and its inclosure of the parsonage appendages, as peaceful and as far from the world as if it had been in distant Devon.

My letter to Mr. Hall led to introductions to Leslie, Harding, Creswick, and several minor painters, all of whom found me attentive to the lessons they gave me on their own excellences and led me no farther, but it also brought me into contact with a painter of a higher and more serious order, J.B. Pyne, one of the few thinkers and impartial critics I found amongst the English painters. Every Sunday I went out to Pyne's house in Fulham, walking the six or seven miles in the morning and spending the day there. Kitchen-gardens and green fields then lay between Kensington and Fulham where are now the museums, and there the larks sang and the hawthorn bloomed. After an early dinner we passed the afternoon in talk on art and artists. Pyne was one of the best talkers on art I ever knew, and a critic of very great lucidity; his art had great qualities and as great defects, but in comparison with some of the favorites of the public of that day he was a giant, and in certain technical qualities he had no equal in his generation except Turner. He had the dangerous tendency, for an artist, of putting everything he did under the protection and direction of a theory--a course which invariably checks the fertility of technical resource, and which in his case had the unfortunate effect of causing him to be regarded as a mere theorist, whose work was done by line and rule. But I had good reason to know that Turner thought more highly of him than the English public, and I am convinced that as time goes on and his pictures acquire the mellowness of tone for which he carefully calculated in his method and choice of material, he will be more highly esteemed than in his own time, and that the careful and systematic technique which characterized his work, and which is so opposed to the random and hypothetically inspired methods that are the admiration of a half-educated public, will find its true appreciation in the future.

Of all the English artists of that day with whom I became acquainted, Pyne impressed me as by a considerable measure the broadest thinker, and, except Turner in his water-color, the ablest landscape painter; old John Linnell in this respect standing nearest him in technical power, with a more complete devotion to nature and her sentiment. In Harding's work I took no interest; his conventions and tricks of the brush repelled me, and generally his work left me cold and discouraged, for this is the effect of wasted cleverness, that it disheartens a man who, knowing that his abilities are less, finds the achievement of cleverer men so poor in what satisfies the artist of feeling. In it I saw an exaggeration of Pyne's defects and the caricature of his good qualities. Creswick had a better feeling for nature, but convention in his methods gave place to trick, and I remember his showing me the way in which he produced detail in a pebbly brookside, by making the surface of his canvas tacky and then dragging over it a brush loaded with pigment which caught only on the prominences, and did in a moment the work of an hour of faithful painting.

A painter who taught me more than any other at that time was Edward Wehnert, mainly known then as an illustrator, and hardly remembered now even in that capacity. Attracted by one of his water-colors, I went to him for lessons, which he declined to give, while really giving me instructions informally and in the most kindly and generous way, during the entire stay I made in London. Among all the artists I have known, Wehnert's life was, with the exception of Sexton's, the most pathetic. His native abilities were of a very high order, and his education far above that which the British artist of that day possessed. He was a pupil of Paul Delaroche, and the German blood he had from his father gave him an imaginative element which the Englishman in him liberated entirely from the German prescriptive limitations, while there was just enough of the German poet in him to give his design a sentiment which was entirely lacking in the English figure painting of that day. He painted in both oil and water-color, with a facility of design I have never known surpassed, making at a single sitting, and without a model, a drawing with many figures. He was at the moment I knew him engaged in illustrating Grimm's stories, for a paltry compensation, but, as it seemed to me, in a spirit the most completely concordant with the stories of all the illustrations I have ever seen of that folk-lore.

Wehnert had several sisters, who had been accustomed to a certain ease in life, and to maintain this all his efforts and those of a bachelor brother were devoted, to the sacrifice of his legitimate ambitions; he was overworked with the veriest hack-work of his profession, and I never knew him but as a jaded man. He was a graduate of Goettingen, widely read and well taught in all that related to his art as well as in literature, and I used to sit much with him while he worked, and most of my evenings were passed in the family. The sisters were women who had been of the world, clever, accomplished, and with a restricted and most interesting circle of friends; but over the whole family there rested an air of tragic gravity, as if of some past which could never be spoken of and into which I never felt inclined to inquire.

Among the memories of my first stay in London the Wehnerts awaken the tenderest, for through many years they proved the dearest and kindest of friends. And the hospitality of London, wherever I found access to it, was unmeasured--the kindly feeling which showed itself to a young and unknown student without recommendation or achievement made on me an indelible impression. I now and then found people who asked me where I had learned to speak English, or if all the people in the section from which I came were as white as I was; but except in a single case, that of a lady who proposed to make me responsible for slavery in the United States, I never found anything but friendship and courtesy, and generally the friendliness took the form of active interest.

Most of my time was passed in hunting up pictures by Turner, and of course I made the early acquaintance of Griffiths, a dealer in pictures, who was Turner's special agent, and at whose gallery were to be seen such of his pictures as he wished to sell,--for no inducement could be offered which would make him dispose of some of them. Griffiths told me that in his presence an American collector, James Lenox, of New York, after offering Turner L5000, which was refused, for the Old "Temeraire," offered him a blank check, which was also rejected. Griffiths's place became one of my most common resorts, for Griffiths was less a picture dealer than a passionate admirer of Turner, and seemed to have drifted into his business through his love for the artist's pictures; and to share in his admiration for Turner was to gain his cordial friendship.

Here I first saw Ruskin and was introduced to him. I was looking at some little early drawings of Turner, when a gentleman entered the gallery, and, after a conversation between them, Griffiths came to me and asked if I should not like to be presented to the author of "Modern Painters," to which I naturally replied in the affirmative. I could hardly believe my eyes, expecting to find in him something of the fire, enthusiasm, and dogmatism of his book, and seeing only a gentleman of the most gentle type, blonde, refined, and with as little self-assertion or dogmatic tone as was possible consistently with the holding of his own opinions; suggesting views rather than asserting them, and as if he had not himself come to a conclusion on the subject of conversation. A delightful and to me instructive conversation ended in an invitation to visit his father's collection of drawings and pictures at Denmark Hill, and later to spend the evening at his own house in Grosvenor Street. After the lapse of forty-eight years, it is difficult to distinguish between the incidents which took place in this first visit to England in 1850 and those belonging to another a little later, but my impression is very strong that it was during the former that I spent the evening at the Grosvenor Street residence, at which I met several artists of Ruskin's intimacy, and amongst them G.F. Watts. I then saw Mrs. Ruskin, and I have a very vivid impression of her personal beauty. I remember saying to a friend, to whom I spoke of the visit just after, that she was the most beautiful woman I had seen in England. As I approached the house there was a bagpiper playing near it, and the pipes entered into the conversation in the drawing-room. On my making some very disparaging opinion of their music, which I heard for the first time, Mrs. Ruskin flamed up with indignation, but, after an annihilating look, she said mildly, "I suppose no Southerner can understand the pipes," and we discussed them calmly, she telling some stories to illustrate their power and the special range of their effect.

At that time Ruskin held very strong Calvinistic notions, and as I kept my Puritanism unshaken we had as many conversations on religion as on art, the two being then to me almost identical and to him closely related. I remember his saying once, in speaking of the doctrine of foreordination (to me a dreadful bugbear), as I was drinking a glass of sherry, that he "believed that it had been ordained from all eternity whether I should set that glass down empty or without finishing the wine." This was to me the most perplexing problem of all that Ruskin put before me, for it was the first time that the doctrine of Calvin had come before me in a concrete form. Another incident gave me a serious perplexity as to the accuracy of Ruskin's perceptions of nature. Leslie had given me a card to see Mr. Holford's collection of pictures, in which was one of Turner's, the balcony scene in Venice, called, I think, "Juliet and her Nurse." It was a moonlight, with the most wonderful rendering of a certain effect seen with the moon at the spectator's back, and I noted in speaking to Ruskin, later on, that no other picture I had ever seen of moonlight had succeeded so fully in realizing it, to which he replied that he had never noticed that it was a moonlight picture; but when I called his attention to the display of fireworks on the Grand Canal, he admitted that it was not customary to let off fireworks by day, and that it must be a night scene.

My acquaintance with Ruskin lasted with varying degrees of intimacy, and some interruptions due to his sympathy with the South during the civil war and bitterness against our government, till 1870, when it was terminated by a trivial personal incident to which his morbid state of mind at that time gave a false color. We separated more and more widely in our opinions on art in later years, and the differences came to me reluctantly, for my reverence for the man was never to be shaken, while my study of art showed me finally that, however correct his views of the ethics of art might be, from the point of view of pure art he was entirely mistaken, and all that his influence had done for me had to be undone before any true progress could be made. What little I had learned from the artists I knew had been in the main correct, and had aided to show me the true road, but the teaching of "Modern Painters," and of Ruskin himself later, was in the end fatal to the career to which I was then devoted, for I was unable to get back to the dividing of the ways.

But the first mistake was my own. What I needed was practical study, the training of the hand, for my head had already gone so far beyond my technical attainment that I had entered into the fatal condition of having theories beyond my practice. My execution was so far in arrear of my perceptions of what should be in the result, that instead of the delight with which I had, untaught, and in my stolen hours, given myself to painting, I felt the weight of my technical shortcomings so heavily as to make my work full of distress instead of that content with which the artist should always work. Everything became conscious effort and the going was too much uphill. I had always been groping my own way, scarcely as much assisted by the fragmentary good advice I received as laid under heavier disabilities by the better knowledge of what should be done. In art education the training of the hand should, I am persuaded, always be kept in advance of the thinking powers, so that the young student should feel that his ideal is just before him if not at his finger's end. That this is so rarely the case with art students in our day is, I am convinced, the chief reason of the technical inferiority of our modern painters and the root of the inferiority of modern art. The artist does not begin early enough. I was already belated, and every advance I made in the study of the theory of art put me farther behind, practically.

The hope of getting much technical instruction from competent masters in England was speedily dispelled. Lessons in water-color I could get at a guinea an hour, and to enter as a pupil with one of the better painters was impossible. Pyne received from his pupils L100 a month. I had calculated how far I could mate my fifty pounds go and put it at six months. By the advice of Wehnert, I applied to Charles Davidson, a member of the New Water-Color Society, for instruction, and went down into Surrey, where he lived, to be able to follow him in his work from nature. He lived at Red Hill, and in the immediate vicinity John Linnell had built his then new home. In the few weeks I lived there I saw a great deal of the old man, one of the most remarkable examples of the old English type I have ever known, and to me as interesting a problem from the religious point of view as from the artistic. Barring differences of the creed, of which I knew and cared nothing (for my own religious horizon had always included all "good-willing men," and I had no conception of the distinctions of creed which would send on one side of the line of safety an Established Churchman and on the other a Nonconformist), we agreed very well, and in the general impression I set Linnell down as a devout Christian of the Cromwellian type, and he certainly was a man of remarkable intellectual powers, both in art and in theology. His Christianity might have taken a form of less domestic sternness, but I remembered my own father too well to find it inconsistent with genuine piety, though not even my mother ever inspired the awe Linnell and his religious severity excited in me.

Linnell's landscape seemed to me the full expression of a healthy love of nature, possible only to a moral sanity in the man--a cheery Wordsworthian enjoyment of her, which as a rule I have never found in perfection out of the English school and its derivatives; the outpouring of a robust nature which prefers to see the outer world with the spectacles of no school, and through the memory of no other man; not self-taught in the sense of owing nothing to another mind, but in the sense that what he had learned he had digested and forgotten except as a chance word in the universal gospel of art; technically weak, slovenly in style, but eminently successful in telling the story he had to tell. Even then, with my limited knowledge of painting, he seemed to me to furnish the antithesis to Pyne,--one too careful of style and running to excessive precision, the other too negligent and running into indecision; and this judgment still holds. Of Davidson, my immediate teacher, there was only to be got certain ways of doing certain things, limited to the elements of landscape; how to wash in the sky, to treat foliage in masses, and those tricks of the brush in which the English water-color school abounds; but no larger views, or more individual, of art itself. What he taught was, perhaps, what I most needed to learn, but

I was already too far on the way to learn it easily.

I made a visit of ten days to Paris and saw with great profit the work of the landscape painters and of Delacroix, the other figure painters in general not interesting me much. I carried a letter of introduction from the Wehnerts to Mademoiselle Didot, the daughter of Firmin Didot, the famous publisher, then an old blind man, but one of the most interesting Frenchmen I ever knew, as Mademoiselle Didot was the most brilliant Frenchwoman. The old man was much interested in what I had to say of America, and he paid us the national compliment of saying that we spoke English more intelligibly than Englishmen in general. As I spoke no French, our conversation was in English, and he understood me perfectly, though he said he rarely could follow without difficulty the conversation of an Englishman, while Americans in general he understood readily. To accomplish all that I did with my fifty pounds it may be easily understood that I had to cut my corners close, and in fact they were so closely cut in my Continental excursion that I landed at Newhaven on my return with one shilling in my pocket, and when, at the end of my stay in England, I took the train for Liverpool, I had only sixpence (my passage being provided for), and my good friend Delf, who saw me off, on finding the state of my purse, insisted at the railway station on my taking a sovereign for contingencies.

This habit of making no provision for accidents had been a part of my moral training, the faith in the overruling Providence never forsaking me for an instant, so that, whatever I set about to do, I made no provision for accidents. To go ahead and do what I thought I ought to do, and let the consequences take care of themselves, has been the habit of mind in which I have always worked and probably still work. If the thing to be done was right, I never thought of what might come after, or even whether I had the means to carry a resolution into effect, taking it for granted that the means would be provided because the thing was to be done. I retain the distinct recollection of an expression of my mother while I was making preparations for this first voyage to Europe, and she was packing my clothes for the voyage and her lips were silently moving and the slow tears running down her cheeks. She said in her low and murmuring voice as if in comment on her prayer, "Oh! no, he is too pure-hearted," and I knew that the prayer was for my protection from the temptations of that world of which she only knew the terrors and dangers from her Bible, and that she was so wrapt in her spiritual yearnings that she had quite forgotten my presence. Poor mother! I never deserved the great trust she had in me, but the memory of that moment has served me in many devious moments to keep me in the path. But if I had no such virtues as those which she attributed to me, I had what was perhaps more potent, the intuitions which I inherited from her, and such as often take a man out of temptation before he is aware of its strength, and before it becomes a real danger; nor can any man remember such confidence on the part of his mother without, from very shame, if no sterner motive should exist, maintaining a higher tone of life.

I did not leave London without a sight of Turner himself, due to the friendly forethought of Griffiths, who so appreciated my enthusiasm for the old man that he lost no opportunity to satisfy it. Turner was taken ill while I was on this visit, with an attack of the malady which later killed him, and I had begged Griffiths to ask him to let me come and nurse him. He declined the offer, but was not, Griffiths told me, quite unmoved by it. One day, after his recovery, I received a message from Griffiths to say that Turner was coming to the gallery at a certain hour on a business appointment, and if I would happen in just before the time fixed for it I might see him.

At the appointed hour Turner came and found me in an earnest study of the pictures in the farther end of the gallery, where I remained, unnoticing and unnoticed, until a sign from Griffiths called me up. He then introduced me as a young American artist who had a great admiration for his work, and who, being about to return home, would be glad to take him by the hand. It was difficult to reconcile my conception of the great artist with this little, and, to casual observation, insignificant old man with a nose like an eagle's beak, though a second sight showed that his eye, too, was like an eagle's, bright, restless, and penetrating. Half awed and half surprised, I held out my hand. He put his behind him, regarding me with a humorous, malicious look, saying nothing. Confused, and not a little mortified, I turned away, and, walking down the gallery, went to studying the pictures again. When I looked his way again, a few minutes later, he held out his hand to me, and we entered into a conversation which lasted until Griffiths gave me a hint that Turner had business to transact which I must leave him to. He gave me a hearty handshake, and in his oracular way said, "Hmph--(nod) if you come to England again--hmph (nod)--hmph (nod)," and another hand-shake with more cordiality and a nod for good-by. I never saw a keener eye than his, and the way that he held himself up, so straight that he seemed almost to lean backwards, with his forehead thrown forward, and the piercing eyes looking out from under their heavy brows, and his diminutive stature coupled with the imposing bearing, combined to make a very peculiar and vivid impression on me. Griffiths afterwards translated his laconism for me as an invitation to come to see him if I ever came back to England, and added that though he was in the worst of tempers when he came in, and made him expect that I should be insulted, he was in fact unusually cordial, and he had never seen him receive a stranger with such friendliness except in the case of Cattermole, for whom he had a strong liking. In the conversation we had during the interview, I alluded to our good fortune in having already in America one of the pictures of his best period, a seacoast sunset in the possession of Mr. Lenox, and Turner exclaimed, "I wish they were all put in a blunderbuss and shot off!" but he looked pleased at the simultaneous outburst of protest on the part of Griffiths and myself. When I went back to England for another visit he was dead.

I may frankly say as to Turner's art, that I enjoyed most the water-colors of the middle period, though the latest gave me another kind of delight,--that of the reading of a fairy-story, of the building of glorious castles in the air in my younger days, that of something to desire and despair of. The drawings of the England and Wales series in the possession of Ruskin seemed to my critical faculty the ***ne plus ultra*** of water-color painting,--especially the "Llanthony Abbey," of which I recall those early impressions with the greatest distinctness[5]. I saw in the Academy Exhibition the last pictures he ever exhibited, some whaling subjects, fresh from his retouching of two days before, gorgeous dreams of color art, but only dreams--the actuality had all gone out. I saw them years after when they had become mere wrecks, hardly recognizable.

I saw also that year a picture by Rossetti and one by Millais, and the latter impressed me very strongly; in fact it determined me in the manner in which I should follow art on my return home. I did not and could not put it on the same plane as the "Llanthony Abbey," but the straight thrust for the truth was evidently the shortest way to a certain excellence, and this of the kind most akin to my own faculties, and I said to Delf, who was with me at the exhibition of the Academy, that

---

5 I saw it again in the Guildhall Exhibition of 1899.

if ever English figure painting rose out of mediocrity it would be through the work of the P.R.B. My impression is that the picture was the "Christ in the Carpenter's Shop," but of this I cannot be sure, though I am certain that it was in the exhibition of 1850. The Rossetti was in the old "National Society," and was either the "Childhood of the Virgin Mary" or the "White Lady." Beautiful as it was, it did not impress me as did the temper of Millais's work, the scrupulous conscientiousness of which chimed with my Puritan education. I left England with a fermentation of art ideas in my brain, in which the influence of Turner and Pyne, the teachings of Wehnert, and the work of the Pre-Raphaelites mingled with the influence of Ruskin, and especially the preconception of art work derived from the descriptions, often strangely misleading, of the "Modern Painters."

I received from my brother, as I had anticipated, the order for a passage on the Atlantic, one of the Collins line of steamers, and one of my fellow-passengers was Jenny Lind, on her way for her first visit to America under the guidance of Barnum. She gave a concert on board for the benefit of the firemen and sailors, and to this the half of Delf's sovereign contributed, the other half going for a bottle of Rhine wine, to return the compliment of my next neighbor at the table, who had invited me to take a glass of wine one day. Thus, as usual, I landed penniless from my venture, but fortunately found my brother on the wharf expecting the arrival of the steamer, her trips having been made with such precision that the hour of arrival was generally anticipated correctly. In those days the steamers were rarely driven, and a voyage of fourteen days was not considered a bad one. A day's run of 336 knots was a triumph of steaming and rarely attained. But we were at the beginning of the contest between the Collins and the Cunard steamers, and up to that time the American line had generally a little the better of it.

The rest of that year and the year following were given to hard and monotonous painting from nature while the weather permitted, and in the winter to working out clumsily the mysteries of picture-making, a work which, as I was without direction or any correct appreciation of what I had it in me to do, became a drudgery which I went through as an indispensable duty, but with no satisfaction. My larger studies from nature (25x30 inches) had attracted attention and had been hung on the line, getting for me the election to the Associateship of Design, and the appellation of the "American Pre-Raphaelite,"--all which for a man so lately embarked in the profession was considered a high honor, as it really was. But the success only confirmed me in my incorrect views of art and carried me farther from the true path. As studies from nature, the fidelity and completeness of them, even in comparison with Durand's, was something which the conventional landscape known then and there had never approached, and to the respectable amateurs of that day they were puzzles. In one of them, a study of a wood scene with a spring of water overshadowed by a beech-tree, all painted at close quarters, I had transplanted a violet which I wanted in the near foreground, so as to be sure that it was in correct light and proportion. This was in the spirit of the Ruskinian doctrine, of which I made myself the apostle. On that study I spent such hours of the day as the light served, for three months, and then the coming of autumn stopped me. Any difficulty in literal rendering of a subject was incomprehensible to me, and in fact in that kind of work there is little difference, for it is but copying, and requires only a correct eye and infinite patience, both of which I had; and it was a puzzle to me rather than a compliment when the veteran Durand said to me of one of my studies, that it was a subject he would not have dared attack on account of the difficulty of the effect of light, for to me it was simply a question of time and sticking to it. It was not art, but the public did not know it any more than I did, and I was admitted to a place which I believe was one of the highest amongst my contemporaries at home in a way that led to little even in its complete success. I influenced some of my contemporaries and gave a jog to the landscape painting of the day, and there it ended, through a diversion of my ambition to another sphere, but there it must have ended; even if I had never been so diverted.

CHAPTER VII
ON A MISSION FOR KOSSUTH

The arrival, in December, 1851, of Kossuth, the Hungarian patriot, on his mission for the redemption of Hungary, set all America in a flame of shallow enthusiasm, and I went to hear his appeals. What he asked for was money to arm his country, to renew the struggle with the House of Hapsburg. His eloquence carried away all deliberation in the Northern States, and even shook the government at Washington; but, in the end, the only practical result was his gain of the dollars which the hearers paid to hear him speak, and which no one regretted who heard him, for such oratory no one in the country ever had heard, even from men to whom the English language was native. Before making his discourse in any town, he took the pains to find out something of the local history, and thus touched the patriotism of his audience in the parish bounds, and the past glories of America were revived in terms of a new and strange flattery. We were like the Athenians after hearing the Philippics of Demosthenes,--all ready to march against the Austrian. Before he left New York I had volunteered to fight or conspire, or take any part in the struggle which might fall to me. I kept my counsel from my family, and when Kossuth went on his westward tour it was settled that, on or after his return to Europe, I was to follow.

His tour of the Northern States was a triumph that caused him to entertain hopes which a man of more sobriety and common-sense would not have conceived. Against the indifference to liberty and the selfishness of the slave States, his flood of eloquence broke in vain. He knew that the North contained most of the capital and energy of America, and he supposed that they ruled, and was late in learning that the South ruled us. At Washington he came into contact with the statesmanship and the demagogy of the republic, and, while the former gave him a magnificent reception, the latter quietly and undemonstratively quenched his hopes. The South had no sympathy with Hungarian or any other liberty, and we felt the chill fall on Kossuth and his eloquence. But, for the politicians, there was something to be made out of him and the naturalized voters, mainly republicans and refugees from the various revolutions which had failed in Europe; so he was not denied the expectation of some private assistance, though the hope that the United States should openly declare Hungary a belligerent, and thus give its moral weight to Kossuth, the recognized governor, was soon seen to be an idle and fallacious one. "Something might be done," said the politicians. So Kossuth waited.

A presidential election was near, and negotiations were initiated between Kossuth and the party leaders for his influence on the foreign vote, and, pending these, he could decide nothing as to his future movements. I was in the habit of going to see him at night, and sometimes waited for the departure of the committees of the politicians who were in discussion with him. One night, when I went in, I found him in a state of nauseated irritation, and he broke out, saying, "Mr. Stillman, if your country does not get rid of these politicians it will be ruined in fifty years." He had just received a Democratic committee, which had formally promised him, in return for the influence he might exert in favor of their candidate, two ships of war ready for service, and a sum of money, the exact amount of which I cannot now remember, but I think it was half a million dollars. Naturally he did not tell me if he had closed with the proposition, but the making of it by the committee was a revelation as to the purity of American politics which he fully understood. This committee had presented itself with the authority of Franklin Pierce, Democratic candidate for the presidency.

The scheme in which he at first proposed to utilize my services was the formation of a deposit of arms and materials of war at a point in the Mediterranean from which he could descend promptly on the coast of Croatia, and this indicated that the two men-of-war of the committee entered into his plans. The desired point he found in the little island of Galita, south of Sardinia, unoccupied and apparently unclaimed by any power, but on which, he told me, the flag of the United States had been hoisted some years before by one of our cruisers; evidently as a joke on the part of some of our sailors. I was to visit it and report on its fitness for his purpose; but negotiations dragged, or there was some hitch, nothing was concluded until

Kossuth's departure for Europe became necessary, and Pulzsky, his *alter ego*, was given full instructions concerning me. I was to follow when affairs were in a certain state of readiness; and, in fact, after a few weeks, I was summoned to London. I received from Pulzsky the clue to Kossuth's quarters, in a quiet street, Bayswater way, if I remember rightly, to which I was to go only late at night, and by some roundabout road, as the Austrian spies were always watching him.

I had a letter to a Madam Schmidt, a German refugee, and an advanced republican, at whose house I used to meet a little assembly of refugees,--German, French, Russian, etc. Every Sunday night we used to meet and discuss the politics of Europe. Of my friends of this circle I remember only one,--a Mr. Norich, a young Russian, with whom I contracted a close friendship, never since renewed. Nothing more was said of the Galita plan, which seems to have depended on the success of the political negotiations with the Americans, and it was finally decided that I should go to Milan and carry the proclamations which Kossuth was to issue to the Hungarian soldiers of the Italian garrison there, ordering them, in case of any revolt, not to fire on insurgent Italians. This was in prevision of the insurrection which Mazzini had determined for the spring of 1853, and with regard to which there were grave dissensions between the two chiefs. Kossuth was not ready for the Hungarian rising, and refused to order it till there was a prospect of success, while Mazzini believed that, even if unsuccessful, the rising was necessary to keep his influence on the Italian population, which was already shaken. Kossuth said to me that he disapproved Mazzini's plans, for he refused "to play with the blood of the nations;" but, if Mazzini persisted, he would give the order to the Hungarian troops not to fire on the people if any rising should take place; more than that he could not do.

Pending the ripening of Mazzini's scheme I waited in London, at the orders of Kossuth, but before the moment came for my undertaking this mission a new one became urgent. When the Hungarian insurrection of 1848-49 had become evidently a failure, and Kossuth was about to escape into Turkey, he decided to conceal, in some place secure from Austrian discovery, the crown jewels, including the crown of St. Stephen, which was considered by the Hungarian people as necessary to the lawful coronation of their king, and with which Francis Joseph had not been crowned; and he and Bartholomew Szemere, one of his colleagues in the ministry--employing for their operations a detachment of prisoners, who were shot after the concealment was complete--buried the jewels at some point down the Danube. Having received information that Szemere, who was then opposed to Kossuth, was about to disclose their hiding-place to the Austrian government, Kossuth determined to remove them, and organized an expedition to this end, of which I was to become the apparent head. The description of the hiding-place was written in a most complicated cipher dispatch, the key to which was contained in a stanza of a song known to Kossuth's correspondent in Pesth. Each letter in the dispatch was represented by a fraction, of which the numerator was the number of the letter in one of the lines of the song, and the denominator the number of the line. This dispatch was then written in four parts; the first, fifth, ninth, etc., letters being put in the first part; the second, sixth, tenth, etc., in the second; the third, seventh, eleventh, etc., in the third; the fourth, eighth, twelfth, etc., in the fourth, and so on to the end. Of these parts of the dispatch, written on the finest paper, I had charge of two; one for myself, and one for a person indicated at Pesth, and the other two were to go by way of Constantinople, one for the confederate who carried it and one for the correspondent who had the song-key. We were to meet and spell out the directions and go to the hiding-place, and, when the jewels were recovered, they were to be hidden in a box of a conserve for which that vicinity was noted, and then carried to Constantinople, from which point I was to take charge of them and deliver them in Boston to Dr. S.G. Howe, the well-known Philhellene.

I folded my portion of these dispatches small, wrapped them in thin gutta-percha, and, going to the most obscure shoemaker in the part of London which I knew, had the heel of one of my boots excavated and the packet deposited in the hole and covered over again by a stout heel-tap. My orders were to take at least six weeks for the journey, to go by a roundabout route, and travel as if for pleasure. From the Austrian territory I was to write to Kossuth all the political information I could collect, the messages being conveyed in a cryptograph in which the form of the letter was to be that of a correspondence between lovers. The words composing the message were to be written on spaces left in a mask of which each had a copy, and the spaces between the words then filled up so that the letter would carry some meaning when read as a whole. Love-letters were supposed to give most room for nonsense. Knowing very little French, I bought a pocket dictionary and a copy of Racine, and, during a ten days' stay in Paris, by diligent use of the former in all my transactions, I picked up enough for the needs of travel, and, spending all my leisure over the latter, I was, before my mission was over, able to converse with considerable fluency and knew my Racine thoroughly.

From Paris I made the journey to Brussels in the company of an American gentleman, Mr. Coxe, of Alabama, traveling with his wife and daughter. At Brussels I made, through the Coxes, the acquaintance of M. Le Hardy de Beaulieu, the leader of a section of the Belgian Liberals, whose father had held a command in the Belgian contingent at Waterloo. My acquaintance with M. Le Hardy lasted many years, he being much interested in America, and having, with his brother, founded a Belgian colony in Alabama. The ancestral estate of the Le Hardys included part of the field of Waterloo, and we visited it in company with M. Le Hardy, who pointed out the trenches made by the heavy artillery of Napoleon still distinguishable on the surface of the fields in spite of the subsequent ploughings. I suppose that his familiarity with the fields from his boyhood gives authority to his assurance that the depressions we saw were the effect of the ploughing of the guns in the wet, soft earth, and did not exist in the natural lay of the land, and the incident brought one very near to the great struggle which fixed for long the position of England in European politics. M. Le Hardy had been, like his father before him, urged to resume the title of nobility which the father had renounced in the warmth of the republican movement prior to the Empire, having burned the patent in the square at Brussels; but, like the father, he had always refused. He was a consistent and, as he would now be classed, a moderate republican.

Visiting Dusseldorf for the sake of the school of art there, I seemed to go into the Middle Ages. We landed from the Rhine steamer in the night, finding the streets deserted even by the police, and dimly lighted by oil lamps hung across them at wide intervals, and I wandered a long time at random with my valise in hand, searching for a hotel, and not meeting a living person to ask guidance of. I blundered at length on a little inn in whose drinking-room still burned a light, and in which I found a night's lodging. Such a primitive state of civilization was to me, fresh from Paris and Brussels, romantic. At Berlin I made the acquaintance of Varnhagen von Ense, through a letter of introduction from Frau Schmidt, my republican refugee friend of London. He treated me with great consideration, and promised me a winter of brilliant social life if I would stay at Berlin. The chief inducement offered was the acquaintance of Humboldt, then absent from the city. Of Varnhagen von Ense I retain the most delightful memory. I found him courteous, genial, and hospitable, with a large-minded outlook on politics and a great interest in America. I saw also the new museum, with Kaulbach at work on his frescoes, and, going by Dresden, reached Prague, where I began my political reports to Kossuth.

Arriving at Vienna, I was beforehand with the famous police, which I found not to merit its reputation for sharpness, and went at once, after establishing myself at the hotel, and before my name was reported to the authorities and a spy put on me, to the address of a republican, known to Kossuth, and to whom I was directed to apply for the identification of some Hungarian resident in the city on whom Kossuth could depend to reestablish communication with the Viennese malcontents, broken by a misadventure of his former agent. This adventure Kossuth recounted to me, I suppose to keep up my courage in the perilous business he was sending me on. One of his agents had been sent on a round tour with instructions for certain officers or soldiers, and, having been detected in communication with the barracks and arrested, a memorandum book was found on him in which, amongst many addresses of persons to whom he had no mission, those to which he was directed were interspersed. All were arrested, among them the Vienna agent, who, ignorant of the reason of his arrest, suspecting treachery, and fearing the disclosures that might be extorted from him by torture, rolled himself in his bedclothes and set fire to them with his candle, the only means of suicide left him. When he felt that the burning was fatal he made an alarm and bade the attendant call the council of war, which immediately met in his cell. He then avowed his complicity in treasonable plans, and, assuring them that nothing more could be extorted from him by any torture they might inflict, that his chief would soon come and make all things right, and that there were thousands more as ready to die as he, he refused to say any more and died in silence.

My business was to find a man to take this agent's place. The individual to whom I was sent was a ribbon manufacturer on one of the main streets, and, pretending a desire to visit his weaving rooms, we went to the manufactory in the upper stories, and then I disclosed, with no preamble, my mission. The good man was in ecstasies, and to show his joy invited me down into his living apartments and introduced me to his wife, daughters, and the lover of one of his daughters, as a messenger from

Kossuth! If my hair did not rise on end, I am certain that at no crisis of my life could it ever have done so. During my ten days' stay in Vienna and the four weeks I afterward passed in Pesth, I never lost a nervous apprehension of the consequences of this singular imprudence, for I was in the enemy's country, on business the slightest suspicion of which meant an obscure prison and complete disappearance from any friend. With cipher dispatches on my person in the handwriting of Kossuth, well known to all the authorities, and with my secret in the possession of five women and two men, the uneasiness I felt for the first two or three days can better be imagined than expressed. I did nothing all day long but walk the streets, drink coffee, and smoke cigars with constant apprehension of an arrest.

But I did not neglect my business. I found a Hungarian whose name Kossuth had given me as the alternative probable medium of the renewed relations with Vienna, but he not only refused to have any relations with the late dictator, but strongly warned me of the possible consequences to myself of the mission I was on, and made me see very clearly that Kossuth overrated his influence on the Hungarians after the ***debacle***, for which he was largely responsible. But it never occurred to me that it was possible to withdraw or do less than obey my instructions. I reported to Kossuth that the only person I could find who was willing to assume the responsibility of entering into relations with him was the ribbon-maker, and then, having acquired the confidence of the American consul, who was a zealous agent of the imperial government, and got his vise for Hungary, I made my way to Pesth.

Once on the scene of my real labors, I discovered how incompetent a conspirator Kossuth was. He had given me the name of his correspondent in Pesth and his residence, in the Karolyisches Haus, as if that were his ordinary residence, without warning me, though he knew it, that he was really in hiding from the police, and probably only to be reached with precaution and indirectly. Adopting the same tactics as in Vienna, and not to attract attention by inquiries, I went at once in a cab to the house. The porter, of course, in reply to my inquiries, being in hearing of the cab-driver, who was probably a spy, denied any knowledge of such a person. I drove back to the hotel, and then went on foot alone and asked again for the individual, but got the same reply, this time angrily delivered. Utterly at a loss what to do, I wrote at once to Kossuth that the person wanted was not at the address indicated. Instead of writing to him to find me and giving him my address, Kossuth only reiterated through the post the former instructions. I repeated the denial, and then waited. In conversation with the hotel people I inquired as fully as was possible without exciting suspicion, about persons of liberal tendencies and such as I conceived that I might make use of, and studied the position as best I could. Pending this study I was summoned to the police headquarters to give an account of myself. This I did in a manner which must have been satisfactory, as they found that I knew little German and was a very stupid and unpractical individual, which I must have really been, to find myself there. I accounted for myself as a landscape painter on his travels, and as I knew nobody and made no acquaintances they dismissed all suspicion of me, our consul's assurance no doubt covering all doubts, and I waited still. But after a few days more a convenient attack of illness gave me a pretext for calling a physician, and I chose Dr. Orzovensky, who I had learned had been chief of the medical staff under the revolutionary authorities. Through him I made such inquiries as were possible about the people to whom I was sent, and then for the first time discovered that they were all under accusation as conspirators and searched for by the police, and of this I had no warning from Kossuth.

But in all this wandering my boot-heel was wearing away, and it was a question of wearing into the packet of dispatches, or putting them in a place of security. I accordingly dug them out, and, hiding them in a convenient corner of the cupboard in my room, where they must soon have been discovered in case of a domiciliary visit, took the excavated boots out to throw them into the river, choosing the earliest darkness of the rainy evening of the same day. I knew that if the bootblack saw the excavated heel he would in all probability report the fact, and my arrest would follow. In my ignorance of the fact that the city was under martial law, and that without a pass no one could be in the streets after 8 P.M., I had waited till 9 to be screened by the darkness, and then, walking down the river on the dike, I slipped down to the water's edge by the path, and gently tossed the boots into the rapid current. Seeing the dangerous articles float away into the dark, I turned to go up the dike to the road running along the top of it, when, to my dismay, I heard a sentinel directly across the road challenge, saw the officer of the guard coming on his rounds, and heard his reply to the challenge. I hurried down the bank, hoping that I had not attracted attention, but feeling that in the contrary case I was in most imminent danger of arrest, and the thought of the dispatches left where they must be found in case of suspicion gave me a moment's anxiety. I hurried back along the water's edge till I judged that I was out of sight from the post, and then walked up on the dike and towards the hotel.

It was very dark and raining slightly, but as I came within the circle of light of one of the street lamps the vigilant eye of the officer of the guard caught me, and he hailed, "Who goes there?" I did not reply, but, acting as if I did not hear, hurried to get directly under the lamp which was near, with a feeling that if the officer saw me there he would see that I was what I pretended to be, a stranger, and also with a feeling that I was safer at a distance if the challenge were followed by a bullet. Under the lamp I stopped for the officer to come up. I was not really frightened, but I cannot deny that I felt very nervous, as he came up, and, in an inquisitorial tone, asked, "What are you doing here?" I replied in German which was certainly comical and not a little shaky, for it was a fragmentary remembrance of the German read in my early college course, and never since revived, that "I was doing nothing--that I was a strangers" (ich bin ein Fremden), and had come out to see the effects on the river, pointing to the glimmering lights; but, fortunately, my German was so funny that he burst out laughing, and after a "sehr schoen, sehr schoen," as I had said "strangers" in the plural, he replied, "When you are a strangers you must stay in the house," and gave me friendly directions as to how to get back to my hotel without falling in with the police, "who wouldn't let you off as I have." I was fortunate enough to arrive without any further notice. The officers of the army hated to do police service, and my inquisitor was no doubt glad not to pass me into the custody of the police. I have always wished to know the name of my protector, for such he was.

I remained in Pesth over a month, exciting an increasing attention and being unable to account for a further delay, as I was doing nothing, not even sketching, which, in the vicinity of a fortress, would have been the surest way of inviting arrest. I profited by the acquaintance of Dr. Orzovensky's family to pass the time agreeably, and, finally, being unable to extort by post further instructions from Kossuth, or explanations in reply to two urgent letters describing the position I was in, and being unable to give any reason for a longer stay, or to find the people I was sent to, I determined to go back to London and start again with fuller oral instructions and a better understanding of the difficulties. I went to Orzovensky and frankly told him my errand, and asked him if I might leave the dispatches in some place known to him, so that he could indicate to some other person, should my mission be taken up by another, where they were to be found. He burst out on me with violence, accusing me of endangering his family as well as himself, and assuring me that if the slightest suspicion of my mission should transpire they would all be thrown into prison, and he be ruined, refusing to have anything to do or say about the dispatches, and breaking off all communications with me on the spot.

I had not, up to that moment, felt any ***real*** fright, though, when I stood under the scrutiny of the officer on the dike, I must confess I felt extremely nervous; but Orzovensky's violence, and his own panic at the thought of having harbored treason so long, making me fear that his anxiety to escape all suspicion might compel him to denounce me, gave me a ***mauvais quart d'heure***. I was instantaneously in an awful funk, and I had a practical demonstration of the "vox haesit in faucibus," for I was unable to reply to the good doctor in anything but the faintest whisper, and my tongue clattered in my mouth, as dry as a stick, in an instant. I threw the dispatches in the sink and took the next train for Vienna, undisturbed by the train running off the track in the night, in the greater anxiety of my position, and, after making at the station of Vienna only a hasty lunch on a boiled sausage and a roll, continued my journey by express until I was out of the Austrian dominions, and stopped to sleep at Frankfort. My panic was as unreasonable as my security had been, for there was no reason to believe that Dr. Orzovensky would warn the authorities, or that I could not have carried the dispatches back to Kossuth in safety. My habitual courage was not the courage of one who realizes his danger and faces it coolly, but that of constitutional inability to realize what the danger is, however clearly it may be shown to him. As a habit the realization of my danger only came to me when the danger itself had gone by, and then I was frightened.

Arrived at London, I went to report to Kossuth, expecting a scene and reproaches, when I was prepared to show him that the failure of the mission was due to his having neglected to inform me that I was going to a man wanted by the police, and in close hiding, so that my failure to find him was probably due to the openness with which I made my approaches, and to his not having then informed his correspondent that I was on the ground expecting to see him, and that he must look out for me. But he only exclaimed, with a tone of regret, "Three months lost!"

yet there was, probably, a reciprocal disapproval of our methods of carrying on a conspiracy; for, while he was most gravely disappointed at getting no result from his work and expenditure, no doubt owing largely to my incompetence for that kind of service, I was equally dissatisfied at being sent on an expedition which put my life in imminent danger, with the minor perils of torture and long imprisonment, provided with information utterly insufficient and needlessly incomplete for the mission confided to me.

If Kossuth had cautioned me that his correspondent was in hiding and wanted by the police, I should not have committed the grave error of going openly to find him, and under the eye of a cabman, who would probably report to the police my act. Had he even after that informed his correspondent where I could be found and who I was (which was perfectly practicable, for he told me himself that he had received letters from the correspondent during my stay at Pesth), there could have been communication at once. Kossuth said that I ought to have sought out the friends at the Tiger cafe, where they were in the habit of meeting publicly, though he knew that the city was swarming with spies, and that the state of siege existed (and of this, even, he did not warn me), and that my chief difficulty was to avoid being brought into contact with suspected Hungarians; nor did he recollect that he had given precise instructions to avoid anything which might lead any one to suppose that I was more than an objectless traveler. I was most reasonably disgusted with having my life exposed in this careless way, and he, perhaps, as reasonably so with my want of resource, and the result was that he decided not to employ me again in such work, and I decided to wait for active insurrectionary movements, in which I could take my place. As it happened, however, the Austrian government had recovered the crown jewels; some one in the secret--Kossuth said Szemere--having learned that Kossuth was sending an expedition to recover them, and, from jealousy of him, disclosed the hiding-place.

Kossuth's practical incapacity for the minutiae of conspiracy in this case was, I judged from what I afterward learned of his compatriots, characteristic of him. He continually neglected the details of important affairs, working by magnificent inspirations, which left out of consideration the defects of human nature. His self-exaltation had offended many patriots who did not fall under his personal magnetism, and his assumption of authority in military matters where he had no knowledge to justify it, alienated the competent officers. The treason of Goergey, as it was popularly considered, was probably due to the perception that Kossuth was an impracticable head for an active revolution, under whose dictature there was no hope of final success while he at the same time refused to abandon his impracticable ideals; and I heard from actual participants that there was great dissatisfaction amongst the officers with his assumption of dignity, out of place, and of command, for which he was incompetent. The fact was that he could not distinguish between the practicable and the impracticable, and though not so visionary as Mazzini, he believed that his power of arousing the wild enthusiasm of the Honveds and masses of Hungarians, due to his marvelous eloquence, was enough to carry on war with, and he would not see that, from the moment that Russia intervened, it was only a question of time when and how the insurrection should end. Then his treatment of the Slavonic element of the population was fatal to the movement. The Serbs only asked to be admitted on an equal footing with the Magyars to the struggle against the centralizing tendency of the German element at Vienna, and Kossuth contemptuously exclaimed, in response to their demand, "These Rascians, who consider themselves a nation and are only a band of robbers," etc.,--a reply hardly calculated to conciliate--one which in fact threw the Slavonic population against the movement and made the Russian intervention inevitable. Kossuth, like Mazzini, was simply an insurrectionary force--the administrative power existed only in great and imposing schemes which lacked adaptation to ordinary human nature and existing circumstances. The personal fascination of the man was beyond anything I have ever known, but his failure as the chief of a state was, I believe, inevitable.

 I took my conge as secret agent, but it was understood that when the renewal of the revolt from Austria, to which he looked forward at no distant time, was at hand, I should take the place to which I had looked forward in the beginning. I saw one of Kossuth's associates subsequently, after the failure of Mazzini's Milan movement in the spring of 1853; and he then told me of the failure, and how the Hungarian soldiers, as had been ordered, refused to fire on the insurgents and had been decimated and sent to Croatia. More than thirty years after, I went to see Kossuth at Turin, and introduced myself as the young man who went to Hungary for him to carry off the crown jewels. He burst out with an impetuous denial of the existence of the expedition. "But," said I, "I have your letters written to me in Pesth." "I should like to see those letters," he replied. I promised to send them, conditionally on his promise to return them; but thinking it over, I sent him only one, inclosed in a stamped envelope directed to myself, with a letter recalling the promise to send it back. I never heard from him again, however, and saw that he only wanted to get the letters to suppress their evidence.

CHAPTER VIII
AN ART STUDENT IN PARIS

I went to Paris to wait for the impending rising in Milan, and meanwhile entered the atelier of Yvon, not to lose my time. My only English-speaking companion in the atelier was a younger brother of Edward Armitage, the Royal Academician; the popular atelier at that time for the English and American students being that of Couture. Yvon had about thirty pupils, to whom his attentions were given gratuitously and conscientiously, three times a week, with rare exceptions of the Saturday visit, by the pupils regarded as the least important. Of the thirty there were not more than a half dozen who showed any degree of special aptitude for their work, and only two were regarded by their colleagues as likely to be an honor to the atelier in the future, and of these, unless they have changed their names, no renown has come in later times. There was a marquis whose income was one hundred francs a month, and a count whose father gave him five sous and a piece of bread for his breakfast when he left home, but the rest were plebeians, with neither past nor future, whose enthusiasm in the face of their weekly failures, and patience in following an arid path, were most interesting as a social phenomenon. I have always found more to wonder at in the failures than in the great successes of artist life--seeing the content and even happiness which some of the hopelessly enthusiastic found in their futile and endless labor. We used to go to work at six in the morning, draw two hours and then go to a little *laiterie* and take our bowl of *cafe au lait* and a small loaf of bread, and then draw till noon, when we went home for the second breakfast. Armitage and myself used to breakfast at the Palais Royal, or some other quarter where the bill of fare was by the rest of the men considered luxurious, and we were dubbed the "aristocrats" of the atelier, my breakfast costing me one franc and a half and my dinner two francs. I had fixed my expenses, as in

London, at the limit of twenty-five francs a week, which had to pay all the expenses of atelier, food, and lodging, and it was surprising how much comfort could then be got for that sum.

I had found a tiny room in the *maison meublee* in the Cite d'Antin where Mrs. Coxe lived, and Mr. Coxe in returning to America had given me charge of his women folk, so that I had a social resource and a relief from tedium which gave me no expense. On Sunday the daughter came home from school, and we all went out to dine at one or another of the Palais Royal restaurants, or made, in the fine weather, an excursion into the environs. Now and then, Mrs. Coxe invited me to take them to the theatre, and thus I saw some of the famous actors, Rachel and Frederic Lemaitre being still vividly impressed on my memory. The afternoons of the week days were given to the galleries and visiting the studios of the painters whose work attracted me, and who admitted visitors. I thus made the acquaintance of Delacroix, Gerome, Theodore Rousseau, and by a chance met Delaroche and Ingres; but Delacroix most interested me, and I made an application to him to be received as a pupil, which he in a most amiable manner refused, but he seemed interested in putting me on the right way and gave me such advice as was in the range of casual conversation. I asked him what, in his mind, was the principal defect of modern art, as compared with ancient, and he replied "the execution." He had endeavored to remedy this in his own case by extensive copying of the old masters, and he showed me many of the copies--passages of different works, apparently made with the object of catching the quality of execution.

In fact, if we consider the differences between the system of education in painting and that in music or any other art or occupation in which the highest executive ability is required, we shall see that we give insufficient opportunity for the painter's hand to acquire the subtle skill we find in the successful violinist or pianist, and which is due to the early and incessant practice in the manual operations of his art. The fact is recognized, that the education of a violinist must begin in the early years, when the will and hand are flexible, and not merely the training, but the occupation, is almost exclusive, for the specialist is made only by a special and relatively exclusive devotion to the particular faculties which are desired to be trained. It is useless to attempt to develop the finest qualities of the draughtsman without the same attention to the condition of training which we insist on in the musician. The theory may come later, the intellectual element may develop under many influences, and healthily, later in life, but the hand is too fine and subtly constituted an implement to be brought into its best condition and efficiency unless trained from the beginning to the definite use imposed on it.

Admitting, therefore, as I do, that the criticism of Delacroix was just, it is evident that, until we give to the modern student of painting a similar training to that which the early one had, we cannot expect him to attain the executive powers of the Italian renaissance, nor can we be sure that he appreciates the subtlety of the work of the masters, any more than the member of a village choir can understand the finesse of the highest order of musical execution, or its first violinist appreciate the touch of a Joachim or a Sarasate. For it is just in the last refinement of touch of a Raphael drawing or the rapid and expressive outline of a Mantegna that we find the analogy between the two arts, in a refinement of touch which is lost on the public, and appreciated only by the practiced student either of music or painting. This final attainment of the hand is only possible to a man who has been trained as a boy to his work. We find it in a water-color drawing of Turner, as in a pencil drawing of Raphael, and in the outlines of the ceiling of the Sistine Chapel, but in modern figure painting never, even in France, where the youth generally takes up the training at fourteen to sixteen. I believe that the reason why this supreme manual excellence is so completely lacking, even in French art, that, so far as I know, only Meissonier amongst them has attained a measure of it, is that the seriousness of life and purpose necessary for any consummate achievement is so rarely found there in conjunction with that early and sound training.

Another acquaintance made in these days, which has always remained a delight to me, was that of Theodore Rousseau, to my mind the greatest of the French landscape painters. Though living and working mostly at Barbison, he had a studio in Paris, and there I used to see him, always received in the friendly and helpful way which was characteristic of most of the French artists of the higher order. Later I went to Barbison, where, besides Rousseau, I knew J.F. Millet, and a minor, but in his way a very remarkable, painter, Charles Jacque. Rousseau was a most instructive talker on art, beyond the sphere of which he hardly seemed to care to go in his thinking. He had never been out of France, had never seen the Alps, and did not care for mountain scenery, but concentrated all his feelings and labor on what he used to call "sujets intimes," the picturesque nooks of landscape one can always find in a highly cultivated country, where nature is tamed to an intimacy with the domestic spirit, or where she vainly struggles against the invasion of culture, as in the borders of the forest of Fontainebleau. In such material, nature withdraws farther and makes a wider margin for art, and the wedding and welding of the two become more subtle and playful.

It has always seemed to me that with all the differences inherent in the antagonism of the characters of the two men, the essential features of the art of Rousseau and Turner were the same; pure impressionism based on the most intimate and largest knowledge of the facts of nature, but without direct copying of them--rather working from memoranda or memories, for neither ever painted directly from nature; the same conception of the subject as a whole, its rhythmic and harmonic unity as opposed to the fragmentary manner of treatment of most of their contemporaries; the lyric passion in line and tint; the same originality which often became waywardness in the conception of subject in itself; the same revolt from all precedent; and the same passion for subtle gradation and infinite space, air, and light--and some of Rousseau's skies were the most vaporous I have ever seen. These are the fundamental agreements of the art of the two great masters, and in those qualities no other man of their countries and epoch has equaled them, but outside of these the contrasts are of the most pronounced. Pyne told me that Turner said he wished he could do without trees; Rousseau worshiped them. Turner loved the mountains; Rousseau never cared to see them and never painted one. Turner, a colorist, reveled in color like a Bacchanal; Rousseau, a tonalist, felt it like a vestal; but both had the sense of color in the subtlest refinement.

Rousseau used to say that if you had not your picture in the first five lines you would never have it, and he laid down as a rule that whenever you worked on it you should go over the whole and keep it together, growing in all parts *pari passu*. Wishing to give me a lesson in values one day as he was painting, he turned his palette over and painted a complete little scheme of a picture on the back of it, suggested by the subject before us as we looked out of the studio window. He showed me his studies from nature, mere notes of form and of local color and pastel. It was to me always a puzzle that, even in the educated art circles of Paris, Corot should have found so great a popularity as compared to that of Rousseau. Without in the least disparaging the greatness of Corot's best work, such for instance as the St. Sebastian and some other classical subjects, the names of which I cannot recall, the range of conception and treatment is limited as compared with that of Rousseau. This alone would give Corot a lower rank, in the absence of a marked superiority in some special high quality--superiority which does not exist, for the picked work of Rousseau possesses technical excellences all its own, as consummate as anything in the world's landscape art, while the range of treatment and subject, so much greater in Rousseau than in Corot, puts the limited and mannered art of the latter as a whole in a distinct inferiority.

Of Millet I saw much less, but enough to know the man and his art, simple and human, the one as the other. His love for manhood in its most primitive attainable types, those furnished by the peasant, was the outcome of his conception of art, such as the Greek of the early schools conceived it, the expression of humanity in a simple and therefore noble state, and of the honest, open, healthy nature of the man himself, averse to all sophistication of society, reverent of an ideal in art, and intolerant of affectations. He conceived and executed his pictures in the pure Greek spirit, working out his ideal as his imagination presented it to him, not as the model served him. The form is of his own day, the spirit of his art that of all time and of all good art, the elaboration of a type and not merely the reproduction of a picturesque model. It is the custom now to class all peasant subjects, emulating the forms of Millet, as belonging to his art. Nothing is more absurd, for the art of Millet was subjective, not realistic; it was in the feeling of the art of Phidias and the Italian renaissance, not in the modern *pose plastique*. The peasant in it was merely incidental to his sympathy with ideal life. Millet was himself a peasant, he used to say, and his moral purpose, if he had any, was the glorification, so far as art can effect it, of his class, the class which above all others in his eyes dignified humanity and held his sympathy. This feeling was with him no affectation, but the deliberate, final conclusion of his life--he reverenced the ***sabot*** and the ***blouse***, the implements of tillage and work, as the Greek did his gods and the implements of war and glory; he saw humanity reduced to its simplest and most noble physical functions and possibilities, as the Greek did the perfection of the physical form, but he lacked the perception of the types of pure beauty of the Greek.

The personal relations between Rousseau and Millet were in the best sense of the word fraternal, and from neither did I ever hear a word to the disparagement of a brother artist, while Rousseau used to talk in the subtlest vein of critical appreciation of his rivals among the landscape painters, the Dupres, Ziem, Troyon, and others, so that I regret that in those days I thought only of my own instruction, and not of the putting on record the opinions of a man whose ideas of art were amongst the most exalted I have known.

A charming nature was that of Troyon, a simple, robust worker, and, like all the larger characters in the French art world with whom I became acquainted, full of sympathy and guidance for those who wanted light and leading. But the lives of these three great painters, like that of Corot (whom I never knew personally), show how completely the French public, so proud of its intelligence of art, ignored the best qualities of it till outsiders pointed to them. Troyon told me that for the first ten years of his career he had never sold a picture, but lived by painting for Sevres; the prosperity of Millet came from the patronage of American collectors, led by the appreciation of a Bostonian painter, William Hunt, and I well remember his famous "Sowers" on the highest line in the Salon, so completely skied that only one who looked for a Millet was likely to see it; while Rousseau, at the time I speak of, was glad to accept the smallest commission, and sold mostly to American collectors. Nor is it otherwise with the Rousseaus, Millets, and Troyons of to-day--the public taste, and the banal criticism of a journalism at its best the tardy echo of the opinions of the rare wise man, find genius only when it has ceased to have the quality of the new and unforeseen.

Yvon, in whose atelier I worked, was essentially a teacher, and his more recent assignment to the directorship of the Ecole des Beaux-Arts put him in his true place, that of a master of style in drawing and the elements of art instruction. He was engaged, when I knew him, on the battle-pieces of the Crimean war, the chief of which were already at Versailles. His was an earnest, indefatigable nature. He was as kindly and zealous a teacher as if he were receiving, like his English confreres, a guinea a lesson. Nothing so strongly marked the difference between the French and the English feeling for art as this characteristic feature of the disinterestedness of the French artist in giving instruction without compensation, while his English colleague of equal distinction gave instruction only at a price impracticable for a poor artist, if indeed he would give it at any price. And even thus, the English drawing-master did not teach art, but facile tricks of the brush. Need one seek any other reason for the curious fact that, with a marked superiority in the occasional highest attainment of rare and original abilities which English art shows, France has become the school of Europe, than that in England the master will teach only on terms which are prohibitive of the formation of a school, while in France, with few exceptions, the most eminent painters regard it as a duty to open their ateliers to pupils often gratuitously, but in any case freely and on terms which are adaptable to the modest means of the poorest class of workers? In how different a position in relation to the art of the world would English art now be in, had Sir Joshua, Gainsborough, Hogarth, Turner, and two or three others who could be named, thrown open their studios to the young enthusiasts who followed them, and the sterling talents which have never been wanting in England been enabled to profit by the experience and art of their elders, instead of groping their way alone to efficiency, or, still worse, going to South Kensington, generally "arriving" too late to succeed fully!

 Waiting the word from Kossuth which should call me to join the ever-impending and ever-postponed insurrection, I passed the winter thus, profiting as I could by all opportunities for the study of art and making acquaintance with the artists. My money was running to an end, but this was a matter in which my faith in Providence did not allow me to borrow trouble, and I made it a rule never to run into debt. That I never borrowed I cannot say, but I never did so except in cases where I was in such personal relations with the lender that if I died without paying the debt, it would neither weigh on him nor on my conscience. I kept up my regular round of economy and work, and one Saturday, when I had paid for my dinner at the Palais Royal restaurant, I found myself with fifty centimes in my pocket, and went on a long walk in the streets of Paris, to meditate on my immediate future. Mrs. Coxe, one of the kindest of friends, would, I knew, gladly lend me what I needed, but I did not allow her to know that I needed, and how to pay for my next day's dinner I did not see. Still, confident that something would turn up, I walked towards my lodgings through the Rue Royale and its arcades, feeling the ten-sou piece in my pocket, when I saw a young girl dart out from one of the recesses of the arcade, dragging after her a boy of two or three years, and then, as if her courage failed, turn and hide herself and him again in the doorway from which she had come. I saw her case at once,--want and shame at begging,--went to her and gave her the ten-sou piece, and went to bed feeling better.

The next day being Sunday and no atelier, I slept late, and was awaked by a knock at my door, when to the spoken "Entrez" came in no other than my friend Dr. Ruggles, between whom and myself there were various communities of feeling which made us like brothers. He sat down by my bedside, and, salutations passed, broke out, "Do you want any money?" His grandfather, just dead, had left him a legacy, and he had come to Paris, artist-like, to spend it. I took from him, as I would have given him the half of my last dollar, a hundred francs, and on this I lived my normal life until, some weeks later, a friend of my brother arriving from New York with instructions to find me out and provide for my wants if I had any, supplied me for any probable emergency, including an order for a free passage home on a steamer of which my brother was part owner. I waited till the spring homesickness made it too irksome to live quietly in Paris, and then finding that the revolution so long waited for had gone by, I went home and to my painting.

In American landscape the element of the picturesque is in a serious deficiency. What is old is the wild and savage, the backwoods and the wild mountain, with no trace of human presence or association to give it sentiment; what is new is still in the crude and angular state in which the utilities are served, and the comfort of the man and his belongings most considered. Nothing is less paintable than a New England village; nothing is more monotonous than the woodland mountain of any of the ranges of eastern North America. The valley of the Mohawk is one of the earliest settled and least unpicturesque sections of the Eastern States, with its old Dutch farmhouses and the winding of the beautiful river; but I had explored it on foot and in every direction for miles around my birthplace, and found nothing that seemed to "make up" save trees and water. I spent one summer after my return amongst these familiar scenes, but found the few subjects which repaid study too remote from any habitable centre to repay the labor needed to get at them. I made long foot excursions through the valleys of the Connecticut and Housatonic; but, after my experience in rural England, it was very discouraging to ransack that still unhumanized landscape for pictures. Everything was too neat and trim, and I remember that one day, when I was on my search for a "bit," I found a dilapidated barn which tempted me to sit down before it, when the farmwife, guessing my intentions, ran out to beg me "not to take the barn yet; they were going to do it up the next week as good as new, and wouldn't I wait?"

An accident drove me to pass one of these summers in as complete seclusion from society as I could find, and where I should be able to do nothing but paint. I had been, two years before, hit in the face by a snow missile, during one of the snowballing saturnalia the New York roughs indulged in after every fall of snow; in this case the missile was a huge block of frozen snow-crust, which flattened my nose on my face and broke the upper maxillary inclosing all the front teeth. I modeled the nose up on the spot, for it was as plastic as clay, but the broken bone became carious, and, after enduring for two years the fear of having my head eaten off by caries, and having resigned the chance of having it shot off in the revolution, I decided to let my brother operate. The bone inclosing the front teeth was taken out with the six teeth, and I was sent into retirement for three months at least, while the jaw was getting ready for the work of the dentist.

I had seen, when last in England, the picture by Millais, "The Proscribed Royalist," which gave me a suggestion of the treatment of a landscape which should be mainly foreground, such as I particularly delighted in. Hoping to find a woodland subject which admitted of this treatment, I went to pass the summer on the farm of an old uncle (where I had caught my first trout), knowing it to be heavily wooded. Of course when one goes out to look for a particular thing he never finds it, nor did I then find the tree subject I wanted, but I found a little spring under a branching beech and surrounded by mossy boulders, and, taking a canvas of my usual size,--25x30 inches,--I gave three months to painting it and carried it home still somewhat unfinished. It was an attractive subject, though not what I had wanted, and was hung in one of the best places in the Academy exhibition, making its mark and mine. It was absolutely unconventional, and the old stagers did not know what to say of a picture which was all foreground. There was much discussion, and, amongst the younger painters, much subsequent emulation; but it did not find a purchaser at my price--$250. Anything so thoroughly realistic that, as President Durand said, "The stones seemed to be, not painting, but the real thing," puzzled the ordinary picture buyer; and the American Art Union, which was the principal buyer of the day, and the ***dernier ressort*** of the young artist, was managed by a committee of ordinary picture buyers. The picture gave rise to a hot discussion when exhibited, the old school of painters denouncing such slavish imitation of nature. As the negative photographic process had just then been introduced in America, I had the picture photographed, and a friend took a print of it to the head of the old school, without any explanation. My antagonist and critic looked at it carefully and exclaimed, "What is the use of Stillman making his pre-Raphaelite studies when we can get such photographs from nature as this!" As I had my brother's generosity to fall back on, I was not obliged to sell, and the picture remained in my studio for two or three years. Later Agassiz saw it and was so delighted with its botany that I decided to give it to him; but when a fellow painter offered--when I was leaving again for Europe--to "raffle it off," I allowed him to do so, and he appropriated the proceeds. I had made a rule of giving the pictures which were not sold in the exhibition to the person who had shown the finest appreciation of them,--a habit which did not contribute to pecuniary success, but which helped my ***amour propre***, and I have always regretted not having sent that picture to Agassiz, who, in later years, became one of my best friends.

CHAPTER IX
SPIRITISM

During the subsequent winter the subject of spiritism occupied the world of the curious and the thoughtful a good deal; and, with my brother Paul, who was a disciple of Swedenborg, I took every occasion that offered to investigate it. Many of my friends were interested in it, and I soon became convinced that it was not the foolish delusion which the scientific world and most religious people pronounced it. In fact, if there be any basis of reality in the phenomena, it is hard to conceive a subject of such vital importance as the determination of the actuality of an individual existence after the physical death. It had always been evident to me that the immense majority of men had no real belief in human immortality, all their pursuits and acquisitions being of a purely material character. My own convictions were ingrained and immovable, but a physical demonstration of their verity seemed to me an eminently desirable result, if attainable, and I entered into the investigation with earnestness and all my patience. Society was largely occupied by the table-tippings and the "rappings." "Circles" were forming amongst all classes, and the mediums became an important element in the world of New York. I very soon came to the conclusion that the professional, paid mediums were, in many cases, the worst kind of impostors, and, in all cases, so far as any intellectual evidence was concerned, of an absurd triviality. Even in the private circles, where no trace of fraud could be suspected, the good faith of all entering them being assured, I found sometimes such extraordinary credulity that the subject would have been offensive to any dispassionate investigator who was not, like myself, determined to get to the bottom of it. The majority of the persons who entered into a circle were ready to believe any extraordinary thing that came to them, and the inanity of the general proceedings, even when fraud was excluded, was sufficient to indispose serious people to take part in them. To me the question had such vital importance that I was determined that neither fraud nor the inconsequent nature of the pretended communications should dissuade me from the most thorough investigation possible.

This investigation lasted several years, and included, to greater or less extent, every form of psychological and physical phenomenon which was offered by spiritism. My experience with the professional mediums was such that I soon ceased to pay any attention to them, finding that, what with the frivolity of their utterances and the evident imposture which, in the case of some of them, invariably marked the display of their powers, the sittings were simply farcical; nor did I ever find, in the doings of the mediums, or in the revelations of the regular spiritistic circles (and I sat in the most important one of them, that over which Judge Edmonds presided, during the two winters) in which no paid medium took part, anything which was not, or could not have been, imposture.

The reason is simple. The professional medium, paid to display certain powers, which are in any case extremely uncertain in their response to the call for them, invariably begins to imitate them when they fail. The mediums are invariably persons of an inferior order of intellect, avid of notoriety, and mostly mercenary, so that the results of the consultations with them were almost sufficient to deter serious-minded people from dealing with them a second time, while the people who formed the regular circles and had made a sect with a devotional character in it, rapidly degenerated into a credulity and materialism which were more discouraging than the most arid skepticism. Physical phenomena which met every demand for absolute guarantee of their genuineness, were very rare, and to meet with them required great patience and persistence, while the scientific student, in the habit of dealing with experiments that had definite results, obeying known or conjectured laws, if entering into an investigation which met at the threshold a frivolous, and possibly fraudulent, "manifestation," threw up the subject, the more readily that in general the student of physical science has no sympathy with psychical research.

Recognizing the correctness of this attitude and the unreliability as well as the utter want of essential importance in the physical manifestations and the invariable inconsequence and silliness of the intellectual results, I withdrew entirely from circles in which mediums took part or in which physical phenomena were sought for, and limited my investigations to the cases in which the good faith of all the company was unquestionable, and the investigation conducted in privacy and sincerity. Here, of course, there was still great uncertainty, and often the most curious triviality and low intelligence, but we were able to check the possible tendency to the simulation of the supra-normal activity. And even so the character of the "manifestation" was generally so trivial and opposed to all preconceived ideas of spiritual intelligence as to justify the conclusion that the departed had left their wits behind them, so that even in those "circles" which included only personal friends and individuals of unquestionable sincerity the results rarely had any intellectual importance. And I came to the conclusion that that form of the phenomena which alone gave any intellectual result, i.e. which manifested ideas in any way transcending the commonplace capacities of commonplace minds, had nothing in common with the physical manifestations, but seemed rather to consist in an exaltation of the intellectual powers of the subject, so that the evidence of any supra-normal power was rather moral than scientific, and had value only according to the relation between the subject and the hearer, and therefore no determinable value to physical science.

The most remarkable of the subjects of this character with whom I became acquainted, which was during the later years of this study, was Mrs. H.K. Brown, the wife of our ablest sculptor of that day. Mrs. Brown was, apart from the peculiar powers she possessed, one of the most remarkable women I have ever known, both morally and intellectually, and the peculiar mental powers she manifested were well known to all the large and thoughtful circle of friends which gathered round her. No physical "manifestation" took place in her presence, and we never "sat" as a "circle," but her telepathic and thought-reading powers in ordinary social intercourse were most surprising. She answered readily any questions proposed in the minds of her interlocutors, often even before they were completely formed, and she possessed the power attributed to Zschokke, of reading, or seeing, past events in the lives of those who were placed ***en rapport*** with her. Bryant, the poet, assured me that she had recounted to him events in his past life not known to any living person except himself, and I had, myself, the evidence that in her presence there was nothing in my past life beyond her perception. On simple contact with a letter from an unknown person she gave me the most remarkable analysis of the character of the writer, and though this evidence is always open to criticism, the disclosures she made were sometimes surprising. I gave her one day a letter of Ruskin without disclosing the authorship, and in the course of a long analysis she said that the writer was not married, to which I replied that in this she was mistaken, and she rejoined, "Then he ought *not* to be." At that time Mr. and Mrs. Ruskin were, so far as I knew, living together, and no rumor of their incompatibility had come about.

Mrs. Brown explained the possession of her occult powers by a voice in the manner of Socrates's demon, which, she said, was always present with her, and which she recognized as entirely foreign to her. She repeated what she heard, word for word as the words came, hesitating and sometimes leaving a sentence incomplete, not hearing the sequence. When she asked who was speaking to her, she received only the reply, "We are spirit," and no indication of personality was ever offered. On one occasion, when Mr. and Mrs. Brown were on a fishing trip into the wild parts of New York State, and, returning, were on their way to the railway station, the wheel of their wagon broke and they had to go to a blacksmith on the road to have it repaired. She said to her husband that they would lose the train, to which the voice replied that they would be in time, for the train was late and they would arrive with a minute to spare. And in fact as they drew up at the station the train came in sight and they had a minute to spare. There were many such instances in which Mrs. Brown showed to the circle of her acquaintances, which was large and included many of the most intellectual minds of the artistic and literary world whose centre was New York, the possession of powers "not dreamed of in our philosophy," but, as she carefully avoided notoriety, they never came under public notice. Her husband implicitly and always followed the directions given her through her demon.

In one of the social gatherings which grew out of the study of spiritism was a lady who, like myself, was a convinced believer in the reality of the phenomena, but skeptical as to the value and personal origin of the communications made in the "circles." Her daughter, a child of seven, was in fact a hypnotic clairvoyant of singular lucidity, and my brother, Dr. Jacob Stillman, obtained from the mother permission to have a private seance, only the mother and child, the doctor, and myself being present. I hypnotized the girl Fanny, and when she opened her eyes in the hypnotic state the doctor made the usual tests for coma, exposing the eyes to the sudden glare of a brilliant light, sticking pins into her flesh, and so forth, and pronounced the coma absolute when, as he stuck a pin in her arm, she spoke, saying, "I wouldn't do that, it might hurt Fanny!" I asked if she felt it, and she replied, "She does not feel it now, but she might when she wakes." "But who are you?" I asked. She replied, "Oh, don't you know? I am Dora." The mother informed us that a young playmate of Fanny's, whose name was Dora Greenleaf, had died some months previously, and that the impersonation through Fanny was always in that name.

The physical test being declared conclusive by the doctor, I asked "Dora" to tell me if there was any spirit friend of ours present, to which she replied that there was a lady there who gave her name as "Kate," and whom she described in terms sufficiently correct to indicate a deceased cousin whose name was Catherine, familiarly called Kate in the family, and this was followed by the names and description of other relatives, all correct as far as names and such identification could go; but to this kind of demonstration I could never attach any importance as to personality, which is indeed a point as to which I have found that reliance can rarely be placed on affirmation, and as to which absolute proof can scarcely be given. As in the case of Mrs. Brown, she replied with lucidity and promptness to every interrogation, and I then began a series of mental questions, being sure at least that the child could not draw from the question matter for an indicated reply. She replied promptly to my questions, and from time to time I explained to my brother what had been asked, that he might follow the conversation. After several relatives had been named, I asked if our brother Alfred was there, to which she instantly replied, "There is a gentleman sitting on the corner of the table by you who says his name is Alfred." The opportunity then occurred to me of asking a "test question," which was, "If Alfred is here, will he tell me when he last saw Harvey?" The relevance of this question will appear from the fact that they were together on the steamer whose boiler burst on the Mississippi, killing my brother and causing injury to the cousin such that he committed suicide a month later. The reply was, "He says he does not remember." At this I remarked guardedly to the doctor, "I asked Alfred when he last saw Harvey, and he replies that he doesn't remember, but he must have seen him on board the boat." To this she instantly replied, with an explosive laugh, "He says that if he did it was all blown out of him!" I will only comment on this reply, that it was quite in accordance with the character of my brother to joke on the most serious subjects--he was an inveterate joker.

At this juncture, and while we discussed the strange reply, Fanny exclaimed, "There is a young gentleman coming through the window; he says his name is Harry--no," she added, holding her ear forward in the direction she indicated as if to hear better, "not Harry, **Harvey**." I then asked, "If Harvey is here, will he tell me if he was with me in Paris, last winter?" She replied, "Yes, he says he was with you in Paris, and that he saw you in the house where you lived with Mrs. Fox--no, not Fox, Coxe--Mrs. Coxe--and he asks if you remember magnetizing Mrs. Coxe at the restaurant?" Mrs. Coxe, as I have said previously, was the lady from Alabama whose acquaintance, as well as that of her husband and their young daughter, I had made when traveling with them through Belgium, on my way to Hungary, and whom Mr. Coxe, when he returned on business to America, left under my protection for the winter. Mrs. Coxe was subject to violent and sudden headaches, which came without warning, and for which during our trip on the Meuse I had once hypnotized her successfully. This led to my being called on subsequently so often that she became an easy subject, and the headaches became less and less frequent and violent. I have before said that it was our custom on Sunday to dine together at some one of the restaurants, and on one of these occasions the headache came on as we sat at the table and I hypnotized her across the table, by simple exertion of my will without passes, and it passed off. The incident was not in my mind, and had, not to cause gossip, never been mentioned by me to any one; my mind was acting at the moment in quite a different direction, and if my thought gave any clue to the answers of Fanny, it would have been in another direction that she would have looked. What was singular and accounted for by no evident circumstance was the manner of the child in listening for the names which she had clearly heard incorrectly--Harry for Harvey, and Fox for Coxe, and after holding her ear forward as would one who heard imperfectly something said to him. No forethought or attempt at deception on the part of a child of seven under the eye of her mother, who was a woman of singular sincerity of character, can be admitted to account for these details in the dialogue, conducted on my part, be it remembered, entirely by mental inquiries.

The evident fatigue of the child put an end to the seance. Neither the mother nor Fanny knew at that time anything of my relatives, our acquaintance being then of recent date, but our intimacy with the family in after years enables me to say that any attempt at deception is out of the question. Fanny died not long after of consumption, as did the mother and two other children, one of whom, an elder sister, had been influenced in the same manner as Miss A., who will be mentioned later, but had never consented to take part in the manifestations, which she regarded with great repugnance. While sitting with us *en petit comite*, she used sometimes to be seized with a convulsive and involuntary effort of her hand to write, but she always refused to submit to the influence. Fanny in her normal state showed no indications of mediumistic powers, nor did the mother.

During the investigation, we heard of a remarkable case in the circle of our own acquaintance which had been kept from public knowledge as far as possible by the aversion to publicity of the father of the subject, my brother's chief foreman. She was a girl of fourteen, of a timid and nervous organization, who had suffered great annoyance by the persistence of the rappings about her wherever she might be; at first in her bedroom, but finally to her great dismay in the class-rooms of the primary public school of New York, in which she held the position of assistant teacher and where she conducted the recitations. The rappings caused such fright amongst the school children that she was menaced with dismissal if they did not cease. She implored the agency which was responsible for the sounds to leave her alone at school and do what seemed best to it at home, and the rappings did actually cease at school. As her father was a man well-to-do in circumstances and annoyed by the occurrence, he silenced the gossip about the matter as well as he could, and gave an inflexible denial to the request for a seance which came from friends who by chance heard of it. My brother Paul, who was a fellow-foreman in the iron works, got permission, however, for a seance at which he and I only were to be present with the girl. The phenomena were so strange that I got permission for a repetition at which only my brother Jacob and myself were present, and we preserved the notes of what passed.

Miss A., as I shall call her, told us in detail the development of the case. After having been for some time troubled by the rappings she began to feel involuntary motions in her right hand which increased to constantly recurring violent exercise of the muscles, when it occurred to her from the character of the motions that the hand wanted a pencil to write and she laid paper and a pencil on the table. Her hand then took possession of the pencil and began to scrawl aimlessly over the paper until, after the interval of many days, the agency seemed to have sufficient control over the muscles to form legible letters. This was a source of amusement to her, and, at the time we made our entry into the investigation, the hand wrote legibly and neatly in reply to mental, i.e. unspoken, questions, she having no control of the muscles so long as the "influence," which was the name she applied to whatever it might be, chose to use it. She knew what was written only when the writing was finished and she read it, as we did; and the writing was, as we found by experiment, quite as regular and well formed when her eyes were bandaged as when she was looking at her work. As a further test of the involuntary character of this we not only tried her with her eyes bandaged, but by my brother talking with her from one side of the table, while she was writing in reply to my mental questions on the other; she talked with him on one subject at the same moment in which she wrote to me on another.

In what was given under these circumstances she wrote for us the replies in conversations with what purported to be the spirits of three deceased relatives, the wife of my brother, my brother Alfred, and cousin Harvey, who had for several years been my most intimate and beloved friend; and the handwriting of the three series of communication was a better imitation of their writing than I, knowing it, could have produced. That of my sister-in-law I was not so familiar with, though my brother recognized it as that of his wife, but that of our brother was a perfect reproduction down to the smallest accidents, and that which was given as the responses of my cousin equally so, and executed with a rapidity of which I was incapable--a large scrawling hand, that of our brother being of a character entirely opposed, slowly and laboriously formed, with occasional omissions of the last line of a final *n*, quite common in his writing. The girl had never known either of these relatives. One of the questions I asked when conversing with Harvey was, "Will you tell me how you died?" to which the only reply was a fixed stare on the part of Miss A., though every other question was answered, by pantomime, affirmative or negative signs, or writing, and always in writing when it was insisted on. Miss A.'s pantomimic powers in this state exceeded anything I have ever seen in professional pantomime, and she employed them largely.

At the conclusion of the questions and replies with Harvey, I asked if he had seen old Turner, the landscape painter, since his death, which had taken place not very long before. The reply was "Yes," and I then asked what he was doing, the reply being a pantomime of painting. I then asked if Harvey could bring Turner there, to which the reply was, "I do not know; I will go and see," upon which Miss A. said, "This influence is going away--it is gone;" and after a short pause added, "There is another influence coming, in that direction," pointing over her left shoulder. "I don't like it," and she shuddered slightly, but presently sat up in her chair with a most extraordinary personation of the old painter in manner, in the look out from under the brow and the pose of the head. It was as if the ghost of Turner, as I had seen him at Griffiths's, sat in the chair, and it made my flesh creep to the very tips of my fingers, as if a spirit sat before me. Miss A. exclaimed, "This influence has taken complete possession of me, as none of the others did. I am obliged to do what it wants me to." I asked if Turner would write his name for me, to which she replied by a sharp, decided negative sign. I then asked if he would give me some advice about my painting, remembering Turner's kindly invitation and manner when I saw him. This proposition was met by the same decided negative, accompanied by the fixed and sardonic stare which the girl had put on at the coming of the new influence. This disconcerted me, and I then explained to my brother what had been going on, as, the questions being mental, he had no clue to the pantomime. I said that as an influence which purported to be Turner was present, and refused to answer any questions, I supposed there was nothing more to be done.

But Miss A. still sat unmoved and helpless, so we waited. Presently she remarked that the influence wanted her to do something, she knew not what, only that she had to get up and go across the room, which she did with the feeble step of an old man. She crossed the room and took down from the wall a colored French lithograph, and, coming to me, laid it on the table before me, and by gesture called my attention to it. She then went through the pantomime of stretching a sheet of paper on a drawing-board, then that of sharpening a lead pencil, following it up by tracing the outlines of the subject in the lithograph. Then followed in similar pantomime the choosing of a water-color pencil, noting carefully the necessary fineness of the point, and then the washing-in of a drawing, broadly. Miss A. seemed much amused by all this, but as she knew nothing of drawing she understood nothing of it. Then with the pencil and her pocket handkerchief she began taking out the lights, "rubbing-out," as the technical term is. This seemed to me so contrary to what I conceived to be the execution of Turner that I interrupted with the question, "Do you mean to say that Turner rubbed out his lights?" to which she gave the affirmative sign. I asked further if in a drawing which I then had in my mind, the well-known "Llanthony Abbey," the central passage of sunlight and shadow through rain was done in that way, and she again gave the affirmative reply, emphatically. I was so firmly convinced to the contrary that I was now persuaded that there was a simulation of personality, such as was generally the case with the public mediums, and I said to my brother, who had not heard any of my questions, that this was another humbug, and then repeated what had passed, saying that Turner could not have worked in that way. After this I did not care to follow the conversation further.

My object in maintaining the mental questioning was, of course, to prevent Miss A. from getting any clue to the meaning of the questions, and I carried the precaution so far as not to look at her while forming the questions in my mind. I also ascertained that she knew nothing of drawing, or of Turner; but while I could not resist the evidence of a mental activity absolutely independent of that of Miss A., I was convinced that there was no question of actual identity. Both the doctor and I were, however, satisfied that on the part of Miss A. there was no attempt at deception, and that the phenomenon, whatever might be the case as to identity, was a genuine manifestation of an intelligence independent of that of the girl. Six weeks later I sailed for England, and, on arriving in London, I went at once to see Ruskin, and told him the whole story. He declared the contrariness manifested by the medium to be entirely characteristic of Turner, and had the drawing in question down for examination. We scrutinized it closely, and both recognized beyond dispute that the drawing had been executed in the way that Miss A. indicated. Ruskin advised me to send an account of the affair to the "Cornhill," which I did; but it was rejected, as might have been expected in the state of public opinion at that time, and I can easily imagine Thackeray putting it into the basket in a rage.

I offer no interpretation of the facts which I have here recorded, but I have no hesitation in saying that they completed and fixed my conviction of the existence of invisible and independent intelligences to which the phenomena were due. The question of the identity of these intelligences--which we may, without prejudging their nature, leaving that to be determined by more complete experiences, consider *disembodied*--with the persons in the flesh whose names they use, is one on which I have great difficulty in forming a conclusion, though, as a rule, my experience in "circles" has been that the imposture was too gross to deceive a person of ordinary intellectual power. The two cases which I have related in the foregoing pages are the only ones in which I have ever been able to find the color of an identification, and of the probability of this I leave the reader to judge. More on the internal than on the external evidence, I consider the probability in the two cases narrated to be in favor of the identity; beyond that I am unwilling to go.

Of the actuality of a disembodied and individual being which, for want of more intelligence of its nature, we call a "spirit," I have no more doubt than I have of my own embodied and individual existence. If, to my philosophic and skeptical critics, this is an indication of intellectual weakness, and excites contempt of my faculties, I cannot help it. I will be honest with myself and the world, have the courage of my convictions, and take the consequences; and I am of the opinion that, if all the cultivated minds which, having studied the subject, agree with me in my conclusions were to be as frank as I am, there would be a large body of witnesses in accord with me. If the inference of a disembodied intelligence, as the source of such phenomena, is difficult of acceptation, that of fraud and collusion is inadmissible, and that of hallucination more difficult than that of the spiritual origin. Of the different hypotheses, then, I take that which seems the most satisfactory one in view of the ascertained facts. But "seeing is believing," and I can fully appreciate the incredulity of reasonable minds as to phenomena which are not in line with our ordinary experience of life, and which, at the same time, are of extreme rarity, and require, for their investigation and actual observation, great patience and the sacrifice of much time and the exercise of much tolerance, surrounded, as the subject is, by gross charlatanry and fraud. But if the beginnings of physical life are worth the years of patient study which science has accorded them, I must believe that the final issue of it is worth the time and study needed to arrive at such results as would, I am convinced, finally crown them. If it were worth while, I could, I am persuaded, define, *a priori*, the lines of investigation along which we should move, but each investigator will choose his own route, and better so.

Two conclusions I draw from my investigations as immovably established, so far as I am concerned. The first is that there are about us, and with certain facilities for making themselves understood by us, spiritual individualities; and, second, that the human being possesses spiritual senses, parallel with the physical, by which it sees what the physical sense cannot see, and hears what is inaudible to the physical ear. And my general and, I think, logical conclusion is that the spiritual senses appertain to a spiritual body which survives the death of the physical.

CHAPTER X
LIFE IN THE WILDERNESS

Under the stimulus, in part, of the desire for something out of the ordinary line of subject for pictures, and in part from the hope that going into the "desert" might quicken the spiritual faculties so tantalized by the experience of the circles, I decided to pass the next summer in the great primeval forest in the northern part of New York State, known as the Adirondack wilderness. It was then little known or visited; a few sportsmen and anglers had penetrated it, but for the most part it was known only to the lumberers. Here and there, at intervals of ten to twenty miles, there were log houses, some of which gave hospitality in the summer to the sportsmen, and in the winter to the "loggers" who worked for the great lumber companies. It was a tract of a hundred miles, more or less, across, mainly unbroken wildwood, cut up by rapid rivers, impossible of navigation, otherwise than by canoes and light skiffs which could be carried from one sheet of water to another on the backs of the woodsmen, around the cascades, and over tracts of intervening land through virgin forests, without roads, and, to a large extent, without paths. I hoped here to find new subjects for art, spiritual freedom, and a closer contact with the spiritual world--something beyond the material existence. I was ignorant of the fact that art does not depend on a subject, nor spiritual life on isolation from the rest of humanity, and I found, what a correct philosophy would have before told me, nature with no suggestion of art, and the dullest form of intellectual or spiritual existence.

One of my artist friends--S.R. Gifford, landscape painter, like myself on the search for new subjects--had been, the year before, to the Saranac Lakes, and gave me the clue to the labyrinth, and I found on Upper Saranac Lake a log cabin, inhabited by a farmer whose family consisted of a wife, a son, and a daughter. There

I enjoyed a backwoods hospitality at the cost of two dollars a week for board and lodging, and passed the whole summer, finding a subject near the cabin, at which I painted assiduously for nearly three months. I passed the whole day in the open air, wore no hat, and only cloth shoes, hoping that thus the spiritual life would have easier access to me. I carried no gun, and held the lives of beast and bird sacred, but I drew the line at fishing, and my rod and fly-book provided in a large degree the food of the household; for trout swarmed. I caught in an hour, during that summer, in a stream where there has not been a trout for years, as large a string as I could carry a mile. All the time that I was not painting I was in the boat on the lake, or wandering in the forest.

My quest was an illusion. The humanity of the backwoods was on a lower level than that of a New England village--more material if less worldly; the men got intoxicated, and some of the women--nothing less like an apostle could I have found in the streets of New York. I saw one day a hunter who had come into the woods with a motive in some degree like mine--impatience of the restraints and burdens of civilization, and pure love of solitude. He had become, not bestialized, like most of the men I saw, but animalized--he had drifted back into the condition of his dog, with his higher intellect inert. He had built himself a cabin in the depth of the woods, and there he lived in the most complete isolation from human society he could attain. He interested me greatly, and as he stopped for the night at the cabin where I was living, we had considerable conversation. He cared nothing for books, but enjoyed nature, and only hunted in order to live, respecting the lives of his fellow-creatures within that limit. He only went to the "settlements" when he needed supplies, abstained from alcoholic drinks, the great enemy of the backwoodsman, and was happy in his solitude. As he was the first man I had ever met who had attempted the solution of the problem which so interested me,--the effect of solitude on the healthy intellect,--I encouraged him to talk, which he was inclined to do when he found that there was a real sympathy between us on this question.

He seemed to have no desire for companionship, but there was nothing morose or misanthropic in his love of seclusion, and I soon saw that, though he had no care for intellectual growth and no longing for books, he thought a good deal in his own way, and that, mingled with his limited thinking and tranquil emotion before nature, there was a large element of spiritual activity, and this had kept him mentally alive. He had heard of spiritism, and his own experience led him to acceptance of its reality. In his solitary life, in the unbroken silence which reigned around him, he heard mysterious voices, and only the year before he had heard one say that he was wanted at home. He paid no attention to it, thinking it only an illusion, but, after an interval, it was repeated so distinctly that he packed his knapsack, took his dog, and went out with the intention of going home. On the way he met a messenger sent after him, who told him that his brother had met with an accident which disabled him from all work, and begged him to come to his assistance. The voice had come to him at the time of the accident. As a rule, however, the voices seemed vagarious, and he attached no importance to them, except as phenomena which interested him slightly. There was nothing flighty about him, no indication of monomania--he reasoned well, but from the point of view of a man who has had only an elementary education, knowing nothing of philosophy; he had no religious crotchets, and apparently thought little or not at all on religious matters--was, in fine, a natural and healthy man, a despiser of alcohol, satisfied with the moment he lived in, and giving no consideration to that which would come after. He had a great contempt for his fellow woodsmen and avoided contact with them.

The backwoods life, as a rule, I found led to hard drinking, and even the old settler with whom I had taken quarters, though an excellent and affectionate head of his family, and in his ordinary life temperate and hard-working, used at long intervals to break bounds, and, taking his savings down to the settlement, drink till he could neither pay for more nor "get it on trust," and then come home penitent and humiliated. About two weeks after I entered the family, the old man took me aside and informed me, mysteriously, that he was going to the settlement for a few days, and begged me to take one of the boats and come down for him on a fixed day, and he would row the boat back. I rowed down accordingly, sixteen miles, and found Johnson at the landing in a state of fading intoxication, money and credit exhausted as usual, and begging some one to give him a half pint of rum "to ease up on." He was "all on fire inside of him," and begged so piteously that I got him a half pint and we started out, he at the oars and I steering. A copious draught of rum, neat, brought his saturated brain to overflow, and before we had gone a mile he was so drunk that I had to guide the oars from behind to insure their taking the water. Then he broke out into singing, beating time on the gunwale of the boat with such violence that it menaced capsizing every minute, and to all my remonstrances he replied by jeering and more uproarious jollity.

It was no joke, for not to talk of him, too drunk even to hold on to the boat, I was a poor swimmer, and in the deep and cold lake water should never have reached the shore swimming, and I found myself obliged to menace violence. I raised the steering paddle over his head and assured him with a savageness that reached even his drunken brain, that I should knock him on the head and pitch him overboard if he did not keep perfectly quiet. There was imminent danger, for the slight boat of that region requires to be treated with the care of a bark canoe, and the menace cowed him so that he quieted down, and watched me like a whipped dog. I tried to get the bottle away from him, but his drunken cunning anticipated me and he put it far behind him, now and then taking a mouthful of rum to keep down the burning. Thus, he pulling and I guiding the oars, we ran through the lower lake, seven miles, to a "carry," where the boat had to be lifted out and carried over into the river above, around a waterfall. Here I fortunately caught the bottle and sent it down the lake, and we labored on through another lake, three miles, and up a crooked river to another carry into the third lake, on which we lived. He was too drunk still to be trusted any further, and, leaving the boat at the landing with him beside it, I carried the load over and waited for him to get sober. After an interval, long enough I thought for him to grow sober enough to carry the boat, I went back and to my amazement he met me, apparently in his right mind, intensely indignant with some one who, having found him in the state of intoxication in which I left him, had given him a drink of what he called "high wines," i.e. common alcohol, the singular effect of which was to bring him immediately to his senses, and we reached home without further incident.

That night, somewhere near midnight, poor Mrs. Johnson awoke me, begging piteously that I would help her and her daughter to search for her husband, who had disappeared from the house. Then she told me that he had the habit of falling into desperate melancholy after his drunken fits, and had even attempted suicide, and they had on one occasion cut the rope by which he had hanged himself, barely in time, and she always expected to find him dead somewhere. We ransacked the house, the loft, the barn, the stable, in all their corners, every shed and nook about the premises and were returning hopeless, to wait for daylight to look for him in the lake, when, as I passed the wood-yard (where the fire-wood was stored and chopped), I heard a groan, and, guided by it, found him lying amongst the chips in the torpor of drunken sleep. The poor wife, with my assistance, dragged him home and put him to bed, and when I saw him the next morning I heard over and over again his vows and resolutions, his sermons against drink, his repentance and pledges never to touch liquor again. When I showed incredulity, he offered to bet with me his best yoke of oxen against one hundred dollars that he never would drink another drop as long as he lived. I thought the bet a safe one for me, at all events, and took it and made him write it down, and it probably kept him from another spree as long as I remained there, but when I saw him again the next summer he was as drunk as ever. I asked him about my oxen, and he leered and jeered and joked with drunken cunning, but said nothing more.

I passed a very happy summer, enjoying my work and wandering in the forest or exploring the streams which flowed into the lake, for subjects. The pure air and the tranquillity of the life, as well as its simplicity, and a certain amount of boating exercise which I went through every day in going to my subject, brought me to the highest point of physical health I had ever known.

The great danger to the uninitiated in the forest life is that of getting lost in this wild maze of trees, with no kind of landmark to serve as a clue. Not a few rash beginners have become bewildered, lost all conception of their whereabouts, and perished of starvation within a short walk of a place of refuge. The houses there were invariably built by the waterways, and the lines of communication were by water, so that there was no necessity for roads. One finds the "runways" or paths made by the deer traversing the woods in every direction,--a perfect labyrinth of byways, ending nowhere and often bringing the incautious wanderer, who supposes them to be paths, back to his starting-place, with the result that he is at once bewildered beyond recovery.

Years before, during one of my college vacations, I had made a fishing excursion to the northern edge of the great woods, in company with a classmate to the manner born, and had learned the need in my excursions of precautions against the bewilderment which follows the loss of one's sense of direction. He told me of one of the inexperienced assistants of a surveying party of which he was a member, engaged in running a township line in the trackless forest, who ventured to leave the line a few minutes, and, before he could recover it, though only a short distance from his party, had become quite insane, and could only be compelled to return with his companions by force. An artist friend who had sketched on the southern border of the Wilderness told me of a similar experience of an English shoemaker who came to settle in a village on the southern edge of the woods, and who, after a short residence, went out to fish in a stream not far from home. He did not return, and, though protracted search was made for him, no trace of him, nor even of his clothing, was ever discovered, except that a resident in a neighboring village said that, a day or two after the stranger had disappeared, a man answering to the description came to his door, his clothes in tatters, and, in a wild and incoherent manner, asked the way to the village from which he had gone, but, before any reply could be made, started off running and disappeared in the woods again. He had contracted the woods madness and so perished.

Of this danger I was well informed, and, beside, I was more or less a child of the woodlands, and had no apprehension of it, having, moreover, an implicit faith in what I considered a kind of spiritual guidance in all I did,--a delusion which at least served to keep me in absolute self-control under all circumstances. It was probably this which kept me during my wanderings from falling into the panic which constituted the real danger, depriving the victim temporarily of the use of his reasoning powers. I had, however, an interesting experience which gave me a clearer comprehension of the phenomenon, which is a very curious one.

One of the woodsmen had told me of a waterfall on a trout stream of considerable size which emptied into a lake near by us, and, in the hope of finding a subject in it, I took the boat one afternoon and began to follow the course of the stream up from the mouth. After a half mile of clear and navigable water it became so clogged with fallen trees that more lifting than paddling was required, and, as its course was extremely tortuous, I occasionally got out and examined the vicinity of the stream bed and the course above, if, perchance, there might be better navigation beyond. On one of the digressions I suddenly came on the stream running back on its previous course and parallel to it. Instantly, in the twinkling of an eye, the entire landscape seemed to have changed its bearings,--the sun, which was clear in the sky, it being about three o'clock, shone to me out of the north, and it was impossible to convince myself that my senses deceived me, or accept the fact that the sun must be in the southwest, the general direction from which the stream was flowing, and that, to get home again, I must turn my back to it, if I had lost my boat, as seemed certain. Then began to come over me, like an evil spell, the bewilderment and the panic which accompanied it. Fortunately, I recognized this panic from the experiences I knew of, and was aware that if I gave way to it I was a lost man, beyond any finding by the woodsmen, even if they attempted to track me.

Fresh wolf tracks were plenty all along the bank of the stream; panthers and bears abounded in that section, and the wilderness beyond me was never explored, and hardly penetrable, so dense was the undergrowth of dwarf firs and swamp cedars. I had one terrible moment of clear consciousness that if I went astray at that juncture no human being would ever know where I was, and the absolute necessity of recovering my sense of the points of compass was clear to me. By a strong effort of the will, I repressed the growing panic, sat down on a log and covered my face with my hands, and waited, I had no idea how long, but until I felt quite calm; and when I looked out on the landscape again I found the sun in his proper place and the landscape as I had known it. I walked back to my boat without difficulty and went home, and I never lost my head again while I frequented the wilderness. I grew in time to know the points of the compass, even when the sky was covered, and often came home from my excursions after sunset without confusion, but I know that I then owed my escape from the most terrible of deaths entirely to my presence of mind, and this I probably owed then, and always, to that supreme confidence in the protection of a superior power which never deserted me.

My studies in spiritism had developed in me another feeling which was kin to this--a belief in a spiritual insight, the possession of which would always, if entire confidence were placed in it, tell one at the moment what should be done; an intuition which would guide him, but only on the condition that it was trusted absolutely. And at that period of my life I followed it with unfaltering trust. A curious illustration of this state of mind and its effect had already occurred to me in the spring, and, as it relates to this topic and involves a very curious psychological phenomenon, I describe it in connection with the so similar experience of the backwoods. I had made an engagement with Mr. Brown, the sculptor, to meet him on the trout brook that ran through my uncle's farm in Rensselaer County, New York, a hundred and fifty miles from New York city, but I lost the last train by which I should have met him at the appointed time,--daybreak of the following day. Determined to keep the engagement, I took a parallel railway, which ran through western Massachusetts and a section of country which was entirely strange to me. From the station at which I left the railway, that of Pittsfield, there was a distance of several miles to the place of rendezvous, which was in the town of Hancock, close to the boundary line between New York and Massachusetts. On leaving the station I inquired the way to Hancock, and was told that as the crow flies, i.e. across an intervening mountain, it was twelve miles without even a footpath; but, by the road around the mountain, twenty, and that, unless I knew the mountain, I could not possibly find my way over it. It was just sunset as I left Pittsfield, and I decided to risk the mountain, and, following a wood road, I climbed the steep declivity, and, going in what seemed to me a nearly direct course, after an hour's walk I recognized a gap in the hill-crest and a distant view with two little lakes reflecting the sky which I had seen the hour before. I had been following a charcoal-burner's road in a circle; daylight had gone, and the mists were coming on heavy as rain, making it impossible to see ten yards before me. There was no recourse, if I was to keep the rendezvous, but to follow the guidance of the inner sense. I determined to obey the monitor, and plunged into the forest, in unhesitating obedience to it. I did not guess, nor did I try to make any kind of calculation. I felt that I must go in a certain direction, and, as the darkness deepened, I had, literally, to grope my way, walk with my hands out before me, not to run against the trees, for, with little exception, the way lay through dense woodland, amidst which were scattered boulders and fallen tree trunks. I could not--and I speak without the least exaggeration--see the trees at my arm's length. The fog was so dense and the trees so wet that every leaf or twig dripped on me till I was soon drenched as completely as if I had been plunged into a lake. I passed the crest of the mountain and began to descend. I felt with my foot before me, and when the foot could find nothing to rest on I drew it back and moved sidewise till I found a step down, hanging on all the time to the branches of the trees. I descended in this way a long distance, then came to a marsh which I recognized only by the croaking of the frogs in it; and, skirting the sound, made my way past it, always keeping the general direction through the divergences made necessary by the nature of the land.

At length I got through the fog and came to an open field, beyond which I saw the outlines of trees against the clouded sky, and, keeping on, came to a road. A few yards further on a light was visible in a roadside cottage, and other houses were near, but all dark, as it was late and all in them were asleep. I knocked at the door where I saw the light and asked the way to Hancock. "Why, you are in Hancock," the man of the house replied; and, on my inquiry as to an inn, he informed me that a hundred yards further on there was an inn, to which I went. The rain had ceased, but I was soaking, and I asked for a fire by which to dry my clothes, and a bed, both of which were quickly prepared; and then the landlord asked me where I came from and by what road. When I told him that I came from Pittsfield by the mountain, he exclaimed in amazement, "Why, there is no place by which a white man could come over in broad daylight;" an exaggeration, as I could testify, but it proved that the passage was held to be dangerous to the ordinary foot traveler. The incident in itself has no importance, but the singular feeling under which I made the passage of a trackless mountain, in complete darkness for the most difficult part of the way, in perfect confidence in a mysterious guidance which justified that confidence, was a mental phenomenon worthy of note, the more that it was in keeping with the invariable feeling which had grown up in me from the cogitations of years. As I am telling the story of my life, and the spiritual influences of my early years are an essential part of that life, it cannot be irrelevant to the general result that I should show how the springs of it acted. While I was on the wood road in the earlier portion of the walk, I followed unhesitatingly the visible path and made no question of guidance; but, when thrown on the occult influence in which I confided, I walked unerringly to my destination with the precision of an animal which nature had never deserted. In the subsequent years, of which a great part was always spent in the wilderness, the fascination of which became absorbing, this occult faculty strengthened, so that I was never at a loss, when in the trackless forest, for my path homeward. I then thought it a newly acquired faculty. I now regard it as simply a recovered one, inherent in all healthy minds, but lost, as many others have been, in civilization.

And in this connection I will deal, once for all, with the gifts to me from this wild nature to which I abandoned myself with all the ardor of a quest. The tendency of the imagination, even healthy, acting in a vacancy, is to create illusions, or, if there be a certain occult mental activity, such as that I have alluded to in my

Pittsfield experience, to intensify its action to such a degree that it finally usurps the function of the senses. In the solitude of the great Wilderness, where I have passed months at a time, generally alone, or with only my dog to keep me company, airy nothings became sensible; and, in the silence of those nights in the forest, the whisperings of the night wind through the trees forced meanings on the expecting ear. I came to hear voices in the air, words so clearly spoken that even an incredulous mind could not ignore them. I sat in my boat one evening, out on the lake, watching the effects of the sky between the gaunt pines which, under the prevalence of the west winds, grew up with an easterly inclination of their tops, like that of a man walking, and thus seemed to be marching eastward into the gathering darkness. They gave a sudden impression of a procession, and I heard as distinctly as I ever heard human speech, a voice in the air which said "the procession of the Anakim." Over and over again, as I sat alone by my camp-fire at night, dreaming awake, I have heard a voice from across the lake calling me to come over and fetch it, and one night I rowed my boat in the darkness more than a mile, to find no one. Watching for deer from a treetop one day, in broad sunlight, and looking over a mountain range, along the crest of which were pointed firs and long level ridges of rock in irregular alternation, the eerie feeling suddenly came over me, and the mountain-top seemed a city with spires and walls, and I heard bands of music, and then hunting-horns coming down with the wind, and there was a perfect illusion of the sound of a hunting party hurrying down into the valley, which gave me a positive panic, as if I were being pursued and must run. I remember also on another occasion a transformation--transfiguration rather--of the entire landscape in colors, such as neither Titian nor Turner ever has shown me. It was a glorification of nature such as I had never conceived and cannot now comprehend.

The fascination of indulgence in this illusory life became such that I lingered every summer longer, and finally until November, when, in that high and northerly locality, the snow had fallen and the lake began to freeze, living only under a bark roof, open to the air and to the snow, which fell on my bed during the night. I can easily imagine the life leading to insanity. Probably my interest in nature and my painting kept me measurably free from this danger, but not from illusions as unaccountable as spiritism, and sometimes more real than the physical facts. I had one evening, when I was lying awake in a troubled state of mind, a vision of a woman's face, utterly unlike anybody I had ever seen, and so beautiful that with the sheer delight of its beauty I remained for several days in a state of ecstasy, as if it were constantly before me, and I remember it still, after more than forty years, as more beautiful than any face I ever saw in the flesh. It was as real while it lasted as any material object could have been, though it was a head without a body, like one of the vignetted portraits which used to be so fashionable in my early days.

In all these years, whether in the wilderness or in the city, I lived a life more or less visionary, and absorbed in mental problems, in the solution of which I passed days of intense thought, and, when no solution appeared to my unaided reason, I used to fast until the solution appeared clear, which was often not until after days of entire abstinence from food of any kind,--the fast lasting occasionally three days,--by which time the diminishing mental energy brought with it a diminution of the perplexity, and I came out of the morbid state in which I had been, and probably found that there was generally an intellectual delusion in the problem. I do not remember the particular character of these perplexities, save that they were generally questions of right and wrong in motive or conduct; but, from the fact that they did not leave a permanent impression, I suppose they were of the ***quisquilioe*** which seem at times to perplex the theological world, the stuff that dreams are made of. Up to this time all the doctrines of my early creed held me in bondage: the observance of the Seventh-Day Sabbath, and the exigencies of the letter of the law, which entirely hid the worth of its spirit, were imperative on me, and out of the complication I derived little happiness and much distress. This kind of Christianity seems to me now of the nature of those burdens which the Pharisees of old laid on the consciences of their day, and it was only years later than the time I am here writing of, when I finally moved to Cambridge and came under the influence of the broadest form of Christianity, that they were removed. I owe it to one of the truest friends of my early manhood,--Charles Eliot Norton, the friend as well of Emerson, Lowell, and Longfellow,--that the real nature of these questions of formal morality was finally made clear to me, and life made a relatively simple matter.

This is an anticipation of the sequence of my development, and given here not to leave occasion to recur to the subject again. On my return from the first summer in the Wilderness, I took a studio again in New York, and entered more formally into the fellowship of the painters of landscape. Being under no necessity of making the occupation pay, I probably profited less than I ought by the regime, and followed my mission of art reformer as much by a literary propaganda as by example. This, as all know who have ventured it, was more or less the effectual obstacle to practical attainment in art.

CHAPTER XI
JOURNALISM

Given a disposition to enter into controversies on art questions, provoked by the general incompetence of the newspaper critics of that day, and the fact that there was at that time no publication in America devoted to the interests of art, it happened naturally that I was drawn into correspondence with the journals on art questions, and easily made for myself a certain reputation in this field. I obtained the position of fine-art editor of the "Evening Post," then edited by W.C. Bryant, a position which did not interfere with my work in the studio. My duties on the paper were light and pecuniarily of no importance, though the "Post" was the journal which, of all the New York dailies, paid most attention to art, and had the highest authority in questions of culture. My relations with Bryant were intellectually profitable to me. He was a man who enjoyed the highest consideration amongst our contemporary journalists,--of inflexible integrity in politics as well as in business affairs. The managing editor was John Bigelow, a worthy second to such a chief. Bryant was held to be a cold man, not only in his poetry, but in his personal relations; but I think that, so far as his personality was concerned, this was a mistake. He impressed me as a man of strong feelings, who had at some time been led by a too explosive expression of them to dread his own passions, and who had, therefore, cultivated a repression which became the habit of his life. The character of his poetry, little sympathetic with human passion, and given to the worship of nature, confirmed the general impression of coldness which his manner suggested. I never saw him in anger, but I felt that the barrier which prevented it was too slight to make it safe for any one to venture to touch it. A supreme sense of justice went with a somewhat narrow personal horizon, a combination which, while it made him hold the balance of judgment level, so far as the large world of politics was concerned, made him often too bitter in his controversies touching political questions; but the American political daily paper has never had a nobler type than the "Evening Post" under Bryant. Demonstrative he never was, even with his intimates, but to the constancy and firmness of his friendship all who knew him well could testify, and, as long as he lived, our relations were unchanged, though my wandering ways brought me seldom near him in later years.

It was about this time that I had become acquainted with the Browns. Of Mrs. Brown I have, in anticipation of events, spoken in connection with spiritism, apart from which she had a remarkable individuality in many ways. She had those instantaneous perceptions of truth in the higher regions of thought, the spiritual and moral, which seem to be either instinct or inspiration. Their house was the meeting place of a school of transcendental thinkers (and I use the word in its full sense) of a very remarkable character. As the Browns lived on the Brooklyn side of the East River, we used to call it the "Brooklyn School," though there were residents of Philadelphia and Boston among the friends who met there. Now and then we had formal *conversazioni*, and at these I soon took a prominent part, though the inquiring spirit strongly predominated over the oracular, which is likely to monopolize such assemblies. I was in that eagerness of early and incomplete knowledge which is more ready in expression than that of riper years, and it is probable that I distinguished myself by fluency of verbiage. It became customary to look to me for the most hazardous reaches of conjecture or inquiry, though certainly Mrs. Brown was worth far more than I was. I had already solved several problems which to-day are not clear to me, and I had always a ready answer to most mysteries. Talk I certainly could, and Mrs. Brown, who had the most sincere friendship for me, and believed in my possibilities if not in my attainment, delighted to put me forward.

One day there was a *conversazione* at which Alcott, the "Oracle of Concord," was to be the chief personage, and, as he had the habit of monopolizing the talk when he took any part, it was suggested that I should try my strength against his. Although Emerson had a high opinion of Alcott, he seemed to me a shallow and illogical thinker, and I have always felt that the good opinion of Emerson was due rather to the fact that Alcott presented him with his own ideas served up in forms in which he no longer recognized them, and so appeared to Emerson as original. Such originality as he had was rather in oracular and often incomprehensible verbiage than in profundity of thought, but, as no one attempted to bring him to book, bewildered as his audience generally was by the novelty of the propositions he made or by their absurdity, he used to go on until suggestion, or breath, failed him. I have forgotten, long ago, the subject of debate, but Alcott started out with one of his characteristic mysticisms, and, after allowing him to commit himself fully, I interrupted him with a question. He was a little irritated at being stopped in the flow of his discourse, and showed it, but this did not disturb me, and I insisted on an explanation of what he had said. He was not in the habit of explaining himself, and replied very much at random, but the training of old Dr. Nott stood me in good stead, and I followed him up with question and objection until he assumed a position diametrically opposed to that from which he started, when I called his attention to the fact that what he then said contradicted what he had at first said. He got angry, and replied that "a man was not bound to be consistent with himself, and that it did not matter." But he lost his thread as well as his temper, and the ***conversazione*** came to a premature end, to the great satisfaction of the conspirators, most of whom had at one time or another been silenced in their attempts to bring him to logical conclusions, by his autocratic way of carrying on the debate without regard to objections, which they had not had the courage to urge.

He seemed to me a shallow philosopher, but I must confess that my treatment of him did not become a man so much younger than he. I felt, however, a certain amount of honest indignation at what seemed to me his charlatanic manner of putting off on people his random and improvised suggestions regarding questions which seemed to me then of vital importance to society. It is easy now to see that I was in the stage of mental evolution at which detail is of supreme importance because large views of life and philosophy have not yet come above the horizon. Alcott was a drawing-room philosopher, the justice of whose lucubrations had no importance whatever, while his manner and his individuality gave to wiser people than I the pleasure which belongs to the study of such a specimen of human nature. He amused and superficially interested, and he no doubt enjoyed his distorted reflections of the wisdom of wiser men as much as if he had been an original seeker. I did not then understand that all knowledge is relative, and that, ***au fond***, his offense was the same as mine, that of thinking he had arrived at finality in the discovery of truth.

It was, perhaps, a natural consequence of all this talking and writing about art that, in the absence of a periodical devoted to it, my friends came to the conclusion that it would be a good and useful thing that I should start an art journal. I had read with enthusiasm "Modern Painters," and absorbed the views of Ruskin in large draughts, and enjoyed large intercourse with European masters, and with Americans like William Page, H.K. Brown, S.W. Rowse, and H.P. Gray, all thinkers and artists of distinct eminence. In this school I had acquired certain views of the nature of art which I burned to disseminate. They were crude rather than incorrect, but they were largely responded to by our public; they were destructive of the old rather than informing of the new, and leaned on nature rather than art. The art-loving public was full of Ruskinian enthusiasm, and what strength I had shown was in that vein. The overweening self-confidence that always carried me into dangers and difficulties which a little wisdom would have taught me to avoid, made me too ready to enter into a scheme which required far more ability and knowledge of business than I possessed. All my artist friends promised me their assistance, and I found in John Durand, the son of the president of the National Academy of Design, a partner with a seconding enthusiasm and the necessary assistance in raising the capital. This amounted to $5000, for the half of which my brother Thomas became security. We doubted not that the undertaking would be a lucrative one, and one of the principal motives which was urged on me by my artistic friends and promising supporters was that it would furnish me with a sufficient income to enable me to follow my painting without any anxiety as to my means of living. We started a weekly called "The Crayon," and at the outset I was able to promise the assistance of most of our best writers residing in New York.

In order to secure the support of the Bostonians I went to Boston and Cambridge, where I was met by a cordial response to my enthusiasm, Lowell becoming my sponsor to the circle of which he was then and for many years the most brilliant ornament. To him and his friendship in after years I owe to a very large degree the shaping of my later life, as well as the better part of the success of "The Crayon." He was then in a condition of profound melancholy, from the recent death of his wife. He lived in retirement, seeing only his most intimate friends, and why he should have made an exception in my case I do not quite understand. It may be that I had a card of introduction from his great friend William Page or from C.F. Briggs (in the literary world, "Harry Franco"), but if so it would have been merely a formal introduction, as my acquaintance with either of those gentlemen was very slight, and I do not remember an introduction at all. My impression is that I introduced myself. But I was an enthusiast, fired with the idea of an apostolate of art, largely vicarious and due to Ruskin, who was then my prophet, and whose religion, as mine, was nature. In fact, I was still so much under the influence of the "Modern Painters" that, like Ruskin, I accepted art as something in the peculiar vision of the artist, not yet recognizing that it is the brain that sees and not the eye. But there is this which makes the nature-worshiper's creed a more exalting one than that of the art-lover, that it is impersonal and compels the forgetting of one's self, which for an apostolate is essential.

It was probably this characteristic of my condition which enlisted the sympathy of Lowell, who, even in his desolation, had a heart for any form of devotion, and who, with the love of nature which was one of his own most marked traits, had a side to which my enthusiasm appealed directly. The mere artist is, unless his nature is a radically religious one, an egotist, and his art necessarily centres on him, nature only furnishing him with material. I was dreaming of other things than myself or that which was personal in my enterprise, and Lowell felt the glow of my enthusiasm. He introduced me to Longfellow, Charles Eliot Norton, R.H. Dana, and other of his friends at Cambridge, and at a later visit to Agassiz, Emerson, Thomas G. Appleton (Longfellow's brother-in-law), Whittier, E.P. Whipple, Charles Sumner, and Samuel G. Ward, banker and a lover of art of high intelligence, the friend of poets and painters, and to me, in later years, one of the kindest and wisest of advisers and friends.

Lowell invited me to the dinner of the Saturday Club,--a monthly gathering of whatever in the sphere of New England thought was most eminent and brilliant,--and here I came, for the first time, into contact with the true New England. It may be supposed that I returned to New York a more enthusiastic devotee of that Yankeeland to which I owed everything that was best in me. In my immediate mission,--the quest of support for "The Crayon,"--I had abundant response in contributions, and Lowell himself, Norton, and "Tom" Appleton, as he was called familiarly by all the world, continued to be amongst my most faithful and generous contributors as long as I remained the editor. Longfellow alone of all that literary world, though promising to contribute, never did send me a word for my columns, not, I am persuaded, from indifference or want of generosity, but because he was diffident of himself, and, in the scrutiny of his work, for which, of course, the demand from the publishers was always urgent, he did not find anything which seemed to him particularly fit for an art journal. Nor would any of those contributors ever accept the slightest compensation for the poems or articles they sent, though "The Crayon" paid the market price for everything it printed to those who would accept. The first number of "The Crayon" made a good impression in all the quarters from which praise was most weighty and most desired by its proprietors. Bryant and Lowell had sent poems for it, but I had to economize my wealth, and could print only one important poem in each number, and to this I gave a page, so that I had to choose between the two. Bryant had sent me a poem without a title, and when I asked him to give it one he replied, "I give you a poem, give me a name;" and I called it "A Rain Dream," which name it bears still in the collected edition of his works. Lowell sent me the first part of "Pictures from Appledore," one of a series of fragments of a projected poem,--like so many of his projects, never carried to completion. The poem was intended to consist of a series of stories told in "The Nooning," in which a party of young men, gathered in the noon spell in the bowl formed by the branches of a pollard willow,--one of those which stood, and of which some still stand, by the river Charles,--were to tell their personal experiences or legends drawn from the sections of New England from which they came. Bryant's greater reputation at that time made his contribution more valuable from a publishing point of view, especially in New York, where Lowell had as yet little reputation, while Bryant was, by many, regarded as the first of living American poets. But my personal feeling insisted on giving Lowell the place at the launch, and to reconcile the claim of seniority of Bryant with my preference of Lowell puzzled me a little, the more that Lowell insisted strongly on my putting Bryant in the forefront as a matter of business. I determined to leave it to Bryant, whose business tact was very fine, and who had as little personal vanity as is possible to a man of the world, which, in the best sense, he was. But I prepared the ground by writing a series of articles on "The Landscape Element in American Poetry," the first of which was naturally devoted to Bryant, and then, taking him the poem of Lowell and the article on himself, I asked his advice as to the decision, saying that I could only print his poem or Lowell's, but that I desired to take in as wide a range of interest as possible. He decided at once in favor of the poem of Lowell and the Bryant article in the landscape series.

The success of "The Crayon" was immediate, though, from a large journalistic point of view, it was, no doubt, somewhat crude and puerile. It had a considerable public, sympathetic with its sentimental vein, readers of Ruskin and lovers of pure nature,--a circle the larger, perhaps, for the incomplete state of art education in our community. That two young men, without any experience in journalism, and with little in literature, should have secured the success for their enterprise which "The Crayon" indisputably did enjoy was a surprise to the public, and, looking at it now, with my eyes cooled by the distance of more than forty years, I am myself surprised. That "The Crayon" had a real vitality, in spite of its relative juvenility, was shown by the warm commendation it received from Lowell, Bryant, and other American literati, and from Ruskin, who wrote us occasional notes in reply to questions put by the readers, and warmly applauded its tone. Mantz was our French correspondent, and William Rossetti our English, and a few of the artists sent us communications which had the value of the personal artistic tone. But I learned the meaning of the fable of "The Lark and her Young," for the general assistance in the matter of contributions, promised me by the friends who had originally urged me to the undertaking, was very slow in coming, and, for the first numbers, I wrote nearly the whole of the original matter, and for some time more than half of it. I wrote not only the editorial articles and the criticisms, but essays, correspondence, poetry, book notices (really reading every book I noticed), and a page or two of "Sketchings," in which were notes from nature, extracts from letters, and replies to queries of the readers.

I remained in the city all the burning summer, taking a ten days' run in the Adirondacks in September. I kept office all day, received all who came to talk art or business, and did most of my writing at night,--not a regime to keep up one's working powers. Durand did some excellent translations from the French, and the late Justin Winsor sent us many translations, both of verse and prose, from the German, as well as original poetry. Aldrich was a generous contributor. Whittier, Bayard Taylor, and others of the lyric race sent occasional contributions, and amongst the women, who were, as a rule, our most enthusiastic supporters, were Mrs. Sigourney, and, not the least by far, Lucy Larcom, the truest poetess of that day in America, who gave us some of her most charming poems. She was teacher in a girls' school somewhere in Massachusetts, and I went to see her in one of my editorial trips. We went out for a walk in the fields, she and her class and myself, and they looked up to me as if I were Apollo and they the Muses; and we went afield in many things. Henry James, the father of the novelist, was also a not infrequent contributor; and, amongst the artists, Huntington, President Durand (the father of my associate), Horatio Greenough, and William Page appeared in our pages, with many more, whose names a file of "The Crayon" would recall.

During the year, Lowell received the appointment of Professor of Modern Languages at Harvard, and on the eve of his sailing from New York we gave him a dinner, to which, besides some of his old friends, such as E.P. Whipple and Senator Charles Sumner, I invited Bryant and Bayard Taylor. I knew that Bryant held a little bitterness against Lowell for the passage in the "Fable for Critics," in which he said:--

"If he stir you at all, it is just, on my soul, Like being stirred up with the very North Pole;"

and I told Lowell how the dear old poet felt, and then put them together at the table. Lowell laid himself out to captivate Bryant, and did so completely, for his tact was such that in society no one whom he desired to interest could resist him; and our dinner was a splendid success. Of all present at it only Durand and myself are now living.

The subscription list of our paper had risen in the first month to above 1200, and the promise for the future seemed brilliant. But, unfortunately, neither of us understood the business part of journalism, or that a paper does not live by its circulation, but by advertisements; and that our advertisements, being a specialty, must be canvassed for vigorously. We did not canvass. Cunning publishers persuaded us that it would be a good thing to take their advertisements for nothing, so as to persuade the others that we had a good advertising list. But the bait never took, and we never got the paying list, and the printer, being interested in our expenditure, never helped us to economize, but played the "Wicked Uncle" to our "Babes in the Wood," and so we wasted our substance. It was, perhaps, fortunate that the funds ran short as they did, for our five thousand dollars could not go far when the subscriptions were all paid in and spent, and the overwork began to tell on me fatally.

With the conclusion of the third volume I broke down and had to give up work entirely.

When I got out of harness, and had no longer the stimulus of the daily demand and habit of work, the collapse was such that I thought I was dying. I gave my share of the paper to Durand, to do as he pleased with, and went off to North Conway, in the mountains of New Hampshire, to paint one more picture before I died. I chose a brook scene, and Huntington and Hubbard--two of our leading painters--and a Duesseldorf-educated painter, by name Post, sat down with me to paint it. I gave six weeks of hard work to a canvas twelve by eighteen inches, and my competitors cordially admitted my victory. Autumn fell on my work with still something to do to it, and it was never finished to my entire satisfaction, but it was one of the successes of the year at the Academy Exhibition. I stayed late amongst the mountains, only thinking of dying, but nature brought me round. There came, towards the end of the season, a newly married couple from Boston, destined in later years to become a large part of my life,--Dr. and Mrs. Amos Binney. Mrs. Binney was one of the earliest women graduates in medicine in America,--an earnest, true woman, whose ministrations to me in body and mind, in those months of dying hopes, flying leaves, and early snowfalls, were full of healing. I had had a skirmish with Cupid that summer, my first real passion, reciprocated by the subject of it, one of the ardent readers of "The Crayon," an enthusiast in art, and like me in Ruskin--an affair which ended in our double defeat under the merciless veto of the mother of my flame. In that affair Mrs. Binney's tact and knowledge of human nature befriended me profoundly, and were the origin of a cordial intimacy which incidentally had on my subsequent life a great influence. Dr. Binney gave me a commission for two pictures, and invited me to come to his home near Boston to paint them.

CHAPTER XII
CAMBRIDGE

I gave up my studio in New York and went to Boston, and, my commissions executed, moved from there to Cambridge, where I made my home, returning thenceforward to the Adirondacks in the late summer and autumn of every year while I remained in America. The following springtime I spent making studies in that classic neighborhood, especially in a favorite haunt of Lowell's,--the "Waverley Oaks,"--a curious group of large white oaks, which had taken root some hundreds of years ago on the foot of a moraine of one of the offsets of the great glacier which, countless thousands of years ago, had covered New England. They were beautiful trees and greatly beloved by Lowell, for whom I painted the principal group, with Beaver Brook, another of his favorite studies, and he lying by its bank in the foreground, a little full-length portrait, not the length of my finger. I painted also a similar portrait of Longfellow, under the most beautiful of the oaks, on an eight-by-ten-inch canvas. It was a good portrait, but Lowell deterred me from finishing it as I wished, saying that if I touched it again I should destroy the likeness. I am half inclined to think that his insistence was mainly intended to abbreviate the martyrdom of Longfellow, whom I conducted every day to the Oaks, to insure pre-Raphaelite fidelity, making him sit on a huge boulder under the tree and even forgetting to carry a cushion for him, so that he sat on the bare stone until at last the discomfort was evident to me, when I folded my coat to cushion his stone seat. So kindly was his nature that he had submitted to the inconvenience with the docility and delicacy of a child, without a sign of impatience.

This absolute unselfishness and extreme consideration for others was characteristic of the man. I saw much of him in the years following, and found in him the most exquisitely refined and gentle nature I have ever known,--one to which a brutal or inconsiderate act was positive pain, and any aggression on the least creature, cause of intense indignation. My recollection of his condescension to my demands on his time and physical comfort remain in my memory as the highest expression of his social beneficence. Longfellow was not expansive, nor do I remember his ever becoming enthusiastic over anything or anybody. One who knew nothing of his domestic life might have fancied that he was cold, and certainly he did not possess that social magnetism which made Lowell the loadstone of so many hearts, and made the exercise of that attraction necessary to his own enjoyment of existence. Longfellow adored his wife and children; but beyond that circle, it seemed to me, he had no imperious longing to know or be known. He had likes and dislikes; but so far as I understood him, no strong antipathies or ardent friendships. He had warm friendships for Lowell, the Nortons, and Agassiz, for example, but I think he had but a mild regard for Emerson, and I remember his saying one day that Emerson used his friends like lemons,--squeezing them till they were dry, and then throwing them away. This showed that he misunderstood Emerson, but perhaps intelligibly, for Longfellow had few of those qualities which interested Emerson, and there could not have been much in common to both. Emerson liked men who gave him problems to solve,--something to learn,--while Longfellow was transparent, limpid as a clear spring reflecting the sky and showing all that was in its depths; and to Emerson he offered no problem. I never saw him angry but once, and that was at his next-door neighbor shooting at a robin in a cherry-tree that stood near the boundary between the two gardens. The small shot carried over and rattled about us where we sat on the verandah of the old Washington house, but showed the avicidal intent, and Longfellow went off at once to protest against the barbarity, not at all indignant at the personal danger, if he thought of any.

His adoration of his wife was fully justified, for rarely have I seen a woman in whom a Juno-like dignity and serenity were so wedded to personal beauty and to the fine culture of brain and heart, which commanded reverence from the most ordinary acquaintance, as in her. No one who had seen her at home could ever forget the splendid vision, and the last time I ever saw her, so far as I remember, was in summer time, when she and her two daughters, all in white muslin, like creatures of another world, evanescent, translucent, stood in the doorway to say good-by to me. In the same costume, a little later, she met death. She was making impressions in sealing-wax, to amuse her daughters, when a flaming drop fell on the inflammable stuff, and in an instant she was in flames, burned to death before help could come. It was then that they found that Longfellow was not the cold man they had generally believed him. He never recovered from the bereavement, and shortly after he became a Spiritualist, and, until he in his glad turn passed the gates of death, he lived in what he knew to be the light of her presence. And certainly if such a thing as communion across that grim threshold can be, this was the occasion which made it possible. There was something angelic about them both, even in this life,--a natural innocence and large beneficence and equanimity which, in the chance and contradiction of life, could rarely be found in wedded state.

One of the most notable personages of that little world, whom I knew in connection with Longfellow, was his brother-in-law,--Thomas G. Appleton,--a most distinguished amateur of art; a subtle, if sometimes vagarious, critic, poet, and thinker: the wit to whom most of the clever things said in Boston came naturally in time to be attributed. The famous saying that "Good Americans, when they die, go to Paris," is generally supposed to be his, though Oliver Wendell Holmes told me one day that he himself was really the author of it; but, if a keen witticism was floating about fatherless in the Boston circles it drifted to Tom Appleton as putative parent. His, too, was a kindly nature, and many a rising artist found his way to a larger recognition by Appleton's unobtrusive aid. He, like Longfellow, was a sincere Spiritualist. One of the most remarkable of this group of men was Professor Peirce, mathematician, of whose flights into the higher regions of the science of numbers and quantities many interesting things were told. He had written a book to show, if I remember right after so many years, that the square root of minus one was a right angle

$$(\sqrt{-1} = 90 \text{ deg.}),$$

which was said to have been read only by a mathematician who presided over an observatory in the Ural Mountains. He had an extraordinary power of making his abstruse results clear to the ordinary intellect, and was in various directions a brilliant conversationalist. One day, going into Boston in the omnibus with him, I questioned him as to the famous problem. To my astonishment he went through a demonstration adapted to my intelligence which made me understand the nature of the substitution and the solution before our half hour's transit was ended. I did not understand the mathematical statement, but he put it in common-sense terms, which I apprehended perfectly, though I never could repeat them.

    My Adirondack experiences and studies having excited the desire on the part of several Cambridge friends to visit the Wilderness, I made up a party which comprised Lowell and his two nephews, Charles and James Lowell (two splendid young New Englanders afterwards killed during the Civil War), Dr. Estes Howe, Lowell's brother-in-law, and John Holmes, the brother of Oliver Wendell, considered by many of the Cambridge set the wittier and wiser of the two, but who, being extremely averse to publicity, was never known in literature. We made a flying journey of inspection through the Saranac Lakes and down the Raquette River to Tupper's Lake, and then across a wild and at that day a little explored section to the head of Raquette Lake, and down the Raquette River back to the Saranacs; the party returning home and I back to the headwaters of the Raquette to spend the summer painting. I built a camp on a secluded bay, which still bears my name amongst the men of the section, and there I worked in a solitude sometimes complete and sometimes shared by my guide, who passed his time between the camp and the settlement at Saranac, whence I drew all my supplies beyond those which the lake and the forest furnished us with. The solitude of the Wilderness at that time can be no longer found anywhere in the vast woodland which, much mutilated and scarred by fires and clearings, still covers the district between the springs of the Mohawk and the rivers which empty into the St. Lawrence. There was one settler on the lake, from whom I could, when necessary, get a loaf of bread, but the solitude for nine days out of ten was not broken by a strange footfall. My camp was a shelter of bark, raised on poles, open in front to the morning sun, just sufficing to shed the rain, while my bed was a layer of the branches of the fir-trees that grew around. Trout from the lake, broiled on the coals of the camp-fire, with a piece of bread, was the usual and sufficient fare, though we now and then killed a deer when Steve, my guide, was with me; at other times the dog was my only company, and in this monotonous life I found the most complete content that my experience has given me. Here wolves abounded, but only on one occasion did they attempt to disturb me, which was when I had left by the lake shore a deer we had killed in the morning, and they came at night to steal the meat. Bears were abundant, but even shyer than the wolves; and though we heard, now and then, the cry of a panther (puma), we never saw one.

Here the morbid passion of solitude grew on me. The serene silence was seldom broken save by the cry of an eagle or an osprey, high overhead, the chirping of the chickadee flitting about the camp to find a crumb, or the complaining note of the Canada jay, most friendly of all wild birds, seeking for the scraps of venison we used to throw out for him. No other birds came to us, and one of the most striking features in the Wilderness was the paucity of bird life and voice. As I sat painting, I would see the gray eagle come down, with his long cycloidal swoop, skimming along the surface of the water, and catch, as he passed, the trout that sunned itself on the surface; or the osprey seizing it with his direct plunge into the lake, from which, after a struggle that lasted sometimes a minute, the only sign of his presence being the agitated water, he would emerge with the fish in his claws and sail aloft, hurrying to escape to the forest with his prey lest the eagle, always watching from the upper air, should rob him of his hard-earned booty. Once I saw the eagle make the mighty plunge from far above, the frightened osprey dropping the fish to escape the shock, and the eagle catching it in midair as it fell. The little incidents of woodland life took the place of all other diversions and left no hour void of interest. I broke up the camp only when the autumn was so far advanced that it was uncomfortable to live in the open air. It is difficult for one who has not had the experience to understand the fascination of this absolute solitude, or the impressiveness of the silence, unbroken sometimes through whole days. I had absolutely no desire for human society, and I broke camp with reluctance, to return to my studio at Cambridge.

The next summer the party was formed which led to the foundation of the Adirondack Club, and the excursion it made is commemorated by Emerson in his poem "The Adirondacs." The company included Emerson, Agassiz, Dr. Howe, Professor Jeffries Wyman, John Holmes,--who became as fond as I was of this wild life,--Judge Hoar (later Attorney-General in the cabinet of President Grant), Horatio Woodman, Dr. Binney, and myself. Of this company, as I write, I am the only survivor. I did my best to enroll Longfellow in the party, but, though he was for a moment hesitating, I think the fact that Emerson was going with a gun settled him in the determination to decline. "Is it true that Emerson is going to take a gun?" he asked me; and when I said that he had finally decided to do so, he ejaculated, "Then somebody will be shot!" and would talk no more of going.

Perhaps the final reason, or that which would in any case have indisposed him to join the company, was his want of sympathy with Emerson. Emerson and he were in fact of antagonistic intellectuality, both in the quality of the exquisite courtesy which distinguished them equally, and in the fibre of intellectual working and the quality of mental activity. Longfellow was of the most refined social culture, disciplined to self-control under all circumstances and difficulties; sensitive in the highest degree to the forms of courtesy, and incapable by nature as by training of an act or word which could offend the sensibilities of even a discourteous interlocutor,-- capable at worst of an indignant silence, but incapable of invading the personality of another; not serene, but of an invincible tranquillity; with no sympathy for mystery or obscurity; supremely above the general and commonplace by the exquisite refinement to which he carried the expression of what the general and commonplace world felt and thought; remote from roughness in the form or the substance of his thought; in short, the *ne plus ultra* of refinement as man and poet. Emerson was too serene ever to be discourteous, and was capable of the hottest antagonism without rudeness, and the most intense indignation without quickening his speech or raising his tone; grasping and exhausting with imaginative activity whatever object furnished him with matter for thought, and throwing to the rubbish heap whatever was superficial; indifferent to form or polish if only he could find a diamond; reveling in mystery, and with eyes that penetrated like the X-ray through all obscurities, and found at the bottom of them what there was to find; arrested by no surfaces, inflexible in his devotion to truth, and indifferent to all personalities or artificial conditions of men or things. Nothing but the roots of things, their inmost anatomy, attracted him; he brushed away contemptuously the beauties on which Longfellow spent the tenderness of his character, and threw aside like an empty nutshell the form to which an artist might have given the devotion of his best art, for the art's sake. In his temper there was no patience with shams, little toleration of forms. It would, I should think, be clear to one who was well acquainted with both men, that there was little in common between them beyond culture, but I never heard Emerson speak of Longfellow, and can only judge by induction that he never occupied himself much with him.

We tried also to get Dr. Holmes to join us; but the Doctor was devoted to Boston, and could not have lived long out of its atmosphere, and with the woods and savagery he had no sympathy. He loved his Cambridge friends serenely, Lowell, Agassiz, and Wyman, I think, above others; but he enjoyed himself most of all, and Boston more than any other thing on earth. He was lifted above ennui and discontent by a most happy satisfaction with the rounded world of his own individuality and belongings. Of the three men whom I have personally known in the world who seemed most satisfied with what fate and fortune had made them,--viz., Gladstone, Professor Freeman, and Holmes,--I think Holmes enjoyed himself the most. There was a tinge of dandyism in the Doctor; not enough to be considered a weakness, but enough to show that he enjoyed his personal appearance and was content with what he had become, and this in so delightful a way that one accepted him at once at his own terms. The Doctor stood for Boston as Lowell for Cambridge, the archetype of the Hub. Nobody represented it as he did. Tom Appleton was nearest him, but Tom loved Paris better, and was a "globe-trotter," as often in Europe as in Massachusetts, while the Doctor hardly left the Hub even for a vacation; there was nothing beyond it that was of great import to him. He was the sublimation of Yankee wit as Lowell was of Yankee humor and human nature, and he made of witticism a study; polished, refined, and prepared his "bons mots", and, at the best moment, led the conversation round to the point at which it was opportune to fire them off. He had a large medical knowledge of human nature and intellectual pathology, but I could never realize that he was a physician; I should not have trusted myself to his doctoring. As with Longfellow, his family affections were absorbing, and his love for his son, the present Mr. Justice Holmes, and his pride in him, were very pleasant to see, and they ran on the surface of his nature like his love for Boston; but I could never feel that his feeling for his outside friends was more than a mild, sunny glow of kindliness and vivid intellectual sympathy. Of course I judge him from a difficult standard, that of the Cambridge circle, in which the personal relations were very warm, and especially comparing him with Lowell and the Nortons, with whom friendship was a religion.

Holmes and Lowell were the antitheses of the New England intellect, and this more in their personality than in their writing. If Lowell could have acquired Holmes's respect for his work, he would have left a larger image in the American Walhalla; but he never gave care to the perfection of what he wrote, for his mind so teemed with material that the time to polish and review never came. Holmes, like a true artist, loved the *limae labor*. He was satisfied, it seemed to me, to do the work of one lifetime and then rest, while Lowell looked forward to a succession of lifetimes all full of work, and one can hardly conceive him as ever resting or caring to stop work. Lowell's was a generous, widely sympathizing nature, from which radiated love for humanity, and the broadest and most catholic helpfulness for every one who asked for his help, with a special fund for his friends. Holmes drew a line around him, within which he shone like a winter sun, and outside of which his care did not extend. The one was best in what he did, the other in what he was. Holmes always seemed to me cynical to the general world; Lowell to have embodied the antique sentiment, "I am a man, and hold nothing human as indifferent to me." Both were adored by those around them, and the adoration kindled Holmes to a warmer reflection to the adorers; Lowell felt it as the earth feels sunshine, which sinks into the fertile soil and bears its fruit in a richer harvest.

Excepting Holmes, Norton, and Longfellow, our company included most of what was most distinct in the world in which we lived, with some who were eminent only in their social relations, and who neither cared to be nor ever became of interest to the general world. The care of arranging the details of the excursion was left to me, and I had, therefore, to precede the company to the Wilderness, and so missed what must have been to the others a very amusing experience. The rumor of the advent of the party spread through the country around Saranac, and at the frontier town where they would begin the journey into the woods the whole community was on the *qui vive* to see, not Emerson or Lowell, of whom they knew nothing, but Agassiz, who had become famous in the commonplace world through having refused, not long before, an offer from the Emperor of the French of the keepership of the Jardin des Plantes and a senatorship, if he would come to Paris and live. Such an incredible and disinterested love for America and science in our hemisphere had lifted Agassiz into an elevation of popularity which was beyond all scientific or political dignity, and the selectmen of the town appointed a deputation to welcome Agassiz and his friends to the region. A reception was accorded, and they came, having taken care to provide themselves with an engraved portrait of the scientist, to guard against a personation and waste of their respects. The head of the deputation, after having carefully compared Agassiz to the engraving, turned gravely to his followers and said, "Yes, it's him;" and they proceeded with the same gravity to shake hands in their order, ignoring all the other luminaries.

I had in the mean time been into the Wilderness and selected a site for the camp on one of the most secluded lakes, out of the line of travel of the hunters and fisherfolk,--a deep *cul de sac* of lake on a stream that led nowhere, known as Follansbee Pond. There, with my guide, I built a bark camp, prepared a landing-place, and then returned to Saranac in time to meet the arriving guests. I was unfortunately prevented from accompanying them up the lakes the next morning, because a boat I had been building for the occasion was not ready for the water, and so I missed what was to me of the greatest interest,--the first impressions of Emerson of the Wilderness, absolute nature. I joined them at night of the first day's journey, in a rainstorm such as our summer rarely gives in the mountains, and we made the unique and fascinating journey down the Raquette River together; Agassiz taking his place in my boat, each other member of the party having his own guide and boat.

The scene, like the company, exists no longer. There is a river which still flows where the other flowed; but, like the water that has passed its rapids, and the guests that have gone the way of all those who have lived, it is something different. Then it was a deep, mysterious stream, meandering through unbroken forests, walled up on either side in green shade, the trees of centuries leaning over to welcome and shelter the voyager, flowing silently in great sweeps of dark water, with, at long intervals, a lagoon setting back into the wider forest around, enameled with pond lilies and sagittaria, and the refuge of undisturbed waterfowl and browsing deer. Our lake lay at the head of such a lagoon, a devious outlet of the basin of which the lake occupied the principal expanse, reached through three miles of no-man's route, framed in green hills forest-clad up to their summits. The camp was a shelter of spruce bark, open wide in front and closed at the ends, drawn on three faces of an octohedron facing the fireplace. The beds were made of layers of spruce and other fir branches spread on the ground and covered with the fragrant twigs of the arbor vitae. Two huge maples overhung the camp, and at a distance of twenty feet from our lodge we entered the trackless, primeval forest. The hills around furnished us with venison, and the lake with trout, and there we passed the weeks of the summer heats. We were ten, with eight guides, and while we were camping there we received the news that the first Atlantic cable was laid, and the first message sent under the sea from one hemisphere to the other,--an event which Emerson did not forget to record in noble lines.

CHAPTER XIII
THE ADIRONDACK CLUB—
—EMERSON AND AGASSIZ

In the main, our occupations were those of a vacation, to kill time and escape from the daily groove. Some took their guides and made exploration, by land or water; after breakfast there was firing at a mark, a few rounds each, for those who were riflemen; then, if venison was needed, we put the dog out on the hills; one boat went to overhaul the set lines baited the evening before for the lake trout. When the hunt was over we generally went out to paddle on the lake, Agassiz and Wyman to dredge or botanize or dissect the animals caught or killed; those of us who had interest in natural history watching the naturalists, the others searching the nooks and corners of the pretty sheet of water with its inlet brooks and its bays and recesses, or bathing from the rocks. Lunch was at midday, and then long talks, discussions ***de omnibus rebus et quibusdam aliis***; and it was surprising to find how many subjects we found germane to our situation.

Emerson has told the daily life in verse in "The Adirondacs," adding his own impressions of the place and time. It is not generally considered among the most interesting of his poems, being a narrative with reflections, and such a subject could hardly rise above the interest of the subject of the narration, which was only a vacation study; but there are in it some passages which show the character of Emerson's intellect better than anything else he has written. His insight into nature, like that of the primitive mind as we find it in the Greek poetry, the instinctive investment of the great mother with the presence and attribute of personality, the re-creation from his own resources of Pan and the nature-powers, the groping about in that darkness of the primeval forest for the spiritual causes of the things he felt,--all this is to me evident in the poem; and it is the sufficient demonstration of the antique mould of his intellect, serene, open-eyed to natural phenomena, seeing beyond the veil they are, to the something beyond, but always questioning, hardly concluding, and with no theories to limit his thought or bend it to preconceived solutions. Knowing that all he saw in this undefiled natural world, this virgin mother of all life (for around Follansbee Pond, at the time we went, there was the primeval woodland, where the lumberer had not yet penetrated, and the grove kept still the immaculacy of the most ancient days), that all this was the mask of things, he was ever on the watch if perchance he might catch some hint of the secret,--secret never to be discovered, and therefore more passionately sought. This seems to me contained in "The Adirondacs" as in no other work of the philosopher. And to me the study of the great student was the dominant interest of the occasion. I was Agassiz's boatman on demand, for while all the others had their personal guides and attendants, I was his; but often when Emerson wanted a boat I managed to provide for Agassiz with one of the unoccupied guides, and take the place of Emerson's own guide. Thus Emerson and I had many hours alone on the lake and in the wood. He seemed to be a living question, perpetually interrogating his impressions of all that there was to be seen. The rest of us were always at the surface of things,--even the naturalists were only engaged with their anatomy; but Emerson in the forest, or looking at the sunset from the lake, seemed to be looking through the phenomena, studying them by their reflections on an inner speculum.

In such a great solitude, stripped of the social conventions and seeing men as they are, mind seems open to mind as it is quite impossible for it to be in society, even the most informal. Agassiz remarked, one day, when a little personal question had shown the limitations of character of one of the company, that he had always found in his Alpine experiences, when the company were living on terms of compulsory intimacy, that men found each other out quickly. And so we found it in the Adirondacks: disguises were soon dropped, and one saw the real characters of his comrades as it was impossible to see them in society. Conventions faded out, masks became transparent, and for good or for ill the man stood naked before the questioning eye,--pure personality. I think I gathered more insight into the character of my companions in our greener Arden, in the two or three weeks' meetings of the club, than all our lives in the city could have given me.

And Emerson was such a study as can but rarely be given any one. The crystalline limpidity of his character, free from all conventions, prejudices, or personal color, gave a facility for study of the man, limited only by the range of vision of the student. How far my vision was competent for this study is not for me to decide; so far as it went I profited, and so far as my experience of men goes he is unique, not so much from intellectual power, for I should be indisposed to accept his as the mind of the greatest calibre among those I have known, but as one of absolute transparency of intellect, perfect receptivity, and devotion to the truth. In the days of persecution and martyrdom Emerson would have gone to the stake smiling and undismayed, but questioning all the time, even as to the nature of his own emotions. It was this serene impassibility in his study of human nature which gave the common impression of his coldness,--an impression which is shown, by the anecdote I have elsewhere recorded of Longfellow, to have been shared by one who might have been supposed to know him well for years. But Emerson was not cold or disposed to make mere subjects of analysis of his friends, as Longfellow thought; he was an eager student of men as of nature, but superficial men he tired of and dropped, nothing being to be learned from them, though where he found what he looked for in a character he never tired of it. His friendships were of the most constant because of this temper, and it was only their serenity and almost impersonality that made them seem frigid to those whose temperament was widely different. Wrong, injustice to man or beast, roused his warmth in indignation,--he could be hot enough on occasion; though the quiet warmth of his affection for his friends was like the sun of May. But undoubtedly his greater passion was for the truth in whatever form he could find it.

Of all the mental experiences of my past life nothing else survives with the vividness of my summers in the Adirondacks with Emerson. The last sight I had of him was when, on his voyage to Egypt, he came to see me at my home in London, aged and showing the decay of age, but as alert and interrogative as ever with his insatiate intellectual activity. And as I look back from the distance of years to the days when we questioned together, he rises above all his contemporaries as Mont Blanc does above the intervening peaks when seen from afar, not the largest in mass, but loftiest in climb, soaring higher if not occupying the space of some of his companions, even in our little assemblies. Emerson was the best listener I ever knew, and at the other meeting-place where I saw him occasionally, the Saturday Club, his attention to what others were saying was far more notable than his disposition to enter into the discussions. Now and then he flashed out with a comment which lit up the subject as an electric spark might, but in general he shone unconsciously. I remember that one day when, at the club, we were discussing the nature of genius, some one turned to Emerson and asked him for a definition of the thing, and he instantly replied, "The faculty of generalizing from a single example;" and nobody at the table could give so good and concise a definition. There is a portrait of him by Rowse, who knew and loved him well, which renders this side of Emerson in a way that makes it the most remarkable piece of portraiture I know, the listening Emerson.

His insatiability in the study of human nature was shown curiously in our first summer's camp. He had the utmost tenderness of animal life and had no sympathy with sport in any form,--he "named the birds without a gun,"--and when we were making up the outfit for the outing he at first refused to take a rifle; but, as the discussion of make, calibre, and quality went on, and everybody else was provided, he at length decided, though no shot, to conform, and purchased a rifle. And when the routine of camp life brought the day of the hunt, the eagerness of the hunters and the passion of the chase, the strong return to our heredity of human primeval occupation gradually involved him, and made him desire to enter into this experience as well as the rest of the forest emotions. He must understand this passion to kill. One Sunday morning, when all the others went out for the drive of the deer,--necessary for the larder, as the drive the day before had failed,--Emerson asked me to take him out on the lake to some quiet place for meditation. We landed in a deep bay, where the seclusion was most complete, and he went into the woods to meditate. Presently we heard the baying of the hound as he circled round the lake, on the hillsides, for the deer at that season were reluctant to take to the water, and gave a long chase; and, as he listened, he began to take in the excitement of the hunters, and finally broke out abruptly, "Let us go after the deer;" and down the lake we went, flying at our best, but we arrived too late,--Lowell had killed the deer.

He said to me later, and emphatically, "I must kill a deer;" and one night we went out "jack-hunting" to enable him to realize that ambition. This kind of hunting, as most people know, is a species of pot-hunting, much employed by the hunters for the market, and so destructive to the deer that it is now forbidden by the law in all the Adirondack country. The deer are stalked by night along the shores, where they come in to feed, the hunter carrying in his boat a light so shaded that it illuminates only the space directly in front of the boat, the glare blinding the animal so that he does not see the boat or the boatman. In this way the deer may be approached within a few yards if the paddler is skillful; but as he stands perfectly still, and is difficult to see in the dim light, the tyro generally misses him. We paddled up to within twenty yards of a buck, and the guide gave the signal to shoot; but Emerson could see nothing resembling a deer, and finally the creature took fright and ran, and all we got of him was the sound of galloping hoofs as he sped away, stopping a moment, when at a safe distance, to snort at the intruders, and then off again. We kept on, and presently came upon another, toward which we drifted even nearer than to the first one, and still Emerson could see nothing to distinguish the deer from the boulders among which he stood; and we were scarcely the boat's length from him, when, Emerson being still unable to see him, and not caring to run the risk of losing him, for we had no venison in camp and the luck of the morning drive was always uncertain, I shot him. We had no other opportunity for the "jack-hunt," and so Emerson went home unsatisfied in this ambition,--glad, no doubt, when he recalled the incident, that he had failed.

The guides--rude men of the woods, rough and illiterate, but with all their physical faculties at a maximum acuteness, senses on the alert and keen as no townsman could comprehend them--were Emerson's avid study. This he had never seen,--the man at his simplest terms, unsophisticated, and, to him, the nearest approach to the primitive savage he would ever be able to examine; and he studied every action. When the dinner was over, and the twilight coming on, he sometimes asked me to row him out on the lake to see the nightfall and watch the "procession of the pines," that weird and ghostly phenomenon I have before alluded to.

More than a generation has passed since then. Twenty-five years afterward I went back to the scene of the meeting. Except myself, the whole company are dead, and the very scene of our acting and thinking has disappeared down to its geological basis, pillaged, burnt, and become a horror to see; but, among the memories which are the only realities left to it, this image of Emerson claiming kinship with the forest stands out alone, and I feel as if I had stood for a moment on a mount of transfiguration, and seen, as if in a vision, the typical American, the noblest in the idealization of the American, of all the race. Lowell was of a more cosmopolitan type, of a wider range of sympathies and affections, accepted and bestowed, and to me a friend, loved as Jonathan loved David; but, as a unique, idealized individuality, Emerson looms up in that Arcadian dream more and more the dominant personality. It is as character, and not as accomplishment or education, that he holds his own in all comparisons with his contemporaries, the fine, crystallized mind, the keen, clear-faceted thinker and seer. I loved more Agassiz and Lowell, but we shall have many a Lowell and Agassiz before we see Emerson's like again. Attainments will be greater, and discovery and accomplishments will surpass themselves as we go on, but to *be*, as Emerson was, is absolute and complete existence.

Agassiz was, of all our company, the acknowledged master; loved by all, even to the unlettered woodsmen, who ran to meet his service as to no other of the company; by all the members of it reverenced as not even Emerson was; the largest in personality and in universality of knowledge of all the men I have ever known. No one who did not know him personally can conceive the hold he had on everybody who came into relations with him. His vast command of scientific facts, and his ready command of them for all educational purposes, his enthusiasm for science and the diffusion of it, even his fascinating way of imparting it to others, had even less to do with his popularity than the magnetism of his presence and the sympathetic faculty which enabled him to find at once the plane on which he should meet whomever he had to deal with. Of his scientific position I cannot speak, though I can see that his was the most powerful of the scientific influences of that epoch in America. When we were traveling it was always in my boat, and we moved as his investigations prompted, wherever there seemed to be a promise of some addition to his collections. We dredged and netted water and air wherever we went, and of course there arose a certain kind of intimacy, which was partly that of a *camaraderie* in which we were approximately equals, that of the backwoods life in which I was, if a comparison were to be made, the superior, and partly that of teacher and pupil; for, with trifling attainments, I had the passion of scientific acquisition, and all that Agassiz needed to open the store of his knowledge was the willingness of another to learn.

The *odium scientificum*, which I notice is no less bitter than the variety *theo-*

logicum, has, in these years, poured on Agassiz the floods of its opprobrium, and even the little dogs of physical science bark at his name; but his greater contemporaries knew and esteemed him better. The revival of the evolutionary hypothesis by Darwin, and the controversies growing out of it, then filled the air, and Agassiz paid the penalty of his eminence and constancy to the system in which he had been grounded by his master, Cuvier. He was attacked and insulted by men who had never made an observation, and, what was more curious, as a panderer to the theological prejudices of the past. But in my mind was still the memory of a former outcry and theological persecution of him, because he had himself laid down what might be considered the forerunner of the doctrine of evolution,--the declaration that the human race could not have been the offspring of one Adam, but must have had a multiple beginning. The result of this was to bring on his head the execrations of the theological world in a storm which no one who had witnessed it was likely to forget or take for other than what it was, the proof of his absolute scientific honesty,--a proof needed by no one who knew him personally, but which, in view of the later animosity shown him, requires reaffirmation.

As I was much with him at this time, and perhaps, out of his family, the one to whom he talked with the greatest freedom and fullness on the subject, owing to my own intense interest in it, it cannot be amiss that I state his exact position as far as he let me see it. It must be remembered that the doctrine of evolution, as he knew it, and in the only form in which it was then stated, was simply and purely that of development by natural selection acting on chance variation, and differing mainly by this from the doctrine of Lamarck, which had long been rejected by the scientific world at large. We have seen since then that this primitive doctrine has been largely supplemented by other theories, and that it no longer stands before the scientific world in the bare simplicity of Darwin's original statement, though even he, at a later date, claimed natural selection not as the only but as the most influential agency of variation of species in creation; repudiating, however, a plan in the universe, and not demanding the influence of the conscious mind on creation. Agassiz's primary objection to the doctrine was that it left the creator out of creation, for it distinctly repudiated the element of design in it; and, though he did not recognize the Creator of Genesis, he could not dispense with the supreme mind.

Myself a convert to the doctrine of evolution, in as absolute a form as it is held even by the materialists, though differently, I am persuaded that if Agassiz had lived long enough to see the latest development of it he would have accepted it, as did Professor Owen, who was, like Agassiz, and possibly even more literally, a believer in the designer of the universe. The fundamental ground for Agassiz's rejection of it is stated by himself in one of the lectures delivered at Cambridge, as follows: "I believe that all these correspondences between the different aspects of animal life are the manifestations of mind acting consciously with intention towards one object from beginning to end. This view is in accordance with the working of our minds; it is an instinctive recognition of a mental power with which our own is akin, manifesting itself in nature. For this reason, more than any other, perhaps, do I hold that this world of ours was not the result of the action of unconscious organic forces, but the work of an intelligent, conscious power." Whatever might have been the process by which the orderly creation was produced (into which he did not inquire), it was the result of a definite plan and the work of design. The immutability of species, **as he defined species**, was the logical consequence of this theory, and that, it seems to me, is the substantial difference between him and Darwin.

But Agassiz was no sectarian, and held no other creed than a belief in the Creator. In the fibre of the man was the consciousness of the immanent deity, rooted, perhaps, in that influence of his early theological environage from which no man can ever escape, though he may rebel against it; and the almost universal deduction by the scientific world from Darwin's theory then was that there could be no divine design in creation. It was this negation of the direction of the great artist in the process of creation against which Agassiz rebelled; and although, at a later phase of the conflict, Darwin himself protested against the implication sometimes drawn from his theory, there can be no question that at that moment the general evolutionary opinion was that the hypothesis of a divine authorship of creation was superfluous. Agassiz maintained the presence of "Conscious Mind in Creation;" Darwin did not deny it explicitly, nor did he admit it.

As a matter of observation, no case of a development of one species from another has ever been noted, and the evidence for it is precisely analogous to that adduced by Agassiz, "that it is in accordance with the working of our minds," still further illuminated by the side-lights which science has thrown on it since Agassiz died. The ultimate decision in the individual mind will be according to the bias for or against the "conscious mind" or automatic creation; and it must not be forgotten that one of the most powerful arguments for a large evolution was the discovery by Agassiz that the embryo of the highest organizations passes through an evolution similar to that of the animal creation. Professor Martins--a leading French scientist and an evolutionist--says of Agassiz: "Another of these precursors of modern science is Louis Agassiz. The oldest fossil forms have a simpler organization than the later ones, and represent some stage of the embryonic development of the latter. This truth, established by Agassiz, has, more than any other, enlightened the history of creation, and prepared for the generalization by which the whole may be comprehended. The oldest fishes known are all more or less related to the sharks and skates; their teeth and scales only, with small portions of the skeleton, have been preserved. Their form, widely different from that of the living species, recalls that of the embryo of our living fishes. This is a truth which Louis Agassiz was the first to proclaim to the scientific world."[6]

But, beyond this question as to the evidence of mutability of species which Agassiz did not find, he took the position "that the hypothesis of the method of creation by evolution exceeded physical science and became theology, which belonged to the province of theology, into which he had no intention of venturing." That was his statement to me during the interval between the two attacks of brain trouble from the latter of which he died. Science, to his understanding, was observation and classification, arrangement, and it had no function in investigating the causes or *modus operandi* through which things became what they were.

Amongst the evolutionists whom I have known there have been several who did not accept without modification the theory of natural selection, and supplemented it by design, amongst whom I may mention the great American botanist, Asa Gray,--one of the most distinguished of Darwinians,--who accepted the method of evolution as the *modus operandi* of the Supreme Intelligence. Professor Jeffries Wyman, the associate of Agassiz in the University, who was one of the doctors of our Adirondack company, accepted in a qualified manner the theory of evolution, but his premature and lamented death set the seal to his conclusions before they were complete, though I have always had the impression that his position was similar to that of Gray. To my question one day as to his conclusions, he replied, with

---

6   *De l'Origine du Monde organique.*

a caution characteristic of the man and very unlike the resolute attitude of Agassiz before the question which the Sphinx proposes still, "An evolution of some sort there certainly was," but nothing more would he say. The loss to American science in his death can never be estimated, for his mind was of that subtle and inductive nature which is needed for such a study, fine to poetic delicacy, penetrating with all the acumen of a true scientific imagination, but modest to excess, and personally so attached to Agassiz that he would with reluctance give expression to a difference from him, though that he did differ was no occasion for abatement of their mutual regard. Wyman's was the poetry of scientific research, Agassiz's its prose, and they offered a remarkable example of mental antithesis, from which, had Wyman lived, much might have been expected through their association in study. Wyman had all the delicacy of a fine feminine organization, wedded unfortunately to a fragile constitution, but the friendship he held for the robust and dominating character of the great Switzer was to the utmost reciprocated.

And Agassiz's disposition was as generous as large. He had absolutely no scientific jealousy or sectarian feeling. The rancor which was shown him by some of the Darwinians never disturbed his serenity an instant; for of the world's opinion of him and his ideas, even when the "world" was scientific, he never took account other than to regret that science was the loser, by running off on what he considered side issues. We had much conversation on the question of evolution and allied topics, in which my part was naturally that of listener and only occasional questioner, and I remember the warm appreciation he always expressed for Darwin and his researches, for his fineness of observation and scientific honesty. He regarded the widespread acceptance of the theory of natural selection as one of the epidemics which have swept the scientific world from time to time, and looked with absolute serenity to the return of science one day to the conception of creation by design.

I am neither qualified nor disposed to pass judgment on Agassiz as a scientist, or institute any kind of comparison of his relative authority, and probably the time is far away at which his comparative eminence can be estimated impartially. I have only to do with his personality as it appeared to me in our relations, and, as the latest survivor of those who enjoyed that greenwood intimacy, to put on record my impression of the great, lovable, magnanimous man. Of his unbounded generosity and indifference to personal advantage, his freedom from scientific jealousy, everybody who came in contact with him was witness. He refused all offers of emolument from any quarter, and spent all his surplus earnings for the aggrandizement of the great natural-history museum he founded at Cambridge. The propositions of the Emperor Napoleon III. he had declined with thanks as soon as made, and without a thought. He had come to America to study natural history, and did not propose to be diverted from this purpose. To a lecturing agent who offered him a very large sum for delivering a course of lectures in the principal cities of the Union, he replied that he had no time to make money; and he died of overwork, insatiate in the pursuit of the completion of his museum and the classification of his observations. I have heard him speak with pain of the animosity shown him by a Swiss associate in his glacial investigations, who had once been his warm advocate, but there was no bitterness in his manner. I am convinced that there was no bitterness in him, and that all personal feeling was overshadowed and minimized by his absolute devotion to scientific truth, with his loyalty to which nothing ever interfered.

His influence even on the business men of the city of Boston and the legislature of the State of Massachusetts was the most remarkable phenomenon of the kind ever witnessed in that frugal and matter-of-fact community, for he had only to announce that he wanted for his museum or department in the University a donation or an appropriation, to obtain either, so absolutely recognized was his unselfish devotion to science by all classes. There are few of us left who can remember the sudden shadow that fell on our community at his unexpected death, and the universal grief that told of the hold he had on the entire nation; and the mourning extended far beyond the circle of personal acquaintance with Agassiz. Even men who had no interest in physical science took it into consideration on account of him, carried away by his enthusiastic advocacy of its advancement. The religious world forgot the indignation at his repudiation of Adam in the refuge it found from absolute atheism in his affirmation of a Supreme Intelligence, as Creator of all things, though to theological contentions he never gave the slightest consideration.

It is needless to say that this was the effect, not of scientific education or of the capacity in the great majority of those who accepted his position to judge of a theory or a scientific line of demonstration, but of the dominance of personal character in the man, his inflexible honesty and disinterestedness. The last time I saw him was when he came to make me a brief visit in a glen of the White Mountains, where

I was encamped near a subject which I was painting, and which was in part composed of huge boulders, dropped in the gorge by a primeval glacier, and brought, perhaps, from beyond Lake Superior. He had then had the first attack of the brain trouble, from which he was recovering, and was making a mountain trip where he could, if possible, study and rest at once. But his want of common prudence in regard to overwork prevented his recovery, and he died just as he was beginning to elaborate his conclusions on the doctrine of evolution, for which he had a colossal plan, cut short in its opening. He was always too hurried in his work, as if he knew that his life would not suffice for its completion, if indeed completion were possible in such work, and he persisted in accumulation of material without pause either to coordinate his ideas or to rest and reflect. I one day said to him that I was intending to write a little book, and he exclaimed: "Oh, I wish I had time to write a little book! All my books come large, and I have not the time to condense them."

CHAPTER XIV
LOWELL

The third magnate of our Club was Lowell, with whose personality the world at large is already well acquainted. In his own day and presence it was impossible to form a satisfactory personal judgment of him, and even now, through the perspective of the years since he died, it is out of the question for me to pronounce a dispassionate judgment. Of all that New England world, so hospitable, so brotherly to me that if I had been born in Cambridge it could hardly have been more kind, Lowell and Norton were those who most made my welcome free from any embarrassment to myself. Norton, almost exactly my contemporary, is still living, and which of us two shall say the last word for the other is in the lap of the gods, but in the Adirondack Club life he does not appear. No kinder or wiser friend have I ever had. Himself the son of one of the most distinguished of the great Unitarian leaders of liberal New England, his broad, common-sense views of sectarian questions first widened my religious horizon, emancipated me from the tithes of mint and cummin, and helped me to see the value of observances, and his hand was always held out to me in those straitened moments in which my impulsive and ill-regulated manner of life continually landed me. I shall not disturb the serenity of his old age by the indiscreet garrulity of mine. But the brotherhood between him and Lowell brought our lives together, and Lowell was the pole to which both our needles swung. Norton's delicate health made it impossible for him to take part in the excursions made by the Club, though he was enrolled as a member.

Of Lowell much has been said by many people, some of whom were less, and others, perhaps, better acquainted with him than I was, but of him I can speak at least without restraint, other than that which love and gratitude impose. And to-day, more than forty years since I found his friendship what it ever remained, the judgment I formed of him at first acquaintance comes up again in one point dominant. He seemed to me a man whom good fortune, and especially the favor of society, had prevented from filling the role that fate had intended for him. There was in not a few of his poems the promise of reaching a height which was attainable only to a man who climbs light. There was in him the possible making of a great reformer, an evangelist, which possibility never became actuality, owing to the weight which social success laid on him.

All through his early poems runs the thread of a fine morality, the perception of the highest obligations of religion and philanthropy, the subtle distinction of the purest Christianity, the defense of the weak and oppressed, the succor of the poor; in fine, the creed of a practical religion which required its adherent to go into the slums and out on the highways to carry out his convictions in acts. In the warfare he waged on slavery when the anti-slavery cause was very unpopular, and, in the case of Garrison and others, brought on its advocates continual danger and occasional violence, Lowell was unsparing in the denunciation of the national sin; but whether because the anti-abolition public which ruled Boston thought denunciation in form of verse had no practical value, or because the personal fascination the man always exercised on all around him was such as to disarm hostility, it happened that he was never made the object of aggression.

> "Men called him but a shiftless youth,
>   In whom no good they saw;
> And yet, unwittingly, in truth,
>   They made his careless word their law.
>
> "Men granted that his speech was wise,
>   But, when a glance they caught
> Of his slim grace and woman's eyes,
>   They laughed and called him good-for-naught."

There was a gracious indolence in him, an imperturbable serenity, which made proclamation in advance of a truce to all forms of brute collision. No doubt if they had hunted him out for a victim of the political animosity which led to so many tragedies in the early days of our anti-slavery agitation, he would have stood up to the stake as gayly as one of the martyrs of old; but the man's nature was repugnant to discords, and shrank from combats ruder than those of the printing-press.

All through his career, the religion of humanity is put forward with point and persistence, and the finest of distinctions in morality are maintained,--the so constantly ignored vital difference between the deed and its motive, as in "Sir Launfal:"--

"The Holy Supper is kept, indeed,
In whatso we share with another's need;
Not what we give, but what we share,--
For the gift without the giver is bare;
Who gives himself with his alms feeds three,--
Himself, his hungering neighbor, and Me;"

so that one might have expected from him the life of a social reformer, so keenly did he feel the outrages of civilization. But, possibly from the fact that in those days human slavery in our country summed up all villainies and crimes, and in the war against that he threw all his surplus energy, he never took part in the crusade then beginning against the more familiar iniquities nearer home. But in his constitution there was, I think, another reason why the author of "Sir Launfal," "Hunger and Cold," "The Landlord," and "The Search" should not have emulated Howard or Miss Fry, and have gone into the realms of destitution to relieve its wrongs. He was extremely fastidious, and anything that offended his taste by vulgarity or crudeness repelled him with such force that the work of practical philanthropy would have been impossible to his temperament. The indolence I have above spoken of--which must not be confounded with slothfulness, but is, as the true meaning of the word indicates, the following of the dictates of the temperament, whether in activity or rest--led him to contemplation rather than action.

The refined idealism of his nature, made more subtle by the indulgence of an idolizing circle of relatives and friends, who saw in him the promise of more even than he ever attained, or than was possible to the smooth prosperity of his life, made it impossible for him to thrust himself into the social conflicts, whether of poverty or of politics, though the finest and most exalted passages of his work were not so fine and exalted as his personality; he was better than anything he ever wrote, and this is understood by all who knew him, and that what he wrote was only the overflow of a mind which never needed a stimulus to divine cogitation. The fascination, the subtle personal glamour he unconsciously threw over those who came in true contact with him, made them always expect more than he accomplished, for in that there was not even the stimulus of ambition. What he did was done with the spontaneousness of the wind or the sunshine. If he had a vanity, it was to be in all points accoutred for his place in society; but even this was so lightly held that few knew him well enough to see it, and it was never a motive power in him.

Knowing all his earlier work before I knew him, I thought I detected a want of that profounder sympathy with humanity and the pathos of life which comes from actual suffering, and I remember saying to one of his admirers, before I saw him, that what he wanted to make him a great poet was suffering. This he had gained somewhat of when I made his acquaintance. His wife had died not long before I went to Cambridge to see him and to enlist his assistance in "The Crayon," and he was in the earliest phase of the reaction from a sorrow which had made him insist on solitude. All his surroundings had kept up the impressions of his bereavement, and all his associates sympathized with and respected it, and I came in with a new life just as he came to need relief from the depression which had become morbid. He has told it in one of his first letters to me:--

> "I am glad you had a pleasant time here. I had, and you made me fifteen years younger while you stayed. When a man gets to my age, enthusiasms don't often knock at the door of his garret. I am all the more charmed with them when they come. A youth full of such pure intensity of hope and faith and purpose, what is he but the breath of a resurrection trumpet to us stiffened old fellows, bidding us up out of our clay and earth if we would not be too late?
>
> "Your inspiration is still to you a living mistress; make her immortal in her promptings and her consolations by imaging her

truly in art. Mine looks at me with eyes of paler flame, and beckons across a gulf. You came into my loneliness like an incarnate inspiration. And it is dreary enough sometimes; for a mountain peak on whose snow your foot makes the first mortal print is not so lonely as a room full of happy faces from which one is missing forever."

The tone of his life at that period is given in the few poems of the time, published later: the "Ode to Happiness," which he read to me unfinished during that first visit; "The Wind-Harp," in which

"There murmured, as if one strove to speak,
  And tears came instead; then the sad tones wandered
And faltered among the uncertain chords
In a troubled doubt between sorrow and words;
  At last with themselves they questioned and pondered,
'Hereafter?--who knoweth?' and so they sighed
Down the long steps that lead to silence and died;"

"The Dead House," "Auf Wiedersehen (Summer)" and the "Palinode (Autumn)," in which the first grief had deepened while losing its acuteness, and the feeling of loneliness had taken largely the place of the first desolation, the wrenching apart of soul and body:--

"It is pagan; but wait till you feel it,--
That jar of our earth, that dull shock
When the ploughshare of deeper passion
Tears down to our primitive rock;"

and some of his friends had tried the folly of condolence, to whom he replies, in the same poem ("After the Burial"):--

"Console if you will, I can bear it;
'Tis a well-meant alms of breath;
But not all the preaching since Adam
Has made Death other than Death."

But the man was too robust in body and mind to linger long in the shadows of melancholy, and though the effects of bereavement--which, in the few years before I knew him, had taken his only boy, who died in Rome, his elder daughter, of whose death "The First Snow-Fall" keeps a touching record, and finally his wife--deepened his character as expressed in his subsequent writing, the buoyancy and elasticity which he found in his enjoyment of nature, and his severe application to the studies of the new position to which the retirement of Longfellow from the professorship of modern languages at Harvard promoted him, restored his old tone of life, while his very happy marriage with his second wife made him, as may now be said without indiscretion, happier than he had ever been.

The second Mrs. Lowell was a woman of the rarest mental, moral, and personal qualities, and her influence on Lowell was of the happiest and sunniest. She was one of three daughters of a merchant of Maine, who had left them without other resources than what their own excellent education gave them, and with the charge of a younger brother, for whose education they provided after the New England way. The other sisters I never knew; but Fannie, Mrs. Lowell, was one of the most remarkable women I ever knew for the combination of resolute and persistent courage and serene religious temperament. She was a Swedenborgian, and probably owed to that form of faith her serenity and imperturbable faith in a Divine Providence; but her unflinching courage in adversity and her extreme sweetness of character were of her New England birth and education. After her father's death she became a governess, and came to Lowell's house in that capacity after the death of his wife; but she had, before that, gone through many vicissitudes of fortune. She told me one day an incident of travel which is worth recording as indicating her character. She had been in a situation in Charleston, S.C., and had accepted another in the valley of the Ohio, to reach which, there being then no railway that traversed the distance, she had to make a long journey by stagecoach, traveling day and night across the Alleghanies. One night she found herself in the coach with a single fellow-passenger, apparently a gentleman, who took his place with her on the back seat, and who, after a time, pretending to be asleep, fell over towards her, so that his head lay on her shoulder, but, correcting himself, sat upright again, to repeat the feint again and again, each time with more abandon, until his arm dropped behind Fannie's waist, with an unmistakable attempt to embrace her. She quietly drew out her shawl-pin and drove it into his arm, without any remark or other attention to him. He sat up instantly, at the next stopping-place took an outside seat, and discontinued his journey at the first town they came to.

Mrs. Lowell fitted her husband as sunshine fits calm, and the gravest sorrow he ever felt with her was her having no children. When, two or three years after the time I am now writing of, I had decided to go to Europe again, and he tried to dissuade me from going, and I, for reasons I could not tell him, persisted, he brought me one day, just before I sailed, six hundred dollars, insisting on my accepting it as a gift, saying: "I shall never want it. I know now that I shall never have another child, and I can well spare it." Lowell had never been wealthy, but he had an income sufficient for all needs in the state of life which he preferred, and his generosity towards his friends who were poorer than he took all the surplus. He rejoiced in the addition to his income in the salary of his professorship, but it added nothing to his own expenditure. And yet I have always felt that if he had been a poor man, compelled to work for his daily bread, he would have occupied a larger place in the world of letters. He was not one of the "intellectual giants buried under mountains of gold," but he was a greater man than he ever showed himself, always cushioned by a sufficiency of fortune for all his needs, and by his tastes inclined to a simple and tranquil life; for, though he became later a political personage, he cared little, *au fond*, for the political world. Perhaps the little was too much for his attainment as a poet, and some of his best friends have always held that his diplomatic life was a disaster for his intellectual completion.

I have elsewhere alluded to his going to Europe to complete the preparations to enter into his professorship, and when he came back from this voyage he said to me, "I must study yet a good deal before I attempt to produce anything more." He finally felt the carelessness of form in his work, and in the succeeding years he worked very hard in his professorial work, which was, perhaps, not the best for his advancement as an author, but it certainly gave more solidity to the production of those years which intervened between his simpler life and his diplomatic career. His lectures before the students and the public (the popularity of Lowell as a lecturer was immense) solidified an education which, as he himself humorously avowed, was often broken by freaks of irrepressible youthful spirit; and the saddening and indelible effects of the war, which came between and sharply divided those phases of his career, had so modified his character for the graver and more profound that I agree with those of his friends who consider his entry into the diplomatic career as a misfortune for American letters, and that his mind flowed to waste in those later years. Nor was he at home in diplomacy. It was a reversal of all the conditions of his habitual existence; but it flattered his ***amour propre*** that the country should recognize the part he had taken in the cultivation of the anti-slavery sentiment of the nation, and the trace of worldly feeling which I have noted grew under the stimulus to a motive in life. His social gifts were very great, and his patriotic pride intensified the pleasure of his successes in a line of life which was really secondary in his nature.

In those years of his diplomatic life we saw little of each other. Our intimate intercourse was suspended by my going to Europe in 1859. We were nearest each other in our Adirondack life, in which he had all the zest of a boy. He was the soul of the merriment of the company, fullest of witticisms, keenest in appreciation of the liberty of the occasion, and the ***genius loci***. One sees through all his nature-poetry the traces of the heredity of the early settler, the keen enjoyment of the fresh and unhackneyed in nature, even of the angularity of the New England farmhouse and the brightness and newness of the villages, so crude to the tastes founded in the picturesqueness of the Old World. Not even Emerson, with all his indifference to the mere form of things, took to unimproved and uncivilized nature as Lowell did, and his free delight in the Wilderness was a thing to remember, and perhaps by none so keenly appreciated as by me, to whom the joy of forest life was a satisfactory motive for living.

CHAPTER XV
THE ADIRONDACK AND FLORIDA

Of the rest of our company in that famous old camp by "Follansbee Water" there is little more to be said which will interest others or recall names known to the world. I painted a study of the camp and its inhabitants, with the intention of making from it, at a future time, a picture which should commemorate the meeting; but, owing to changes in my plans, it remained a study, and was purchased by Judge Hoar, the most eminent of my companions still to be described. He had been a justice of the Superior Court of Massachusetts,--a man as well known for his intellectual fibre and sympathy with letters as for his judicial abilities. He was one of the most brilliant members of the old Saturday Club, of which ours might be considered the offspring and succursal; of wit the most spontaneous and electric, whose sallies burst in the merriment of our *al fresco* camp dinners with the flash and surprise of rockets, and left behind them the perfume of erudition as did no others of the company, not even Lowell's. In my study the party is divided in the habit of the morning occupations: Lowell, Hoar, Binney, Woodman, and myself engaged in firing at the target; Agassiz and Wyman dissecting a trout on a tree-stump, while Holmes and Dr. Howe watch the operation; but Emerson, recognizing himself as neither a marksman nor a scientist, choosing a position between the two groups, pilgrim-staff in hand, watches the marksmen, with a slight preference as between the two groups. My own figure I painted from a photograph, the company insisting on my putting myself in; but it was ill done, for I could never paint from a photograph.

When the company left me I returned to my painting, and remained in camp as long as the weather permitted. On my return to Cambridge I became affianced to Miss Mack, the eldest daughter of Dr. David Mack, with whom I had been boarding while I was occupied in painting the various pictures of the Oaks at Waverley.

The excursion had been so satisfactory that when the whole company had come together again, in the autumn, at Cambridge, the formal organization of the Club was called for, and to the number of those who had been at Camp Maple there was a large accession of the most prominent members of the intellectual society of Boston and Cambridge. It was decided to purchase a tract in the Adirondack Wilderness, the less accessible the better, and there to build a permanent club-house, and I was appointed to select the site and lay it out. The meeting was late in the autumn, and the winter had set in with heavy snow before I had my orders. I caught a severe cold at New York,--a trivial matter to notice, but one which very narrowly escaped the gravest consequences to me; for the cold became aggravated to a bronchial attack, disregarding which I pushed on into the Wilderness, and drove from the settlements in to the Saranac in a storm, facing a northwesterly wind which, filling the air with a cold fog as penetrating as the wind, crystallized on every tree and twig, and made the entire forest, as far as the eye could reach, like a forest of frosted silver. It was a spectacle for a lifetime, and has never been offered to me again; but I reached Martin's, where we had to put up, dangerously chilled.

Next day, however, I had all the guides of the neighborhood in for consultation as to a certain tract which I had fixed on from report and general knowledge of the region, and we planned a survey in the snow. It was fourteen miles from any house to the lake I had fixed on,--that known as the Ampersand Pond; but, fortunately, there were, amongst the guides called in, some who had been assistants in the official survey, and, with their practical knowledge and memory of the lines, I was enabled, without leaving the inn, to draw a map of the section of a township which included the lake, and determine its exact position, with the fact that it had been forfeited to the State at the last tax sale, and was for sale at the land office in Albany. We bought the entire section, less 500 acres, taxes on which had been paid, for the sum of $600,--thus securing for the Club a tract of 22,500 acres. My cough was increasing alarmingly, and, when I consulted a physician at New York, he advised me to get home and to bed as quickly as I might; so, returning to Boston, I called together the executive committee of the Club to dinner, made my report, drank a glass of champagne to the future lodge, and went to bed in the early stages of pneumonia, which kept me prostrate six weeks.

I owed it to the fortunate and intelligent woodcraft of my guides that I was not caught in the depth of the forest by the increasing lung trouble, probably never to return to civilization. It was the closest shave to death that I have ever had, and the actual survey of the tract, buried four feet deep in snow, without a shelter or other bed than the ground, would in all probability have finished me, for I barely escaped as it was; but I was determined to finish my work, animated by the same incomprehension of, rather than indifference to, the danger before me which had obtained in my Hungarian expedition and in many other circumstances of my life. Something of the splendid physical health I brought back with me from the Wilderness helped me, no doubt, through the attack of pneumonia and pleurisy, which released me in the early spring, when I was ordered off to Florida to recuperate. Being advised not to occupy myself with painting while there, I bought a photographic apparatus, and learned photography as it was practiced in 1857,--a rude, inefficient, and cumbersome apparatus and process for field work, of which few amateurs nowadays can conceive the inconveniences.

This trip--for the means to make which I was indebted to Norton, my illness having exhausted my resources, and the great crisis which had broken over New York the year before having swept off the fortune of my brother--gave me a sight of the South before the war, with slavery and the patriarchal system at its perfection. I went up the St. John's River, and took board at a plantation called Hibernia, one of numerous similar establishments on the river, hotels proper not existing there. The owner of the plantation, old Colonel Fleming, was one of the traditional patriarchal planters, and the experience I gained there certainly agreed with the views of the institution of slavery entertained by the great majority of Southern people I have known. I never heard of the punishment of a slave, or saw a discontented negro; the black children were the jolliest little creatures I ever saw in clothes, and the adults seemed to do as much or as little work as they pleased.

I had carried my rifle with me, and young Fleming and I used to go hunting for alligators, still abundant in the river. The thickets of palmetto and the groves of magnolia filling the air with new and cloying fragrance, alternating with other unaccustomed odors which made the grove resemble an orchestra of perfumes, were to me a new and delightful experience. There was a mythical wild turkey in the woods around, and the hope of a shot at him carried me many a mile, though he proved only a myth; but of rattlesnakes and copperheads there was no lack. As I was collecting specimens for the natural-history museum of Cambridge, I canned the largest snakes that I came across, and I secured one rattlesnake which measured nine feet; but the fear of his kind never damped my enthusiasm for the luxuriant forest. Into the great cypress swamps, with their centennial trees, swarming with reptiles of infinite variety, there run devious inlets which they call "creeks," and up these I used to paddle my skiff, and lie and watch the teeming life, wishing I were a naturalist. I spent a week at the ancient (for America) town of St. Augustine, on the Atlantic coast,--then the sleepy watering-place of a few Southern invalids,--and enjoyed greatly its local color, so different from that of all other American towns, its picturesque fortress of the days of Spanish rule, and its Spanish fishermen, in their undiluted nationality and costume. I here poisoned myself dreadfully, rubbing with my legs some poison plant as I shinned up the trees for epiphytal orchids, new to me and an irresistible attraction.

To naturalists, this part of Florida must have been a most interesting field before the bird-slaughterers had invaded it to the extermination of its myriad population of feathered winterers from the Northern regions. The geological formation is a concrete of shells of enormous thickness, which has hardened to the only semblance of rock which the coast affords, and the low dunes have shut off from the Atlantic long lagoons which swarm with life, marine and aquatic creatures occurring in numberless species and orders; alligators lie in wait for their prey, and schools of porpoises come in by the inlets in pursuit of other schools of fat mullet which swarm in the water. Such teeming life I had never before any conception of. In the surf the sharks lurked and coasted up and down, watching us as we waded in fishing for bass, if by chance we should give them an opportunity for a bite; the sharp, warning fin showing in the hollow green of the combing breaker ever and anon as we stood thigh-deep in the foam. It made one shudder to see that silent terror patrolling up and down the margin of the deep water, waiting for an incautious venture of the bather beyond the shallows, into which the shark dared not come.

I went with a fishing party down the coast to Matanzas, an abandoned fort of the early Spanish days, and passed there the most impressive open-air night in my recollection. We camped on the beach, and my shelter was a gauze mosquito netting stretched over four poles, about three feet high, driven in the sand, and as wide as high, and my bed was the sea sand, no covering being required. Through the gauze the sea breeze blew gently; on one side of the long, narrow beach the great Atlantic breakers roared a monotonous bass, and on the other there came from the lagoon the many-toned murmur of a thousand bird voices, some familiar and some strange, whooping of cranes and chattering of coots, ducks, and divers, cries of pelicans, and now and then the sound of flapping wings, as if some great bird had been routed out and had changed his feeding-ground. Around me on the sand ran and crawled the host of crabs, some pulling curiously at the gauze of my shelter; and now and then a huge spider crab climbed up the netting like a squirrel and danced an infernal jig over my head, skipping about on the very tips of his claws, until I tired of his frivolity and hit him from underneath, when he scuttled away, and after half an hour, more or less, was succeeded by another, as if they found an intoxication in dancing over my head. The gnats sang their monody, and the midges put in their treble, but the meshes of my gauze were too fine to let them pass; and after hours of this strange pandemonium I fell asleep, to be waked in the morning by the sun streaming over me from the broad Atlantic.

It is worthy to note here, in justice to the old days of the Floridian society, a society now utterly extinct, and a subject of history, that the kindliness to the slaves was universal on the St. John's River. At nightfall they used to gather in their quarters and sing; and they had a peculiar yodel, which, starting from one plantation, was caught up by the others, and ran round and off along the river into the distance and back, going and coming again and again with a peculiar fascination, like the voice of a happy and careless common life. It was a kindly and indulgent community, and that it was a slave-holding society never forced itself on the attention. The lazy social virtues had, no doubt, their lazy vices, but we never saw them on the surface. The negro quarters were as merry as the day was long, and the negro was a more important and better appreciated element of social life than in the North. The whole valley joined in unreserved malediction of a planter, one of our neighbors, who had profited by the accidental burning of the free papers of a black family which had been bought out of slavery by the father, with money earned as pilot to the steamers of the United States Army during the Seminole War, to compel him to purchase himself and his wife and children again, and the thief was spoken of as the meanest of white men, out of the social pale of self-respecting folk; cheating a slave being far worse than cheating one of his own class. The old scoundrel was the reproach of the whole community; but no more formal indictment of the system of slavery, as established in the United States, is required than the fact that a former master could recall to slavery an emancipated slave family, the head of which had paid in hard cash for himself, his wife, and all his children, because his free papers had been burned, in a fire of which, moreover, the neighbors accused the former owner of being the incendiary. While those papers were in existence the negro could legally sue and be sued; but without them he had no more legal rights than a dog. The life which honest people lived in that primitive community was Arcadian, and it is probable that even in Arcadia they had slaves. Certainly, in my experience of living in many countries and under various systems, I have not found that the most primitive system secures the largest personal liberty; rather the contrary.

I returned to my painting with the early summer, and, when the season came, to the organization of the Club and the inauguration of its club-house and grounds. It was certainly the most beautiful site I have ever seen in the Adirondack country,--virgin forest, save where the trappers or hunters had cut wood for their camp-fires, the tall pines standing in their long ranks along the shores of a little lake that lay in the middle of the estate, encircled by mountains, except on one side, where the lake found its outlet; and the mountains were cloaked to their summits in primeval woods. In a little valley where a crystal spring sent its water down to the lake, and a grove of deciduous trees gave high and airy shelter, I pitched the camp,--a repetition slightly enlarged of that on Follansbee Pond. As usual I preceded the Club party, accompanied by S.G. Ward and his son, and also the son of Emerson, to prepare the ground. The solitude of the locality may be judged from the first hunt. We had arrived late in the day, and had no food except the bread we took with us, and the next morning we had to kill our breakfast before we could eat it. I took Mr. Ward and the boys in my boat and paddled down to the foot of the lake, where was a wide beach, on which we found a two-year-old buck grazing. I paddled to within fifty yards of him, and, though I found that my rifle would not go off and had to change it for another, with considerable movement, the deer took no notice of us, and I dropped him in his tracks with a feeling of compunction only overcome by the fact that we had no breakfast if he went away. So peaceful was our realm! I have often paddled within easy shot of a deer on other waters, but only by remaining motionless when he was looking round, for the movement of a hand would send him flying in panic; but this poor deer might have been reared in Eden.

The meeting of the Club that year was a most successful one; and when it was over, and I was left alone to my painting, I selected a subject in which, for the first time, I introduced a dramatic element. I supposed that a hunter and a buck had had a hand-to-horn fight, and, during it, had fallen together over a ledge of rocks, at the bottom of which both lay dead. A perpendicular ledge of granite, about twenty feet high, mosses and ferns clinging in its crevices, overhanging a level space covered with a heavy growth of luxuriant fern, furnished the background. There I laid the first large buck I killed, and painted him with extreme care, and then painted my guide with his arms locked in the antlers of the deer. The hour was the late afternoon, when the red sunlight slanted through the trees and fell in broken masses on the face of the cliff, catching the leaves here and there in its path. All this was painted carefully from the scene, with as much of the details of the forest as the time permitted, on a canvas twenty-five by thirty inches, on which I worked about two months, till the lake began to freeze and the snow fell. The thermometer was about zero Fahrenheit before I broke off, early in November.

I never enjoyed so entirely the forest life as that autumn. I had laid a line of sable traps for miles through the woods, and caught several "prime" sable which I intended as a present to my fiancee, and the long walks over the line in the absolute silence of the great forest, the snowfall, and the gorgeous autumn were more fascinating than ever before. The bears left their tracks around me, and several pumas made themselves heard, but of wolves, which I had heard in other parts of the woods, I heard none. Returning in the gloaming from my traps, one day, I heard at a distance a wailing cry like that of a woman in distress, to which I replied by hallooing at the top of my voice. After a few minutes I heard the cry again, approaching me, and again responded. The cry continued, still nearer and nearer, but slow in its approach; and, wondering why so slow, I finally fired my rifle three times rapidly, which is the conventional signal for help, and at the same time a reply to the call for help; and it was only when this evoked no further call that I remembered that the cry was that of a puma.

As usual I lived alone, save for the weekly visit of my guide bringing me bread and my post. It was with the greatest reluctance that I obeyed the necessity to return to the state of civilization, and took leave of that most charming retreat of the natural man from the artificial life. That was my last serious experience of woodland life. The uneasy and thriftless spirit which drove me out, like the possessed of the Scripture, to wander in strange places at times, again drove me that winter to England, putting, as it happened, against my intention or prevision, an end to the American period of my life.

CHAPTER XVI
ENGLAND AGAIN

I have generally been happy at sea; and when not so, it has been from reasons apart from the sea itself,--preoccupations which kept me insensible to the old charm, or mental troubles which made me insensible to everything beside them. On this voyage I had the company of an old friend of the days of "The Crayon," one of our most thoughtful and successful portrait painters, George Fuller, and a young friend of his, a Mr. Ames. We sailed just before Christmas, in an old sailing ship of about eight hundred tons burthen; for, unless time is of importance, I prefer a sailing ship to a steamer, and one pleasant companion is worth a shipload of commonplace fellow-voyagers. A stiff westerly blow caught us off Sandy Hook, and never left us till we were halfway across the Atlantic, increasing in violence every day, until it gave me, what I had always longed for, but never seen, a first-class gale on the open ocean.

I had said to the captain (one of the old sort of Cape Cod sailors, still a young man, however) that I wanted to see a real gale; and one day, after we had been out nearly a week, he called me up on deck, saying, "You wanted to see a gale, and now you may see it; for unless you get into a tornado you will never see anything worse than this." I went on deck, obliged to hold firmly to the rails or some part of the rigging, for the wind was such as to have carried me overboard if I had attempted to stand alone on the quarter-deck. We were running with the wind dead abaft, under a reefed fore-topsail and a storm jib, everything else having been taken in the night before. The studding-sail boom of the foreyard, which had been carelessly left out, had been broken off short in the earing, from the pressure of the wind on the bare spar. The roaring of the wind through the rigging was such as only one who has heard it can conceive.

I gripped close the quarter-deck railing, and drew myself aft to the shelter of the wheelhouse, where, securing myself from being blown away like a piece of paper, I watched the sea. It rose behind us in huge mountains, the summits of which were always combing over and sliding down the weltering flanks of the wave,--not like the surf on a shore, but pushed over like snow; and as a wave overtook us lying in the bottom of the valley, it so overhung that it seemed impossible that when it broke it should not bury us; but the stern was always caught by the forefoot of it, and the old ship began to rise, and went up, up, up, until I was dizzy. Then we hovered on the summit a moment, looking out on such an expanse of gigantic waves as I had never pictured to myself, the distance lost in the driving spray; and, while I looked, the wave passed from under us, and we went down and down with a rapidity of descent which was almost like falling from a balloon. Then, after another moment's rest in the valley, came the shuddering half apprehension of the next wave as it rose above us, threatening again, and then, after again soaring aloft, down again into the driving of the spray; the old ship rolling, plunging, and now and then quivering, as some side wave struck her, with a complication of motions, sidelong and headlong, the huge waves flying before us and yet carrying us on,--wild motions, rolling, pitching, sinking down the long green slope into the valley, to be flung up into the tumult of wind and wave again. In all this complexity of forces we were as helpless as feathers in the wind, cut off from mother earth as much as if we were carried away on the clouds; the feeling of absolute insignificance growing on one as the ship drove on, the creaking of the ship and the hissing rush of the waters hardly audible for the shrieking of the gale through the rigging. In all my life I have never so understood the utter impotence and triviality of humanity as I felt it then.

The ship, though not in measure with the colossi of later times, was yet a huge mass as measured by the man, and she was no more than a cork on the tide. Up and down she went, like a child's swing,--wallowing and rolling, with the sea breaking over the side till the channels were full, and pouring over the bows in green torrents, and then in blinding deluges of spray and water over the stern; tearing along ten knots an hour, and yet always seeming to be left behind by the waves that tore by us,--the great waves, that obeyed the wind only to be crushed down again by it, spurting up here and there fitfully in pinnacles which were instantly driven off in foam and froth; no combing waves, such as the land dweller sees, for no wave could rise enough to comb,--only great hills of water, crystalline with wavelets, streaked with spun foam, heaving as if from a blind impulse, and leaving us, in a contemptuous toleration, to keep afloat if we could. And now and then two great waves raced each other, as they will at long intervals, till they ran close to each other and united, and we were thrown aloft a little higher, to see nothing more than a wild waste of foam, spray, and watery chaos which defies human language to express it.

This was the sea as I had wanted to see it, and as no painter has ever painted, or probably ever will paint it, and as very few could ever have seen it; for in seventy thousand miles of sea travel I have seen it only once. For three days and nights our captain never left the bridge to rest. Of two other ships that left New York the same day that we did, one was dismasted to the south of us, and the other had her quarters stove in and barely escaped foundering just to the north of us. The gale blew out and left us in a dead calm, which lasted a couple of days, when another gale of three days drove us in the direction we wanted to go, and dropped us off Torquay in the morning of what seemed a delicious spring day, all sunshine and south wind. We hailed a fishing boat and went ashore. We had left a land buried in snow and ice, and we reached one in early spring, though it was still January, the gorse in odorous blossoming, and in the hedgerows the early wild flowers in profusion. But we learned, on landing, that the recent gales had strewn the shores of England with wrecks, with great loss of life. It had been one of those terrible winters which have helped make the British sailor the sea dog he is.

I took lodgings in Charles Street, Middlesex Hospital, near Wehnert, and worked hard. I had brought my "Bed of Ferns," a large study from nature on Saranac Lake, and one or two smaller studies. I had visits from Dante Rossetti, Leighton (then in all the glory of his Cimabue picture, and in the promise of even a greater career than he finally attained), Millais, Val Prinsep, and Boyce. I had brought letters from Lowell to Tom Hughes, from Norton to Arthur Hugh Clough, from Agassiz to Professor Owen. Hughes introduced me to the Cosmopolitan Club, where I made the acquaintance, amongst others whom I do not remember, of Millais and Monckton Milnes.

The artists who came seemed to be interested in my work, especially in the "Bed of Ferns," of which Rossetti--whose opinion I valued more than any other, for he was very honest and blunt in his criticisms, and not at all inclined to flattery--

expressed himself in strong terms of praise. As it was the first thing in which I had attempted to introduce a human interest in the landscape, I was naturally inclined to consider it my most important work, and I was dismayed when Ruskin came to see me, and, in a tone of extreme disgust, said, pointing to the dead deer and man: "What do you put that stuff in for? Take it out; it stinks!" My reverence for Ruskin's opinion was such that I made no hesitation in painting out the central motive of the picture, for which both subject and effect of light had been selected. Unfortunately, I habitually used copal varnish as a medium. When Rossetti called again, he asked me, with a look of dismay, what I had done to my picture. I explained to him that on Ruskin's advice I had painted out the figures, and exclaiming, "You have spoiled your picture!" he walked out of the room in a rage. However, I sent it to the Academy as it was, and had it back, "Not hung, for want of room," or something equivalent. I then tried to remove the pigment which hid my figures; but the varnish was refractory, and, after a vain attempt, I finally cut the picture up and stuck it in the fire.

The incident, though it cost me the work of three months, and was in fact the only important outcome of the summer's study, did not diminish my confidence in Ruskin's judgment and correct feeling for art. It required a still more severe experience. As all the world knows, that knows anything of Ruskin's ways with artists, he was blunt and outspoken in his criticisms, and not in the least tender of their feelings, unless indeed they happened to be women. Knowing this, I took his praise for certain studies and drawings I had brought with me as a patent of ability; and though I was never extravagant in my opinion of my own capacities for art, his approbation of some things that I had done, and his assurance of a respectable attainment if I followed the best methods of study, encouraged me, and I took it without question that the methods were his, and it was a costly experience which undeceived me.

Of the people with whom I made acquaintance in London at this visit, those who most interested me were Clough and Owen. Of the artists I saw little, as they and myself had other things to do than to frequent one another's studios; but by the Rossetti family I profited largely, as I had been more or less in intimate relations with William since he undertook the correspondence of "The Crayon" from England. Of Dante, indeed, I saw little at that time, as he lived by himself; but with

William my relations were constant and cordial, and he was for many years my most valued English friend. Through his extreme honesty and liberality, and his extensive knowledge of and wide feeling for art, there was great community of appreciation between us, and our friendship lasted long beyond the direct interest I had in English art matters.

Of Christina I saw a good deal, for the hospitality of the Rossetti family was informal and cordial. She was then in excellent health, and, though she was never what would be, by the generality of tastes, considered a beautiful woman, there was a noble serenity and dignity of expression in her face which was, as is often said of women of the higher type of character, "better than beauty," and in which one saw the spiritual exaltation that, without the least trace of the **devote**, dominated in her and made her, before all other women of whom I know anything, the poetess of the divine life. The faith in the divine flamed out in her with a mild radiance which had in it no earthly warmth. She attracted me very strongly, but I should as soon have thought of falling in love with the Madonna del Gran Duca as with her. Being myself in the regions of dogmatic faith, I was in a position to judge sympathetically her religion, and, though we differed in tenets as far as two sincere believers in Christianity could, I found in our discussions of the dogmas a broad and affectionate charity in her towards all differences from the ideal of credence she had formed for herself. I do not remember ever meeting any one who held such exalted and unquestioning faith in the true spiritual life as was hers. From my mother, who was in most respects the most purely spiritual woman I have ever known, Christina differed by this serenity, which in my mother was often disturbed by the doubts that had their seeds in the old and superstitious Calvinism mingled with the ground of her creed, and from which she never could liberate herself.

Christina believed in God, in heaven, in the eternal life, with an unfaltering constancy and fullness which left no questionings except, it might be, concerning her fulfillment of her religious obligations. And while I thought her belief in certain dogmas, such as transubstantiation, and in the fasting and ritual of her High Church observances, to be too trivial for such a really exalted intellect, so near the perception of the essential truth, she held them with such a childlike and tranquil faith that I would sooner have worshiped with her than have disturbed her tranquillity in it. She gave me a demonstration of doctrinal charity which was to me a novelty, and showed me that tenets which are to me, and those trained like me, idle formalities were in reality the steps of a ladder by which she must climb to the realization of the abstract good. Dogmas and observances apart, I felt that her religion was so much loftier than my own that, though it would have been impossible for me to profess acceptance of it, it was equally impossible to argue with her about it,--that it was so woven into the fibre of her existence that to move it in the least would be impossible, or, if possible, only at the cost of mental and spiritual dislocation. But, with all this, there was not in her a trace of the assumption of a religious superiority which I have so often found in the driest non-conformist, or the putting me apart with the creatures that perish and are doomed which I have oftener found in Catholic friends, with whom I have felt that they regarded me with a sort of pitiful friendship, as one certain to be damned, and so only worth a limited regard, lest love should be wasted. In after years I saw her not infrequently, and when illness and grief had touched her, and I saw always the same serenity and the same wide personal charity.

Much of Christina's character one could see in her mother, a noble and worshipful woman, in whom the domestic virtues mingled with the spiritual in a way that set off the singleness of life of Christina singularly, as if it were the same light in an earthen vessel. Mrs. Rossetti was what one often hears spoken of as "a dear, good woman," whose motherly life had absorbed her existence,--one of the witnesses (martyrs) of the practical Christianity, who go, unseen and unknown, to build the universal church of humanity, and whom we reverence without naming them. Of Maria, the elder sister of Christina, I saw less, but enough to know that the same ardent, beautiful religious spirit burned in her, mute. In the years when I, later, saw most of the family, Maria lived in a sisterhood. She had none of the genius or the personal charm of her sister, but possessed the same elevation and serene religious sentiment.

Of Clough I saw a good deal, though his occupation in a government office left him not much leisure; and it seemed to me that, of all public officials I ever knew, he was the most misplaced at an office desk. Of fragile health and with the temperament of a poet, gentle as a woman can be, he often reminded me of Pegasus in harness. I had a commission from Norton to paint a small full-length portrait of him, and had several sittings; but it did not get on to suit me, and his being compelled to go to Italy for his health before I had finished with it, for well or ill, put an end to it. He left me in occupation of his house while they were away. Of all the people of the poet's temper I ever knew, Clough was the least inclined to talk of poetry, and but for the sensitive mouth and the dreamy eye, with a reflective way he had when talking, as if an undercurrent of thought were going on while he spoke, one might have taken him for a well-educated man of business, a poet-banker, or publisher. Perhaps it is in the memory more than it was in the life, but as I recall him there seemed to be in him an arcanum of thought, something beyond what came into every-day existence,--a life beyond the actual life, into which he withdrew, and out of which he came to speak. I should have liked to live beside him and know him always, for in that phase of him was infinite study. What I did see, however, left on me the impression of a man who was able only to sketch out the life he would have lived,--a life of far greater capabilities than anything accomplished could indicate.

In giving me the letter to Tom Hughes, Lowell had remarked that, though he had never seen him, yet, as Hughes had edited his "Biglow Papers," he thought he might assume an acquaintance sufficient to warrant a letter of introduction. He was not mistaken, for Hughes did the fullest honor to his letter; and as long as I was in London, and indeed for many years after, our relations were of the most cordial, and not long before his death he made me a visit at Rome. Very much of the enjoyment of that winter in London was due to the hospitable and companionable welcome of the author of "Tom Brown," and one of the most enjoyable items was the introduction to the evenings at Macmillan's, where the contributors to the magazine used to meet on Thursday evenings, if I remember rightly, and where I saw the Kingsleys,--Charles only once, but Henry often enough to contract with him a pleasant friendship. Hughes was one of the largest and most genial English natures I knew,--robust, all alive to all his human obligations; and in those troublesome days when the American question was coming to the crisis of our Civil War he was a consistent friend of the North, when the dominant feeling in English society was hostile to it, and this was a strong bond between us.

Owen I saw frequently, and, though my scientific education was, and is, superficial, he interested me greatly; for he had, like Agassiz, the gift of making his knowledge accessible to those who only understood the philosophy and not the facts of science, and I knew enough of the former to profit by his knowledge. Then he was a warm friend of Agassiz, and we used to talk of his theories and studies, of which I knew more than of any other scientific subject. Like Agassiz, he had at first resisted the theory of natural selection, but had, unlike Agassiz, come to recognize the necessity of admitting the idea of evolution in some form, like Asa Gray and Jeffries Wyman. How far he finally went in recognizing the agency of natural selection as the sufficient element in this I do not know, for at that time the battle waged over that phase of the question; but that he did not accept the solution proposed by Darwin as final I have reason to believe, from the fact that, the last time I saw him, he assured me that he was confident that if he could have seen Agassiz again before he died he could have persuaded him that evolution was the solution of the problem of creation, though knowing that Agassiz could never have accepted the doctrine of natural selection in its bareness, absolutely convinced as he was of the agency of Conscious Mind in creation. And I had the further declaration of Owen himself in his expressed conviction that the process of evolution was directed by the Divine Intelligence. One statement he made struck me forcibly in this connection, viz.: that he believed that the evolution of the horse reached its culmination synchronously with the evolution of man, and that the agreement was a part of the divine plan, while Darwin refuses to admit a plan in creation. I have heard amongst evolutionists much bitterness expressed concerning Owen for what they considered his yielding to the pressure of public opinion, and adopting the theory of evolution in contradiction to his real convictions; but I saw enough of him to be certain that he really believed in evolution subject to the dominance of the Divine Intelligence, nor did any of the accusations I heard against him persuade me of the least insincerity in his acceptance of the theory with that qualification,--a position, I am convinced, held by many, even then, who did not openly support it, not caring to go counter to the very general advocacy of natural selection.

The teaching of Owen completed my conversion to the theory of evolution as a general law, not on grounds of physical science, the demonstration by which is and must remain forever incomplete, but on the philosophical ground, which I was more capable of measuring; and with the acceptance of evolution disappeared, logically and, in the subsequent years, completely, the influence of the old anthropomorphic religion, with its terrible dogmas of the inheritance of Adam's transgression and an angry God with His vicarious punishment of His only son, with all the puzzles of miraculous intervention and the perplexities of an infallible revealed word which continually contradicts itself. The conception of Deity thus liberated from the fetters of a materialistic faith rose to a dignity I had never before comprehended, and brought me the new perception of a spiritual religion and life, which was more consoling and vivifying by far than the old belief.

It is possible that the impressions of that time have been modified by my subsequent intercourse with scientific men in England; but they are that the very wide and rapid acceptance of the theory of evolution by natural selection was largely due to the relief it offered from the incubus of the old theological conception of the Deity as a personal agency, always interfering with the course of events,--an infinite, omnipotent, and omniscient stage manager,--a conception under which the Christian world at large lay when Darwin announced his solution of the problem. The religious world had been, up to that time, chained to the anthropomorphic conception of Deity, and it was even less due to the purely scientific faculty than to the philosophic that Darwin came as a liberator from a depressing superstition,--the belief in the terrible Hebrew God, ingrained in the conscience of every reverently educated boy, and become in his growth inseparable from the maturer beliefs. The evolution of the human mind itself had finally reached the point at which this anthropomorphism became a thing impossible to maintain reasonably any longer, and the magic word was spoken by Darwin which broke the spell and set us free--who wished to be free--from a mental servitude grown dangerously dear to our deepest faculties, those of reverence and devotion. That evolution took hold slowly with some who finally adopted it was owing to the fact that, with them, that servitude had never been slavish, but always held less sway than pure reason. And contemporaneously with this evolution of the human mind had come the liberation from religious persecution, either inquisitorial, legal, or social; and, perhaps for the first time in the history of the religious dogma, a man might openly dispute the fundamental ideas of a dominant religion and suffer no penalty for his skepticism.

CHAPTER XVII
SWITZERLAND

Though my "Bed of Ferns" was sent back from the Academy, one of my large studies was exhibited at the British Society, and the result of the year's work was, on the whole, satisfactory. Ruskin invited me to go to Switzerland with him for the summer, finding in some of my studies and drawings the possibility of getting from me some of the Alpine work he wanted done. Unfortunately for both of us I could not draw well in traces, and he did not quite well know how to drive, and the summer ended in disappointment, and finally in disaster. I was too undisciplined to work except when the mood suited, and our moods rarely agreed: he wanted things which were to me of no interest, and I could not interest myself vicariously enough to do them to his satisfaction. He preceded me some weeks, and it was arranged that I should come to meet him at Geneva early in June. Certainly I owe to him my earliest and most delightful memories of the Alps and of Switzerland. More princely hospitality than his no man ever received, or more kindly companionship; but, as might have been expected, we agreed neither in temperament nor in method, if indeed the mainly self-taught way in which I worked and thought could be called method.

He met me with a carriage at Culoz, to give and enjoy my first impressions of the distant Alps, and for the ten days we stopped at Geneva I stayed with him at the Hotel des Bergues. We climbed the Saleve, and I saw what gave me more pleasure, I confess, than the distant view of Mont Blanc, which he expected me to be enthusiastic over,--the soldanella and gentians. The great accidents of nature,--Niagara and the high Alps,--though they awe me, have always left me cold; and all that summer I should have been more fruitfully employed in some nook of English scenery, where nature went undisturbed by catastrophes and cataclysms.

Our first sketching excursion was to the Perte du Rhone, and, while Ruskin was drawing some mountain forms beyond the river, he asked me to draw some huts near by,--not picturesque cottages, thatched roofs and lichen-stained walls, but shanties, such as the Irish laborers on our railways build by the roadside, of deal boards on end, irregular and careless without being picturesque, and too closely associated with pigsty construction, in my mind, to be worth drawing. When Ruskin came back I had made a careless and slipshod five minutes' sketch, not worth the paper it was on, as to me were not the originals. Ruskin was angry, and he had a right to be; for at least I should have found it enough that he wanted it done, to make me do my best on it, but I did not think of it in that light. We drove back towards Geneva in silence,--he moody and I sullen,--and halfway there he broke out, saying that the fact that he wanted the drawing done ought to have been enough to make me do it. I replied that I could see no interest in the subject, which to me only suggested fever and discomfort, and wretched habitations for human beings. We relapsed into silence, and for another mile nothing was said, when Ruskin broke out with, "You were right, Stillman, about those cottages; your way of looking at them was nobler than mine, and now, for the first time in my life, I understand how anybody can live in America."

We went to Bonneville to hunt out the point of view of a Turner drawing which Ruskin liked, but, needless to say, though we ransacked the neighborhood for views, we never found Turner's; and then we went on to St. Martin, the little village opposite Sallanches, on the Arve. For a subalpine landscape with Mont Blanc in the distance, this is the most attractive bit of the Alpine country I know, with picturesque detail and pleasant climbing up to 7000 feet. The view of Mont Blanc, too, is certainly the finest from below which can be found. In fine weather the mountain is hidden to the summit by clouds which clear away at sunset, and from the little and picturesque bridge over the Arve we saw the huge dome come out, and glow in the sunlight, when we were all in shadow. It was to me new and startling, this huge rosy orb, which at its first appearance suggests a huger moon rising above the clouds, until, slowly, the clouds below melt away, and the mountain stands disclosed to its base. If anything in the Alps can be called truly picturesque, it is the view of the Aiguille de Varens which overhangs the village of St. Martin, with the quaint and lichenous church and cemetery in the foreground, and I made a large drawing of it from the bridge, intending to return and work it up after Ruskin had left me. The little inn of the village was the most comfortable *auberge* I was ever in, and its landlord the kindest and most hospitable of hosts. Twenty years later I went back to the locality, hoping to find something of the old time; but there was only a deserted hostel, the weeds growing over the courtyard, and the sealed and mouldy doors and windows witnessing ancient desertion.

Hardly had I become interested in my drawing when Ruskin decided to move on to Chamounix, where we might hope to get really to work. When the first sublime and overpowering impression of Chamounix and the majesty and gloom of its narrow valley wore off, it began to oppress me, and long before we got away I felt as if I were in a huge grave. The geological interest was great, and the sublimity overpowering. But to my mind sublimity does not suffice for art; the beautiful must predominate, and of the beautiful there is little in the valley. The sublime rendered on a small scale is not satisfactory; the beautiful loses nothing by reduction.

I was disappointed in the High Alps,--they left me cold; and after visiting the points of view Turner had taken drawings from, we went up to the Montanvert, where Ruskin wished me to paint for him a wreath of Alpine rose. We found the rose growing luxuriantly against a huge granite boulder, a pretty natural composition, and I set to work on it with great satisfaction, for botanical painting always interested me. Ruskin sat and watched me work, and expressed his surprise at my facility of execution of details and texture, saying that, of the painters he knew, only Millais had so great facility of execution. We were living at the little hotel of the Montanvert, and he was impatient to get back to the better accommodation of the valley hotels; so that when the roses and the rocks were done we went back, the completion of the picture being left for later study. From Paris, in the ensuing winter, I sent it to Ruskin, the distance being made of the actual view down the valley of Chamounix; and he wrote me a bitter condemnation of it, as a disappointment; for he said that he "had expected to see the Alpine roses overhanging an awful chasm," etc. (an expectation he should have given expression to earlier), and found it very commonplace and uninteresting. So it was, and I burnt it after the fashion of the "Bed of Ferns." As Rowse said of him later, "he wanted me to hold the brush while he painted." But our ideas clashed continually, and what he wanted was impossible,--to make me see with his eyes; and so we came to great disappointment in the end.

I was very much interested in his old guide, Coutet, with whom I had many climbs. He liked to go with me, he said, because I was very sure-footed and could go wherever he did. He was a famous crystal-hunter, and many of the rarest specimens in the museum of Geneva were of his finding. There was one locality of which only he knew, where the rock was pitted with small turquoises like a plum pudding, and I begged him to tell me where it was. There is a superstition amongst the crystal-hunters that to tell where the crystals are found brings bad luck, and he would never tell me in so many words; but one day, after my importunity, I saw him leveling his alpenstock on the ground in a very curious way, sighting along it and correcting the direction, and when he had finished he said, as he walked past me, "Look where it points," and went away. It was pointing to a stratum halfway up to the summit of one of the aiguilles to the west of the Mer de Glace, a chamois climb. He told me later that he found the crystals in the couloir that brought them down from that stratum. A dear old man was Coutet, and fully deserving the affection and confidence of Ruskin. Connected with him was a story which Ruskin told me there of a locality in the valley of Chamounix, of which the guides had told him, haunted by a ghost which could be seen only by children. It was a figure of a woman who raked the dead leaves, and when she looked up at them the children said they saw only a skull in place of a face. Ruskin sent to a neighboring valley for a child who could know nothing of the legend, and went with him to the locality which the ghost haunted. Arrived there he said to the boy, "What a lonely place! There is nobody here but ourselves." "No," said the child, "there is a woman there raking the leaves," pointing in a certain direction. "Let us go nearer to her," said Ruskin; and they walked that way, when the boy stopped, saying that he did not want to go nearer, for the woman looked up, and he said that she had no eyes in her head,--"only holes."

The valley of Chamounix finally became to me the most gloomy and depressing place I was ever in. We made excursions and a few sketches; but I had little sympathy with it, though I tried to do what Ruskin wanted, and to get a faithful study of some characteristic subject in the valley. Every fine day we climbed some secondary peak, five or six thousand feet, and in the evenings we discussed art or played chess, mainly in rehearsing problems, until midnight. Sundays no work was done, but we used to climb some easy hilltop; and there he spent the afternoon in writing a sermon for a girls' school in which he was much interested, but not a hue of drawing would he do. To me, brought up in the severity of Sabbatarianism, the sanctity of the first day of the week had always been a theological fiction, and the result of the contact with the larger world of thinkers and the widening of my range of thought by the study of philosophy had also made me see that the observances of "new moons and fast-days" had nothing to do with true religion, and that the Eden repose of the Creator was too large a matter to be fenced into a day of the week. This slavery to a formality in which Ruskin was held by his terrible conscience provoked me, therefore, to the discussion of the subject.

I showed him that there was no authority for the transference of the Christian weekly rest from the seventh to the first day of the week, and we went over the texts together, in which study my Sabbatarian education gave me an advantage in argument; for he had never given the matter a thought. Of course he took refuge in the celebration of the weekly return of the day of Christ's resurrection; but I showed him that the text does not support the claim that Christ rose on the first day of the week, and that the early fathers, who arranged that portion of the ritual, did not understand the tradition of the resurrection. "Three days and three nights," according to the gospel, Christ was to lie in the tomb,--not parts of three times twenty-four hours. But the women went to the tomb "in the end of the Sabbath, as it began to dawn toward the first day of the week," and they found that he had already risen and was gone. Now, as by the Jewish ritual the day began at sunset, the first day of the week began with the going down of the sun on Saturday, and, therefore, as Christ had already risen, he must have risen on the seventh day. And the reason of this twilight visit was in the prohibition to touch a dead body on the Sabbath, and the zeal of the disciples sent them to the sepulchre at the earliest possible moment. And I showed him how careless or ignorant of the record the redisposition of the sacred time had been, in the fact of the total disregard of the words of Christ, that he should lie in the earth three days and three nights; for they assumed him to have been crucified on Friday, while he must have lain buried Thursday, Friday, and Saturday, and was therefore buried on Wednesday, just before sunset. And this is confirmed by the text which says that the disciples hastened to bury Christ on the day of crucifixion, because the next day was the day of preparation for one of the high Sabbaths, which the early church, which instituted the observance of the first day, confounded with the weekly Sabbath, not knowing that a high Sabbath could not fall on the weekly Sabbath.

To this demonstration Ruskin, always deferent to the literal interpretation of the gospel, could not make a defense; the creed had so bound him to the letter that the least enlargement of the stricture broke it, and he rejected the whole tradition,--not only the Sunday Sabbath, but the authority of the ecclesiastical interpretation of the texts. He said, "If they have deceived me in this, they have probably deceived me in all," and he came to the conclusion of rejecting all. This I had not conceived as a possible consequence of the criticism of his creed, and it gave me great pain; for I was not a skeptic, as he, I have since learned, for a time became. It was useless to argue with him for the spirit of the gospel; he had always held to its infallibility and the exactitude of doctrine, and his indignation was too strong to be pacified. He returned somewhat, I have heard, to his old beliefs in later years, as old men will to the beliefs of their youth, and his Christianity was too sincere and profound for a matter of mistaken credence in mere formalities ever to affect its substance, and the years which followed showed that in no essential trait had the religious foundations of his character been moved. For myself, I was still a sincere believer in the substantial accuracy of the body of Christian doctrine, and the revolt of Ruskin from it gave me great pain. My own entire liberation from the burdens of futile beliefs had yet to come, and at that time he went further than I could go with him. But we never discussed theological matters any more.

I finally found a subject which interested me in a view of the foot of the Mer de Glace from the opposite side of the river, looking up the glacier, with the bridge under the Brevent, and a cottage in the foreground, and set to work on it energetically. Ruskin used to sit behind me and comment on my work. My methods of painting were my own, for I had never painted under any one except the few months with Church, whose method had taught me nothing; and I had a way of painting scud clouds, such as always hang around the Alpine peaks, by brushing the sky in thinly with the sky-blue, and then working into that, with the brush, the melting clouds, producing the grays I wanted on the canvas. It imitated the effect of nature logically, as the pigment imitated the mingling of the vapor with the blue sky; but Ruskin said this was incorrect, and that the colors must be laid like mosaic, side by side, in the true tint. Another discouragement! I used to lay in the whole subject, beginning with the sky, rapidly and broadly, and, when it was dry, returning to the foreground and finishing towards the distance; and Buskin was delighted with the foreground painting, insisting on my doing nothing further to it. In the distance was the Montanvert and the Aiguille du Dru; but where the lines of the glacier and the slopes of the mountain at the right met, five nearly straight lines converged at a point far from the centre, and I did not see how to get rid of them without violating the topography. I pointed it out to Ruskin, and he immediately exclaimed: "Oh, nothing can he done with a subject like that, with five lines radiating from an unimportant point! I will not stay here to see you finish that study." And the next day we packed up and left for Geneva.

At Lausanne I made some careful architectural drawings, which he praised,--some pencil sketches on the lake; and then we drove across country to Freiburg, and finally to Neuchatel, where I found a magnificent subject in the view from the hill behind the city, looking over the lake towards the Alps, with Mont Blanc and the Bernese Alps in the extreme distance. In the near distance rise the castle and its old church, which Ruskin drew for me in pencil with exquisite refinement of detail, for in this kind of drawing he was most admirable. As we should stay only a few days, I could not paint anything, and spent all my time, working nine hours a day, hard, on the one subject in pencil. We still spent our evenings till late in discussions and arguments, with a little chess, rarely going to bed before midnight; and the steady strain, with my anxiety to lose none of my time and opportunities, finally told on my eyes. One day, while working hard on the view of Neuchatel, I felt something snap behind my eyes, and in a few minutes I could no longer see my drawing; the slightest attempt to fix my vision on anything caused such indistinctness that I could see neither my work nor the landscape, and I was obliged to suspend work altogether. In a few days we went to Basle, and, after a rest, my vision came back partially, and we went to Laufenburg, where Turner had found the subject for one of his Liber Studiorum engravings. Here the subjects were entirely after my feeling, and, as my eyes had ceased to trouble me, I set to work on a large drawing of the town and fall from below. In the midst of it the snapping behind my eyes came back, worse than ever, and that time not to leave me for a long time. It was followed by an incessant headache, which made life a burden, with obstinate indigestion. Here Ruskin suddenly found that he must go back to England, and I returned with him as far as Geneva, and thence went to St. Martin, where I spent the rest of the autumn, as helpless for all work as a blind man.

My summer with Ruskin, to which I had looked for so much profit to my art, had ended in a catastrophe of which I did not then even measure the extent. It was nearly two years before I recovered from the attack at Neuchatel enough to work regularly, and these circumstances threw me still further from my chosen career. More exciting and absorbing occupation called me, and I obeyed, whether for better or worse it now matters not. When I was free to return with undivided attention to my painting my enthusiasm had cooled, and human interests claimed and kept me. Ruskin had dragged me from my old methods, and given me none to replace them. I lost my faith in myself, and in him as a guide to art, and we separated definitely, years later, on a personal question in which he utterly misunderstood me; but, apart from questions of art, he always remains to me one of the largest and noblest of all the men I have known, liberal and generous beyond limit, with a fineness of sympathy in certain directions and delicacy of organization quite womanly. Nothing could shake my admiration for his moral character or abate my reverence for him as a humanist. That art should have been anything more than a side interest with him, and that he should have thrown the whole energy of his most energetic nature into the reforming of it, was a misfortune to him and to the world, but especially to me.

At St. Martin I waited the return of my vision. I climbed, and tried chamois-hunting with no success so far as game was concerned, though I saw the beautiful creatures in their homes, and now rejoice that I did not kill any, though I fear I wounded one mortally, where we could not retrieve him. One of my excursions was to the summit of the Aiguille de Varens, by a path, in one place cut in the face of a precipice, only wide enough for one's feet, with sheer cliff above and below, and nothing to hold by. I have a good head, but to follow my guide on that path was something which only *mauvaise honte* brought me to. I was ashamed to hesitate where he walked along so cheerily. We arranged to spend the night at a chalet where a milkmaid with the figure of the Venus of Milo tended a remnant of the herd, most of which had already descended to the valleys below. As the sun was setting I walked out to the brow of the aiguille, which from below seemed a point, but was in reality only the perpendicular face of a mass of mountain which in the other direction sloped away towards Switzerland for miles. The view of Mont Blanc, directly opposite, then bare of clouds from the base to the summit, with the red sunset light falling full on the great fields of snow, of which I had never realized the extent from any other point, was by far the most imposing view of the great mountain I have ever found. I stood at an elevation of about 7000 feet, halfway to the summit of Mont Blanc, with the whole broad expanse of glacier and snowfield glowing in the rosy twilight; and, while I watched the sun set, at my feet lay the valley of the Arve, with the town of Sallanches and its attendant villages in the blue distance of gathering night, thousands of feet below me. As I looked, enchanted, the chimes of the convent below rang out a Gregorian air, which came up to my heights like a solemn monition from the world of dreams, for nothing could be distinguished of its source. We started a chamois, and saw him race across the broad field of snow like the wind, while I could only follow, laboring knee-deep in the snow, like a tortoise after a hare. We slept that night buried in the hay. I am glad to say that the hunt in the morning was without other result than a delightful walk, for my guide was a better climber than huntsman.

 A few days later, I made, with another guide, an excursion to the Col des Fours, on the other side of the valley. The guide was an old professional hunter, and knew the habits of the chamois well. We climbed up leisurely in the afternoon, and slept in the hay of a deserted chalet; for from there the cattle had already been all driven down. While the guide prepared the supper, I walked out to the edge of the cliffs to get the view. The landscape had become a sea of mist,--a river, rather; for the whole valley was filled with a moving, billowy flood of fog flowing from Mont Blanc, and enveloping mountain and valley alike in a veil of changing vapor, melting, forming, and flowing beneath my feet, hiding every object in the landscape below the cliffs I stood on. It made me dizzy, for I seemed to be in the clouds. And while I waited there came a transfiguration of the scene,--the mist began to grow rosy, and deeper and deeper, till it was almost like a sea of blood. No source of light was visible from my point of view, but, of course, the phenomenon, though seemingly mysterious, was evident. The sun, in setting, illuminated the fields of snow at the summit of the mountain beyond, which reverberated its flaming light into the vapor below, penetrating it down to my feet, but the mountain itself was, from my elevation, invisible. It passed like all glories, and quicker than most.

The next morning we went to take our posts for a chamois drive. A friend of the guide, whom he had picked up to profit by my coming, took one side of the valley, and I the other, while a boy with an umbrella went down the valley to drive the chamois up to us. Having posted me, the stupid guide crossed the line of the drive between me and the meadow where the chamois would come to feed, and took his post, hiding nearer the peaks where they had passed the night. Soon after sunrise they made their appearance on a field of snow which sloped down into the Val,-- nine, young and old. I shall never see anything prettier than the play of those young chamois on the snow. They butted and chased each other over the snow, frolicked like kittens, standing on their hind legs and pushing each other, until, probably, they grew hungry, and then came down to the grass to feed. This was the moment for the driver to come in, and he came up the valley waving his arms and umbrella and shouting. The chamois came in my direction till they crossed the track of the old hunter, scenting which they halted, sniffed the air, and then broke in panic, the majority running back past the driver and within a few yards of him, so that if he had had a gun he could easily have killed one, and went down the valley out of sight; three came up the valley, taking the flank of the almost perpendicular rocks, within shot of me, but at full gallop, and I fired at the middle one of the group. They passed behind a mass of rock as I fired, and two came out on the other side. If I hit one I could not know, for the place was inaccessible, but I hope that I missed. I have often thought of the possibility that I might have hit the poor beast, and sent him mortally wounded amongst the rocks to die, and I never recur to the incident without pain. It becomes incomprehensible to me, as my own life wanes, how I could ever have found pleasure in taking the lives of other creatures filling their stations in the world better than I ever did. The late educated soul pays the penalty of earlier ignorance, but there is no atonement to the victims.

I stayed at St. Martin while the plebiscite and annexation to France took place. It was a hollow affair, the voting being a mockery, but the Sardinian government had never made itself seriously felt in Savoy, for either good or ill; the people were a quiet and law-abiding race, and while I was in the country I never heard of a crime or a prosecution. The regiments of Savoyard troops went into the French army with ill will, and there was a bloody fight between them and the French soldiers at Lyons when the former went into the barracks there.

I was at St. Martin when the Emperor and Empress made their tour through the new possession. The state carriages had to be left at Sallanches when the sovereigns went up to the great ball offered them at Chamounix, and, when they returned, the little mountain carriages which brought them down halted under the windows of the *auberge* of St. Martin, in which I lived, to wait for the state carriages to come across the river. They had to wait about half an hour, and as they walked up and down in the road under my window, beside which stood my loaded rifle, I thought how easily I could change the course of European politics, for I could have hit any button on the Emperor's clothes, and I hated him enough to have killed him cheerfully, as an enemy of mankind; but regicide has always seemed to me a great mistake, as it would have been in that case, for it would only have placed the young Prince Imperial on the throne, under the regency of the Empress. I was then a radical republican, with all the sympathies of a Parisian Red, for I had not learned that it is less the form of the government than the character of the governed which makes the difference between governments. I did not spare the life of the Emperor from any apprehension of consequences to me, for I had none. I knew the paths up the mountain at the back of the hotel, and before the confusion should have been overcome, and a pursuit organized, I could have been beyond danger, on my way to the Swiss frontier, for the pine woods came to the back door of the hotel; and beyond that, I never had the habit of thinking of the consequences of what I proposed to do. When I returned to Paris, after the autumn had passed, I told the story to an artist friend, an ultraradical, how I stood at my window with a loaded rifle by my side, and the Emperor twenty feet below, and he shouted with fury, "And you didn't kill him?" Time and fate have punished him more fitly than I should have done, and wise men leave these things to time and fate.

CHAPTER XVIII
PARIS AGAIN THE CIVIL WAR IN AMERICA

I remained in Paris all that winter, and took a studio with an American friend,--Mr. Yewell,--but I could do no work; the headache never left me, and, though I could draw a little, my vision failed when it was strained, and I seemed to have lost my color sense. I was desperate, and, when Garibaldi set out on the Marsala expedition, I was just on the point of sailing to join him when I received a letter from the father of my fiancee, telling me that her perplexities and distress of mind over our marriage had so increased that they feared for her reason if she were not set at rest. I took the next steamer, and ended the vacillation by insisting on being married at once. Nothing but a morbid self-depreciation had prevented her from coming to a decision in the matter long before, and there was no other solution than to assume command and impose my will. We were married two days after my landing, and returned to Paris a few days after. When the spring opened we went down into Normandy, and there, returning to the study of nature and living in quiet and freedom from anxiety, I slowly and partially recovered my vision, and began to regain in a measure the power of drawing. The landscape of the quiet French country suited me perfectly, and I made two or three good studies, but without getting into a really efficient condition for painting, which I only did a year or two later at Rome.

Our winter in Paris had been greatly brightened by the acquaintance of the Brownings, the father and sister of the poet. We lived in the same section of Paris, near the Hotel des Invalides, and much of our time was passed with them. "Old Mr. Browning" we have always called him, though the qualification of "old," by which we distinguished him from his son Robert, seemed a misnomer, for he had the perpetual juvenility of a blessed child. If to live in the world as if not of it indicates a saintly nature, then Robert Browning the elder was a saint: a serene, untroubled soul, conscious of no moral or theological problem to disturb his serenity, and as gentle as a gentle woman,--a man in whom, it seemed to me, no moral conflict could ever have arisen to cloud his frank acceptance of life as he found it come to him. He had, many years before we knew him, inherited an estate in Jamaica, but on learning that to work it to profit he must become a slave owner he renounced the heritage. And, knowing him as we knew him, it is easy to see that he would renounce it cheerfully and without any hesitation. A man of a rougher and more energetic type might have tried the experiment, or questioned the judgment, at least have regretted his own integrity, but Browning could have done neither. The way was clear, and the decision must have been as quick as that of a child to reject a thing it abhorred. His unworldliness had not a flaw. So beautiful a life can never have become distinguished in the struggles and antagonisms which make the career of the man of the world, or even the man of letters, as letters are now written; for he was a man, and the only one I ever knew, of whom one would say that he applied in the divine sense the maxim of Christ, "Resist not evil,"--he simply, and by the necessity of his own nature, ignored it.

He had a curious facility in drawing heads of quaint and always varied character, which character he could not foresee when he began the drawing. They were always in profile, and he began at one extremity and ran his pencil round to the other, always bringing out an individuality, but without any intention as to what that should be; and he named it, when it was done, according to the type it offered, generally in character, with a trace of caricature, and, for the most part, subjects from the courts of law,--a judge or a puzzled juror, a disappointed or a triumphant client, etc., etc. He would draw a dozen or twenty in an evening, all different and all unforeseen, as much to him as to us, and he was as much amused as we were when it turned out more than usually funny. His chief amusement was hunting through the bookstalls along the quays, and I have, amongst my old books, an early life of Raphael, which he gave me, with his name on the fly leaf.

Of Miss Browning, who still lives, I will not speak; but what she told me of the poet's mother may, I think, be told without indiscretion. She had the extraordinary power over animals of which we hear sometimes, but of which I have never known a case so perfect as hers. She would lure the butterflies in the garden to her, and the domestic animals obeyed her as if they reasoned. Robert had been given a pure-blooded bulldog of a rare breed, which tolerated no interference from any person except him or his mother, and which would allow no familiarity with her on the part of strangers; so that when a neighbor came in he was not permitted to shake hands with her, for the dog at once showed his teeth. Not even her husband was allowed to take the slightest liberty with her in the dog's presence, and when Robert was more familiar with her than the dog thought proper he showed his teeth to him. They one day put him to a severe test, Robert putting his arm around his mother's neck as they sat side by side at the table. The dog went round behind them, and, putting his feet upon the chair, lifted Robert's arm off her shoulder with his nose, giving an intimation that he would not permit any liberty of that kind even from him. They had a favorite cat, to which the dog had the usual antipathy of dogs, and one day he chased her under a cupboard, and, unable to reach her, kept her there besieged and unable to escape, till Mrs. Browning intervened and gave the dog a lecture, in which she told him of their attachment for the cat, and charged him never to molest her more. If the creature had understood speech he could not have obeyed better; for from that time he was never known to molest the cat, and she, taking her revenge for past tyranny, bore herself most insolently with him, and when she scratched him over the head he only whimpered and turned away, as if to avoid temptation. An injury to one of his feet made an operation necessary, and the family surgeon was called in to perform it, but found him so savage that he could not touch the foot or approach him. Mrs. Browning came and talked to him in her way, and the dog submitted at once, without a whimper, to the painful operation. She had been long dead when I knew the family.

We had planned to go together--the elder Browning, Robert and Mrs. Browning, Miss Browning, my wife, and myself--to pass the summer at Fontainebleau, and we were awaiting the arrival of Robert and his wife from Florence when the news came of Mrs. Browning's illness, followed not much later by that of her death. The intrusion even of a friend was too much for this catastrophe, and we saw little more of the Brownings until years after, when other and many changes of fortune had come over us, and we met again in Italy.

Out of a quiet and happy life in Normandy I was aroused by the complications of our Civil War. An intimate friend living in Paris, the late Colonel W.B.

Greene, a graduate of West Point, had applied for the command of a regiment of Massachusetts troops, and offered me a position on his staff if he got it and I would come. We agreed to go together, but his impatience carried him away, and he sailed without giving me notice. I followed by the next steamer, and, leaving my wife with my parents, I went on to Washington and to Greene's headquarters. I was too late for Greene, and I could not pass the medical examination, which was then very rigid, for all the North was volunteering. "Go home," said Greene; "we have already buried all the men like you. We have not seen the enemy yet, and we have buried six per cent. of the regiment. It is no place for you." But I had no choice; there were 800,000 men enlisted, and further enlistments were countermanded. I tried to get some position with Burnside,--who was fitting out an expedition to North Carolina,--even as cook; for I could not pass for the rank and file, and Burnside, as a friend of my friends in Rhode Island, might, I thought, help me. He replied that he had already nine applications for every post at his disposal. As a last resource, I went up into the Adirondacks to raise a company of sharpshooters. My backwoodsmen were all ready to go, but they wanted special rifles and special organization, for they meant to go to "shoot secesh," not to be regular infantry. Their ambition was not reconcilable with the plans of the military authorities, so that the company was never raised, and I then turned to my plan for the consulate.

I suppose that there are few now living who knew by personal investigation and remember clearly the condition of the country at that epoch. We had suffered the defeat of Bull Run, and the country at large was in a state of flaming patriotism; but sober people had many doubts whether the government was strong enough to carry through the plans of the President, and he also had, I was told by some one who knew him, been very uncertain whether the population at large would respond, even when he made the first call for 75,000 volunteers. Persons in positions of great influence were of the opinion that the North had no right to coerce the South. General Scott, the commander-in-chief, urged separation peacefully, and Horace Greeley, the most influential member of the press in the country, opposed coercion, while the mass of the Democratic party were either on the fence or openly in favor of the South, and this opposition of the Democrats was probably what gave Lincoln the most serious consideration. Some of the most earnest and patriotic people I knew had grave doubts if the Northern people had any conception of the work they had undertaken, and if they would be constant when they came to realize it.

While I was in Washington I saw Lincoln and some of those around him, and my opinion is that, but for his faith in the Supreme Providence and in the destiny of our Republic, his courage, and with it the whole scheme of defense, would have broken down. Future generations will not understand the difficulties before him,--perhaps he himself did not. The administration of Buchanan had prepared for the secession, and Buchanan as minister to England had already established the opinion of the governing class in that country in the certainty of impending separation,--a fact which should be remembered when we judge the attitude of England; the fleet had been dispersed to the ends of the earth, and the officers of the army were mainly Southerners. The support of New York and Massachusetts was of the gravest importance. The former was largely under the influence of Seward, and he was inclined by nature to conciliation; in the latter State, General Butler, a Democrat, and of seriously questioned loyalty, had an influence which might easily become the dominant one and carry the State over to the Democratic opposition, which was in the country at large distinctly opposed to coercion. The government and the ruling class in England were clearly hostile to the North, and the position on that side was menacing.

Had the South then been content with separation on the lines of "Mason and Dixon's line," I am convinced that it would have taken place without a struggle, if the position could have been defined without bloodshed. But this was what the most sagacious of the Southern leaders did not desire. It became evident that the majority in the South did not desire separation, and the leaders knew that a peaceful separation would be followed by reconstruction on something like the old lines, for the South could not stand alone industrially; so that they had not concealed their determination to invade the Middle and Western States, and carry them forcibly over to the new Confederacy, "leaving out New England." It was generally known that Pennsylvania and New Jersey were Democratic and lukewarm for the old Union, and that Ohio and the West would not resist if there were a successful beginning of a movement and a military invasion. So far as the sentiments of the politicians were concerned, the South had a very correct idea of the probabilities of the situation; what they were utterly ignorant of was the spirit of the masses in the North, which they thought to coerce easily. There they were mistaken, and there Lincoln saw his strength, and that saved the country; for, with the firing on Fort Sumter and the open insult to the flag, the Northern masses took fire, and the conflagration burned out the roots of sympathy for the South. Butler was given a command in the field; others of the same class were given commands, and the dangerous demagogue class was enlisted for the war.

When I landed, the entire able-bodied population of the North was seeking to enlist, and the troops were pouring by thousands into Washington, and only the most uncertain and prudent of the Northern leaders doubted of victory, though no one dreamed what it would cost. And, looking at the corruption of American politics to-day, the venality and the indifference to the true interests of the nation of most of the men who control the political life at its most important centres, and the general tendency of our politics, it needs a serene and far-reaching faith in human progress to enable a citizen of the United States, who believes in a political ideal, to regard the sacrifices then made as having been profitable. I see things dispassionately and as an old man removed from the chance of personal gains or losses, and, but for a faith in human progress being the result of an eternal and inevitable law, I should say that the blood of that war had been wasted. It is a painful conviction to die with,--but I expect to die with it,--that generations and unparalleled disasters must pass before my country reaches the goal its founders believed to be its destiny.

Having exhausted every appliance to open a way into the army, I made my appeal to Dr. Nott, and received by return of the Washington post my commission as consul at Rome, as I have told in a previous chapter. I went on to Cambridge to get information and advice, and, at Lowell's, met Howells for the first time. We could, each of us, offer condolence for the other's disappointment; for Howells had asked for Dresden and was appointed to Venice, while I had asked for Venice, intending to write the history of Venetian art. But Rome had always been given to an artist; and, though there was no salary, but fees only, it seemed to have been a much-sought-for position, and I accepted.

Leaving my wife at home, for her confinement, I sailed for England, **en route** for Italy, just when the capture of Mason and Slidell had thrown the country into a new agitation; for it was foreseen that England would not submit to this disrespect to her flag, though the step was in strict accordance with her own precedents. Seward and the more prudent part of the public were in favor of releasing the prisoners at once, and before any demand could be made by the English government; but it was said that Lincoln and the West were in favor of holding them, and letting England do her worst. It is possible that he thought that a foreign enemy would decide all the wavering minds, and possibly open the way to a pacification between the North and South. I left New York before we had heard of the reception of the news in England, and found the agitation there intense. The consul at Liverpool told me that he could not go into the Exchange for the insults offered him there, and American merchants were insulted on the street. In London, at the restaurants where I dined, the conversation turned altogether on the incident, and the language was most violent.

As I was in the service of the government I waited on Mr. Adams, the minister, and remained in London until the question was settled, in daily communication with him. He thought the danger of war still great, as Lincoln had not decided to accept the ultimatum, and the English ministry was, in Adams's opinion, desirous of having a *casus belli*, or at least a justification for recognizing the Southern Confederacy. That war had not already become inevitable he considered due entirely to the attitude of the Queen, who resisted any measure calculated to precipitate a hostile solution, and had refused her assent to a dispatch demanding the release of the envoys, and worded in such peremptory terms that Lincoln could not have hesitated to repel it at any cost,--an outcome which, in the opinion of Mr. Adams, was what Palmerston, Gladstone, and Lord John Russell wanted. But, on the insistence of the Queen, the offensive passage was struck out, and peace was preserved, though at that moment the reply of our government had not been received, and Adams did not consider that, even in its modified form, the demand of the English ministry might not be rejected. As the crisis was still undecided, I waited until the solution was definite. The favorable reply came by the next steamer. To the peace-loving heart of the Queen mainly, and next to the tact and diplomatic ability of Mr. Adams, the world owes that the war most disastrous possible for the civilization of the west was avoided. Put at rest with regard to this danger, I continued my journey and entered upon my functions as representative of my government at Rome.

I have since heard various versions of this crisis and its solution, but the above is, I believe, substantially the truth. I have heard that the English dispatch was referred to the French Minister of Foreign Affairs, and that he advised against it; but this is impossible. The Emperor of France was more determined even than Palmerston to destroy the United States, if possible, as his Mexican enterprise showed, and we knew from other sources that he was pressing the English government to recognize the belligerency of the South. Day by day I heard from Mr. Adams of the position, and he said to me emphatically that he did not consider the declaration of war impossible until he received the reply of Lincoln to the English ultimatum; and it is impossible that such a transaction as that of the consultation with the French government should have taken place without Adams knowing of it, for his information from the surroundings of the Queen was minute and incessant. He said to me, without the slightest qualification, that the preservation of peace was due solely to the insistence of the Queen, strengthened by the advice of Prince Albert, on the demand for the release of the envoys being made in terms which should not offend the ***amour propre*** of the North.

CHAPTER XIX
MY ROMAN CONSULATE

The convenient road from London to Rome, when I went there as consul, was via Paris to Marseilles, and thence by sea to Civita Vecchia. It was December when I left London, and the journey from Paris to Marseilles, in a third-class carriage, took twenty-six hours. The Mont Cenis tunnel had not been opened yet, and the voyage by diligence was tedious, costly, and at that season uncomfortable on account of the cold. I arrived at Rome shortly before Christmas, when the city was astir with the preparations for the great ceremonies which were then the principal attraction for foreigners there, but the number of visitors was very small compared with that which now gathers to their diminished religious and spectacular interest. The foreign quarter was limited to that immediately about the Piazza di Spagna, and only the artist folk lived in the remoter quarters, where they found cheap and commodious apartments in the palaces of fallen nobility, glad to let their upper stories; and there were few or no new houses.

Rome was given up to art and religion; it was still decaying, picturesque, pathetic, and majestic. Where now we find the prosperous and hideous new quarters,--the Via Nazionale, and the expanse of structures to the east of it, the region between the Coliseum and the Lateran, the 20 Settembre, Via Veneto, and the vicinity where were the Ludovisi gardens, and now are long streets of ugly houses, with the entirely new quarter of the Prati, were then expanses of vineyards and gardens, and we used to cross the Tiber by a ferry to visit the farm of Cincinnatus, now buried under twenty feet of rubbish, on which are built the palaces of the Prati, huge, ugly barracks; and even the Campagna has lost much of its desolate beauty. Down the Tiber, where the ghastly embankment walls in the yellow stream, there was then a picturesque riverbank, with a delightful foreground in every rood of it. Where now is the Piazza delle Terme and the great railway station, we used to go to get studies of the ruins of the baths of Diocletian, one of the most picturesque objects of the region.

Political or social life there was none, and the foreign element, whether the regular or the transitory, was divided by its nationalities, and cut off absolutely from the Roman. Only the English and American mingled to any extent, the foreign Catholics finding their way, with such Protestants as gave hope of conversion, into the clerical world, which, from all that I could see of it, offered little attraction to the fugitive visitors. Wide-eyed, hurried Americans came, saw, and bought a picture, and went away again; English sightseers came for Christmas or Easter, and bought a few old masters; but the mass of those who stayed for long were invalids, who settled down and tried to keep as much in the sun as possible, for the universal belief then was that to live out of the sunshine was to contract mortal malaria. It was the most unreal world I have ever lived in, whether we use the word unreal in the sense of shadowy or poetical.

Rome was in fact at that time a spectacle never before or since seen in the world. Ruled by an absolute government, theocratic and therefore considering its authority beyond all human attack, but besieged on all sides by an invading liberalism, which had already captured all its outposts and undermined its position at the centre, it, still defiant, refused to make a single concession to the spirit of the epoch, and bade defiance to diplomacy and insurrection alike. All its former allies from north and south were in refuge within the walls of the city, the King of Naples and all his court offering the daily spectacle of a parade of their downfall as they drove through the streets. Rome itself was a huge cloister in which the only animation was in the processions of priests and students of the theological seminaries, or the more melancholy funerals in which the hooded and gowned friars added gloom to the mystery of our common lot,--no industry except those of jewelry and art and that of ecclesiastical apparatus. The principal revenues were the charity of the outside world,--St. Peter's pence. Government was not by law, but by the arbitrary decisions of the most incompetent of officials, enforced by the bayonets of a foreign army, the soldiers of which despised the population, and lived in the most complete separation from it. The Pope himself had little affection for his French protectorate, which urged, and sometimes effected, certain improvements which he regarded as innovations and invasions.

I had, soon after my arrival, a case before the lower tribunal which showed how the administration of justice was regarded. Having a relapse into the malady that had followed my breakdown in Switzerland, which was exaggerated by the heat of Rome, I was ordered by my physician to Ariccia to recruit, and I left my apartment, which was also the consulate, and took quarters at the little Ariccian inn which was the resort of the artists at that date.

As I could not absent myself from the office longer than ten days at a time without permission of the government at Washington, I had to return ***pro forma*** at that term, when, to my surprise, I found my apartment in possession of a stranger. I intimated his dislodging, to which he replied that he had taken the rooms and paid his rent and would not go. At that time there was a temporary occupation-- merely nominal, however--of the legation by ex-Governor Randall of Wisconsin. The minister had taken an apartment where he could mount the arms of the Republic, and had then gone off on his European tour, leaving me in occupation of the post as charge d'affaires and in care of his rooms. As I had thus another place to sleep in, I evacuated the consular quarters not unwillingly, removing all my effects except a set of silver spoons which my mother had given me on my leaving home, and which were heirlooms. The spoons were being cleaned, the landlady said, and would be ready the next day. I called for them again, and was again deferred, when I went at once to the tribunal and made a claim for my spoons. On statement of the case, the judge gave an order for the immediate and unconditional delivery of the plate; but when I went to get them at the tribunal, he said it was lucky for me that I came when I did, as the landlady had come in the afternoon and applied for an order against me to pay another month's rent (always paid in advance), and that if she had come first he should have been obliged to give it to her. I explained that I had been driven out of the apartment by another occupant; but that, he said, made no difference, the first applicant for justice would alone have been heard.

Not long after, a similar case called for my more or less official recognition. My colleague the consul at Florence had come for a visit to Rome, and had taken a cab to make the rounds of the sights, and, making his visit to the church of Ara Coeli, he of course left the cab at the foot of the stairs. He found little which interested him in the church, and, returning sooner than the cabman expected, he found no cab there. In the course of the day he went to the police court and asked for a punishment for the cabman for having deserted him on his round. The cabman was summoned and fined accordingly; but the magistrate remarked to my friend when he came to give evidence that it was fortunate for him that he complained first, for the cabman had come later in the day and asked for his fare for the night which he had passed at the foot of the stairs waiting for the return of the ***forestiero***; and he added that if the cabman had come first, my friend would have been obliged to pay the claim. It was simple and expeditious, first come being first served, but hardly good civil administration.

At the time of the expedition of Garibaldi which ended at Aspromonte, the excitement in the city was intense, and the panic on the part of the ecclesiastical population so great that they mainly took refuge in the convents and villages of the mountain country. I had occasion to see the Pope at that time, and found him in profound despondency, evidently persuaded that Garibaldi would come to Rome. He said to me that he was convinced that the great day of tribulation prophesied for the church had come, and it would have its fifty years of oppression, after which it would arise again more glorious than ever; but there was no question that in his mind the French garrison was not for the moment an efficient protection. The Italian party in the city was very small, but active, and in those days especially so. The priests were insulted and menaced whenever it was possible to reach them covertly, and finally one was stabbed in a crowd. Many arrests were made, and amongst those arrested was an exile who had ventured into the city to visit his friends. He was put on trial for the stabbing, and, though he proved an alibi, he was condemned to death, for "some example must be made," they said. There was not the slightest evidence against him except that he was an exile who had no right to be in the city, and he was executed. Every day the police had to obliterate rebellious inscriptions from the walls, and a constant correspondence was kept up with the patriots in Florence. To belong to the order of Freemasons was punishable by death, but a lodge was in full activity, and when Lincoln was assassinated it sent me, for his widow, a letter of condolence. It was given me by Castellani, who, not being initiated, had received it from a brother known to him. About the same time, the revolutionary committee decided to contribute a stone from the ***agger*** of Servius Tullius to the Washington monument at Washington, and got out one of the largest, had it dressed and appropriately inscribed, and forwarded it to Leghorn for shipment to America, the bill of lading being sent to me for transmission.

The police regulations were extremely severe against heresy, but brigandage was common, and the darker streets were unsafe at night to strangers. People were not infrequently robbed in their own doorways, and there was a recognized system of violent robbery known as "doorway robbing." The streets were very badly lighted, and the entrance halls on the ground floor were scarcely ever lighted, so that we always carried wax tapers to light ourselves up to our rooms, or to visit our friends. Incautious foreigners, ignorant of this need for precaution, entering the dark passages, were sometimes seized by robbers hidden behind the door, gagged, and stripped of all valuables without a possibility of assistance unless a friend happened to enter the house at the moment, for the police were never seen about the streets at night. I had, in the second year of my residence, a very narrow escape from capture by brigands, which might have been a serious matter. I was making, with my wife and son, our *villeggiatura* at Porto d'Anzio, then a miserable fishing village, but, except Civita Vecchia, the only convenient seaside locality in the States of the Church where one could find lodgings. With an American lady friend staying with us, we planned to make an excursion by boat to the Punta d'Astura, where are the ruins of a villa of Cicero; but when half way there we were driven back by a passing shower. On the same day a party of Roman sportsmen, out quail shooting, were "held up" in the ruins and obliged to pay a ransom of five thousand scudi. The brigands of the kingdom of Naples were constantly given refuge and sustenance on our side the frontier, and on a visit to Olevano, in the Sabine hills, I was witness of a band of over two hundred taking refuge from the Italian troops in the Papal territory, and being furnished with provisions and refreshments as at a festa. Artists out sketching were never molested, not because the Papal influence protected us, but because the brigands knew their poverty, and had a tinge of sympathy with the arts.

The ecclesiastical authorities were so severe on heresy that a friend of mine, who had married an English lady who remained a Protestant, was brought before the Inquisition (the "Holy Office") and put under the severest pressure to compel his wife to abstain from attending the English church outside the Porta del Popolo. He escaped ulterior consequences only by appealing to the French authorities, he being a surgeon in the service of the French garrison. For common morality there was little care. The sexual relations were flagrantly loose, and the scandal even of some of the great dignitaries was widespread. Antonelli's amours were the subject of common gossip, and most of the parish priests were in undisguised marital relations with their housekeepers; nor was this considered as at all to their discredit by the population at large. One of the leading Liberals, permitted to remain in the city on account of the importance of his industry, one of the great goldsmiths' works, told me that the Liberals never permitted the priests to frequent their houses, as they invariably conspired to corrupt the newly married women, unmarried girls being unmolested. In the lower circles of the bourgeoisie it was a matter of common knowledge that the husbands openly made a traffic of the virtue of their wives; and in my personal acquaintance amongst the artists, I knew of a number of cases in which the artist had the wife as a mistress for a fixed compensation to the husband.

For this kind of immorality the police had no eyes, and, admitting enormous exaggeration in the common report of the conduct of the younger priesthood and the students of the theological schools (and there is no smoke without some fire), the conditions of morality amongst the younger Italian clergy was a gross scandal. Houses of ill-fame were notorious, and it used to be said that when Pius IX. was urged by the French authorities to put them under control and license he replied that "every house was a brothel, and it was useless to license any." There was another saying which I heard often, that "if you wanted to go to a brothel you must go in the daytime, for at night they were full of priests." How far this was justified I do not know, but I remember that two American acquaintances went one night to one of the best recognized houses of the kind, a place of the most common notoriety on the Corso, and they were told at the door that there was no room,--"every place was occupied."

Let me not be charged with making of this state of things an accusation against the Catholic religion. The English, Irish, and American students, who were those with whom I principally came in contact, were ardent and enthusiastic devotees, as earnest in their religious observances as any of the most devoted members of any other church I have known. Indeed, it is my personal experience that so far as regards the younger men, I have never found so many animated by the true apostolical spirit as amongst the students of theology of British and American birth whom I then knew at Rome. At the head of all the Catholics of all nations whom I have ever known are the English, in respect of sincere and ardent devotion to their church, with the minimum of animosity towards other creeds, and the most healthy morality. With the great majority of Italian ecclesiastics, on the contrary, religion is a mere formality, and its influence on the life is inconsiderable and unconsidered. It was, therefore, not because it was a Catholic city that the morality of Rome was so low, but because the energies of the hierarchy were so occupied with the difficulties of the position of a government of priests unused to civil administration and by their own education disqualified for it, that the ordinary functions of government were impossible to it. The situation was made still worse by the Italian constitutional indifference to questions of common morality. As the government of the church lies in the hands of the Italian clergy, it will be forever impossible for a government organized on the principles of the Papal temporal power to be other than that which has been suppressed by Italy. To the majority of the higher Italian ecclesiastics, the church has become merely a political instrument, into the management of which the spiritual interests of the people do not enter, and the efforts of the Catholics of other countries to bring about a reform will never succeed while the power is in the hands of the Italian clergy, which it will be as long as the Papacy is an Italian institution; and as the Pope is Pope merely because he is the Bishop of Rome, it is difficult to see how the situation can be made different.

Pius IX. was personally a most sincere and devout, though worldly, man, and it is difficult to believe that any other than a devotee could now be elected to the Holy See, for even the most corrupt civil or ecclesiastical intellect must see the importance of a reputation for sanctity in the Pontiff, while, as the influence of the Papacy is no longer of vital importance to the government of any country in the world (though doubtless of considerable utility to several), there is little political importance in the personality of the Pontiff, and slight motive for foreign governments to exercise influence on the election. If removed from Italy and established in a seat surrounded by a population like that of the masses in France (out of Paris and the large cities), amenable to purely spiritual influences, the church would revert to its normal functions and abandon politics,--a result never to be hoped for while it remains Italian. I have no sympathy with its creed, or any other of the creeds, for

I conceive no healthy conformity of belief possible to men and women differing in intellectual and spiritual capacities; but I have seen good work done by the Catholic church in many quarters, and I have many and admirable Catholic friends, and, to be frank, I do not believe that the creed makes much difference in the religion.

As to Pius IX., I am convinced that he was not only a devout man, but an excellent and admirable man, as men go, a genuine believer in the divine direction of his pontificate, and incapacitated for civil government simply because no one could carry on a civil government on ecclesiastical principles. He loved his people, and, personally and generally, was beloved by them; but the progress of liberalism and democracy had driven out of the Papal States, or into a mute and inflexible opposition, all the most active and potent intellects amongst them, and the clergy without them could not administer the government; so that, wishing to do good to his subjects, he could not improve their political condition without inviting those elements of liberalism which he considered the inexorable enemies of the church, which was to him the highest interest of humanity, He reposed his faith on the abilities of clerics who knew nothing of human nature or practical politics, but comprehended only a paternal control, absolute, and to be enforced by the rod, actual or figurative; or on those of civilian devotees and fanatics less intelligent even than the clerical functionaries.

As I was, for the greater part of my term, in charge of the legation interests and duties, I saw Pius IX. often and liked him much. One day when I was having an audience in his little room, the windows of which looked west, there came up a great thunder storm, with frequent flashes of lightning, at each of which he crossed himself and devoutly said a prayer. His conversation convinced me that he felt profoundly convinced of his divinely appointed function as the vicegerent of God on earth, and his sincerity inspired me with great respect for the man; but, naturally, with little for his intellect. His **bonhomie** was remarkable, and he had a keen sense of humor, which led him to make sarcastic, and often telling remarks, on men and things, in which he was sometimes the reverse of diplomatic. He had, for my advantage, many jibes at our past ministers, of some of whom he had diverting memories, and especially of Major Cass,--of whom he always spoke as "quel Cass," who had curious habits of night wandering and adventure seeking, or, as Pius put it, "could not be quiet of nights." Either he or his predecessor, I forget which, had insisted on putting his horse through a ride round the parapet of the Pincian balustrade, where a slip or a yielding stone meant death to the rider, which might have been of no importance, but to the horse also, which would have been a pity. And the old man liked a sly thrust at any of us who had made a blunder.

While thus in charge of the diplomatic relations of my government without its recognition, the Department sent out a chaplain, an ex-chaplain of the House of Representatives, who, having served his time in that capacity, was entitled to a vacation in Europe, and came with recommendations to me. Protestant worship was forbidden within the walls of Rome, but to induce the English Protestants to come to Rome and spend their money there, they were allowed to worship in a sort of warehouse outside the Porta del Popolo. This was repugnant to our democratic ways, and the new chaplain insisted on having his chapel inside the walls. So I "put on cheek" and hired in the name of the legation an apartment with a huge reception room close to the Piazza di Spagna, put up the arms of the United States of America, and opened the reception room for public worship as the chapel of the legation,--the first instance in recorded time of Protestant worship in the Papal city. The sequel was amusing, for as Sunday was my only holiday, and I always spent it on the Campagna, the chaplain cut me dead for not attending his services and keeping Sunday.

I expected some admonitory allusion to this achievement when next I saw the Pope, but no notice was ever taken of it either by the superior or the lower authorities, and so far as I know the church of my planting flourished as long as the city remained under the Papal rule, but with no more of my watering. The Pope was, I am persuaded, quite indifferent to it, for, devout and unquestioning believer in his own divine authority as he was, he was not a bigot, and not of a persecuting disposition, but he was only a part of an immense and intricate machine, over the movements of which neither he nor any other Pope could have much control. He had every possible disposition to be that ideal ruler, a benevolent despot, but even in that little realm the details of government were impossible of control by the most competent head of a government; they were necessarily left to the incompetent, bigoted, and zealous administrators chosen by the secondary chiefs of the departments, all the most conservative of men, with a reverence for the abuses and usages of the old regime. It was personal government down to the lowest grade of responsibility. The

Pope presided and bore the responsibility of the proceedings, but Antonelli was the real ruler of the States of the Church.

And Antonelli was the very impersonation of unscrupulous and malignant intellect, subtle with all the Italian subtlety, and unscrupulous as any of the brigands from the community in which he had his origin. He was in those days a cardinal of the order of deacons, and only in his later career a priest, which fact is sometimes made the excuse for his frank and notorious disregard of the rule of chastity, nor did he seem to be concerned that his amours were the common gossip of Rome. I was one day in his anteroom waiting for an audience when a lady came to visit him, and when she was announced he flew to receive her with the ardor of a boy in love, and with such open and passionate expressions of affection as could be seen only in a southern nature. But he had none of the slowness of action or decision which we attribute sometimes to the languor of tropical natures. In business, as in love, he lost no time, and never was at a loss for his expedient, but came at once to a decision, and gave it on the spot. When the cruise of the Alabama gave rise to diplomatic correspondence, and our government protested against her receiving such treatment from neutrals as would facilitate her career, I was, amongst my colleagues under similar obligations, charged to protest against her being admitted to the privileges of a national man-of-war in the port of Civita Vecchia. Antonelli replied to my communication of the protest that she would be admitted to the port with the same privileges as a man-of-war of any other nation, and the reply was given with almost explosive promptness and vivacity. But until a request for relaxation of the passport regulations in favor of Southerners was made by some one professing to speak on behalf of our own government, which was in my second year, he never permitted the least bending of them, and only in important cases, where strong personal influence was brought to bear, issued passports of the Foreign Office for Southern Americans to leave the city.

Antonelli had a face which gave one an idea of the expression "beaute du Diable," for a more perfect type of Satanic intelligence and malignity than it showed at times I cannot conceive. If I had been a figure painter, I should certainly have painted him as Mephistopheles, as he appeared in the audience room in his close-fitting purple costume with scarlet trimmings, his long coat-tails flying behind him when he moved like the fringe of a flame. He was the most curious contrast to the

Pope, with his humorous and kindly manner, that it is possible to conceive, for the Cardinal was nothing if not sardonic and serious. The very slightest trace of humor would have transformed him completely.

Unique as was the government, so was the position of a consul. It had something of the exterritoriality of the same position in the Turkish empire. The arms of my government over my door were a protection against legal process, and I imagine that my predecessor had so employed it, for when I had my first clothes made the tailor refused to send them to the consulate till they were paid for. I had a right to carry arms and shoot anywhere in the territory of the Pope, and I had an absolute control over the passports, i.e. over the movements of my fellow citizens, for no one who had come to Rome with the passport of the United States of America could leave it without my visa, and I could sequestrate the passport whenever I saw fit. But on the part of my own government the consideration afforded was the minimum of its kind. I had no salary, and my compensation was in fees, viz. those on passports and the few invoices of goods sent to America, with such notarial business as might arise. The late consul had resigned, and gone home to fight for the Confederate cause, leaving the consulate in the hands of a French secretary, an old and needy teacher of his native language whenever he could find a pupil. He was satisfied with the pittance my own means allowed me to give him, and he wrote, in a much better French than mine would have been, the dispatches to the Vatican. I could talk French fluently if not correctly, and that sufficed. Before leaving Washington, I had received a hint from a friend in the Department of State that the fewer dispatches I troubled them with the higher would be my favor in the department, so that, with the exception of my quarterly accounts, I had little official writing to do; but when I came to Rome again in 1882, I was told by my successor of that date that my file of dispatches to the department was the only one which existed in the consular archives of the Papal occupation of Rome.

Rome was in those days the Lotophagitis of our century, whose population lived in an artificial peace, a sort of dreamland--artists who, whether German, French, English, Americans, or Russians, were more or less imbued with the feeling of the old art, and who found their *clientele* in people who believed, as I have heard some say, that *any* picture painted in Rome was better than any picture painted elsewhere! There was, therefore, a continual exportation of copies, good and bad, of the old masters and a few landscapes for the remembering of localities, but the quality of the art was of trifling importance to the buyers--it was "done in Rome," and that sufficed as merit. The Cafe Greco, haunt of the race of artists since Salvator Rosa, was in its original and charming, if rude, simplicity, and there came all the artists to take their after-dinner cup. Old John Gibson, though not the oldest of the habitues, was the chief of our Anglo-American community; Randolph Rogers, Mosier, Reinhart, Story, and two or three other sculptors, whose names I have forgotten, and two or three American landscape painters, of whom Tilton was chief at the time of my arrival, had the monopoly of American patronage, and every wealthy American who came conceived it his duty to patronize American art, while our government had the tradition of always sending an artist to Rome as consul.

Charlotte Cushman, a famous actress of her day, was the nucleus of a little clique of women sculptors, Miss Stebbins, Harriet Hosmer, and one or two others of lesser fame. Accordingly, she made war on sculptors of the other sex in all the curious ways of womanly malice, in order to the exclusive reaping by her protegees of the golden harvest. I had known her years before, when she was still on the stage and I the dramatic and art critic of the New York "Evening Post," and, as our relations had then been cordial, it was natural that she should "take me up" on my arrival. Her hospitality was large--dinners, musical evenings, etc., and she had a "salon," to all which I was a welcome guest, and the cordiality lasted until she thought it time to make use of me. She then proposed to me to undertake the demolition of the fictitious reputations of the leading American sculptors, especially Story, Mosier, and Rogers, and, when I replied that I had then the intention of returning to the occupation of a landscape painter, and that in that position, as well as in that of consul and in a manner the protector of all my countrymen, it would be inconsistent with the position to publish criticisms on my fellow artists, the thermometer of her regard fell at once, and I had instant evidence that I was out of her list of friends.

Her coolness was changed to active hostility by another case of conflicting interests. The recognition of passports issued before the rebellion having been interdicted by the government, the consuls received an order to cancel all such as had been issued prior to the order, and to issue new ones only on the oath of allegiance being taken by the recipient. There was also a charge of five dollars for the passport, which was to be renewed after a year. Charlotte was, amongst her other qualities, avaricious, and though wealthy and ostentatious she rebelled at expenditure which did not show, and when it came time for her to leave Rome for the summer, and her passport came for visa, I stopped it and notified her to take out a new one. She refused, and confiding in the friendly personal relations which had existed between her and Seward, she wrote to the department protesting against my action and making formal complaint of my discourtesy. Seward replied that I was obeying my orders and that the passport must be taken and paid for. From that day war was open and malignant. Of course I was interdicted from responding in any way to her attacks, but I found them of no great importance; though when I was sent to Crete, four years later, she had influence enough to get her nephew appointed consul in succession.

In the years when Miss Cushman was on the stage I had understood her pretty well, and, though she had done what was possible to give me a good impression of her, I do not think I was ever much persuaded of her goodness or surprised at the enmity she showed when I came into collision with her interests. I think she possessed an utterly selfish nature, was not at all scrupulous in the attainment of her purposes, and was, in effect, that most dangerous member of society, a strong-willed and large-brained woman without a vestige of principle. She had a diabolical magnetism which in her best part, Meg Merrilies, had a sensuous attraction I have never known so powerful in another woman. Her Queen Katherine was a failure, and she could not play the part of a refined woman, but into that of Meg Merrilies, an adaptation of her own of Sir Walter Scott's novel, she put her whole nature--it was her very self as far as she would let herself be seen.

When I had a studio in New York I had as next-door neighbor an artist who was scene painter to the company in which Charlotte used to play at the old Park Theatre, and the stories he told me of her in that connection were terrible. My friend had never dared to speak of her openly, and only did so to me with a caution that if what he told me got to Miss Cushman's ears she was quite capable of silencing him in the most effective manner. I am of opinion that he judged her correctly, for she must have been a tiger when her passions were aroused, capable of anything, and I was careful never to give her more serious cause of offense than the doing of my official duty. Over those whom she chose to fascinate, she had an extraordinary power, and I have known young women who were so completely under her control as to be unable to escape from it when they found out her real nature except by flight.

If she had been beautiful she might have set the social world topsy-turvy. I think she was the cleverest woman I ever knew. Her tact was extraordinary, and she never failed to impress the visitors to Rome with her sincerity and benevolence, though she really possessed neither of those qualities. She was an immense illustration of a maxim of Dante Rossetti to the effect that artists had nothing to do with morality. She was always on the stage--in the most familiar act and in the presence of strangers she never lost sight of the footlights, and the best acting I ever saw her in was in private and in the representation of some comedy or tragedy of her own interests. She played with a marvelous power one part, and all others were but variations of that or failures--it was not art which dominated her, but the simulation of nature, and that her own, which is not the same thing as art, as we all ought to know.

Between herself and the sculptor Rogers, who was, in his way, as clever as she, there was an implacable war, veiled by the ordinary forms of civility, which both were careful never to break over. Miss Cushman had begun her career as a singer, but, her voice failing, she had to be content to remain on the stage of the theatre; but she always retained a certain dramatic quality of voice, and, within a very limited register, she sang with great power and pathos. Two of her favorite songs were Kingsley's "The Sands of Dee" and the "Three Fishermen," which, as she sang them, rarely failed to affect those who heard them for the first time to tears. Rogers was an admirable mimic and sang those songs with such a close rendering of the voice and manner (for Miss Cushman's voice was rather that of a man than one belonging to her own sex), with just a touch of burlesque, that he brought out roars of laughter; and when the two cordial enemies met in society somebody was sure to ask Rogers to sing "The Sands of Dee," which he did with good will, and Miss Cushman was obliged, to her intense anger, to applaud the caricature of her best performance. It was cruel, but he was merciless, and spared no exaggeration of her voice, her dramatic manner, and a way she had of sprawling over the piano, producing an ensemble which made it impossible to hear her again in the same songs without a disposition to laugh.

An incident occurred at this time which made Miss Cushman's position in regard to the quarrel with the consulate still more difficult. It was not long after the advent of the famous horse-tamer John S. Rarey, of whom she had been a pupil in America when he first came out. A person professing to be Rarey was touring Europe and teaching his manner of breaking horses, beginning at Copenhagen and following the seashore to Naples, whence he came to Rome and was received with great enthusiasm by Miss Cushman, for at that time, and while the war was in its critical stage, American lions were very rare in Rome. The horse-tamer was, on her authority, made the guest of the American community, breakfasted, dined, and feted, and a large subscription was made for a class in horse-breaking. At this juncture I heard of a performance of the *soi-disant* Rarey at Naples, in which he had nearly killed a beautiful young mare, and, knowing that the system of Rarey did not include cruelty, I began to doubt the identity of the tamer. I called for the passport with which he had come, and which was, as usual, deposited at the police office, and discovered that it was issued by a "vice-consul *pro tempore*" at Dresden, an officer not recognized by our regulations, bad and loose as they were, and a man whose name, moreover, was not on the consular list, though the passport was on a regular form. I at once wrote to the police, requesting them to cause the said John S. Rarey to prove his identity.

The summons to the police office brought him to the consulate the next morning before I was out of bed (the office and my bedroom constituted the headquarters of the government of the United States of America at Rome), with a petition to me to request the police to delay the examination until the next day, as he had two friends who would identify him, but who were that day (it was Sunday) at Tivoli for the day. As an escape was impossible, and he was in a nervous trepidation which, it was clear to see, was awful funk, I wrote the note desired; and, before the day was out, he had gone to my English colleague, the amiable Severn, and confessed that he was an impostor, a Canadian, and asked for English protection. Severn replied that without my consent he could do nothing for him; he had come with an American passport and must abide by it, unless I gave him up. He was wilted, in such a fright as I never saw a man in before or since, and he had good reason, for the penalty of coming to Rome with a false passport was imprisonment in St. Angelo. Meanwhile Miss Cushman had gone into heroics over the insult I was offering so distinguished a man as to suspect his identity, and all her clique were united in abusing me; but on Monday the impostor slipped out of Rome by the connivance of Severn, the police, and myself, after I had attached the amount of the subscriptions for his class, which were still lying at the bankers', and pledged him to abstain in future from any similar impersonation. As Miss Cushman had stood sponsor for him, she having been a pupil of the real Rarey, his confession was a mortification which she visited on my head, but as it disarmed her I was tranquil over the consequences.

I was continually at war with the Confederate Americans, galled to extreme bitterness by the right I had of compelling them to take the oath of allegiance before renewing their passports. Amongst them was a very beautiful woman, a Virginian, and the wife of a commodore in the navy of the United States of America, then on service in the Potomac. She refused to take the oath, and insulted me in the grossest manner and in public, as an insulter of ladies, *etc., etc*. But all the influence she could bring to bear could not get her passport from the police without my visa; and at last, despairing of escape from Rome, she came to make her peace, meeting me at the bank, but unwilling to accept the degradation of coming to the consulate. "You are not going to make me come to your dirty little consulate, are you?" she said; to which I replied, "Oh, no; my secretary shall administer the oath to you in your bedroom, if you choose;" but, in the end, she had to take the oath and sign it, as did many of her compatriots. Amongst the Southerners who came under my administration was the wife of General Winfield Scott, commander-in-chief of our army, who actually died under my care, without a friend or relative near her.

This social warfare, the consequence of my official position, had the effect of giving me occupation and excitement, and I was sustained cordially by the loyal Americans in Rome, so that the position, though unremunerative, was rather pleasant than otherwise. In the course of the summer after my arrival, ex-Governor Randall of Wisconsin came as minister, his appointment being intended to "keep the place warm" for General Rufus King, a personal friend of Seward, to whom the place was promised whenever he should be tired of fighting, or qualified by glory for future political contests. Randall was a mere party hack; he knew nothing of diplomacy or good manners, or of any language but Western American. I took for him the house on the Pincian now known as the House of the Four Winds, a magnificent situation for the summer. He saw the sights, generally in a carriage, with a paper of fruit on the front seat and me as cicerone; was presented at the Vatican, presented me as charge d'affaires, and, having his leave of absence in his pocket, departed for a tour of Europe, bequeathing to me the honor of paying his bills, rent, etc., down to the washing bill, to be settled on his return, and never appeared again. I was left to pay out of my empty pocket; and I never heard from him, though, a long time after, I succeeded in recovering from the Treasury the amount of those bills I had paid for Randall for which I could show vouchers; those for which I had none I had to put to account of profit and loss, which was, as long as I was in Rome, largely to the loss account, drafts on my brother making up the deficiency. I was also, until it suspended publication, Roman correspondent of John Bright's paper, which I think was called the "Star."

After an interregnum of some months came another bed-warmer for General King, this one a New York politician, also a friend of Seward's, an ancient politician, who had recently married a young wife desirous of a stay in some European capital, and, if possible, at the expense of the government. These at least were gentlefolk, and paid their bills without doing anything to scandalize the Romans. They spent the winter and went home, and finally came General King.

Finding that my fees and sales of pictures (for I had taken up my painting again and had sold a few small pictures) amounted to about six hundred dollars a year, and were slowly increasing, I decided to go home and bring my wife and child out. I had been absent more than a year, and several months after being in Rome had the news of the birth of a son. It was near being my death, for, on the evening of receiving the news, I had gone to make a call on an English lady who lived in the Villa Negroni, where the railway station now is, and close by the prison where all the political offenders were kept, and which was guarded by French soldiers. I was in a vein of profound meditation on the news I had just received, and absorbed to that extent that I kept on my course along the sidewalk in front of the prison, walking towards the sentry, and did not hear his challenge till it had been repeated three times, when I heard his rifle rattle as it came down to the take aim, and suddenly became conscious that I had heard a sound, the meaning of which must be "Qui vive?" I sung out lustily, "Ami" and was told that if I was a friend the other side of the road was my place.

I had discovered that the consular agent left by my predecessor at Civita Vecchia was engaged in a system of espionage on behalf of the Papal authorities, and had been issuing American passports to spies whom they were employing in Italian territory, and I at once dismissed him and informed the Italian government through Mr. Marsh, our minister to Italy, and received a letter of thanks from that government. From Washington a new consular agent was sent, and, putting him in charge of the consulate, I started for home, going by way of Turin, to see Mr. Marsh, and by diligence over Mont Cenis. Subsequent events brought me much in contact with that admirable diplomat and scholar, at that time the one bright feature of our diplomatic service on the Continent. Our government received great credit for sending such a man abroad to represent us, but the chance of it was in the fact that he was closely related to Senator Edmunds of Vermont, whose influence with the administration was sufficient to secure any single nomination he insisted on, and who did insist on the maintenance of Marsh in the diplomatic service. As Marsh had been conspicuous in the advocacy of the Italian cause during the unitary movement, he was designated by the circumstances for the American legation to Italy, in which he honored his appointment as few of our representatives at that epoch had done.

In fact, with the exception of Adams, at London, and Marsh, at Turin, we had hardly a representative abroad, either consular or diplomatic, who was a credit to the country. As the war continued, the importance of being respected in Europe became more evident, and a change took place; but the few men of respectable standing who were in foreign countries representing the United States of America were appointed on account of political pressure, and not on their merits. My colleague at Venice, Howells, one of Mr. Lincoln's most fortunate appointments, owed his position, not to his literary abilities, which were then unknown to the country at large, but to his having written a campaign life of Lincoln, a service which was always considered by the successful candidate as entitling the biographer to some appointment. A term of consular service was and is still considered the reward for campaign services, personal or vicarious, and at the next change of administration the consul was superseded by another, equally crude, and with all to learn in his business.

What the character of the Americans as well as of the government, as such, has suffered of derogation abroad from this political huckstering with public offices, no one can know who was not much abroad in the years preceding our war. Marsh was honored and beloved at Rome by both King and people, as was Adams by the Court of St. James, but the dead weight which the standing disrepute of our diplomacy imposed on both those distinguished men can hardly now be estimated. My predecessors at Rome, and the ministers before my time, had left a bad odor behind them. One of them was notorious for his devotion to a form of dissipation much and scandalously known at Naples during the reign of the Bourbons as a springtime sport, and which has since been the occasion of a noted crusade in England led by Mr. Stead. Of a minister of the United States of America found drunk in the streets of Berlin by the police, and a charge d'affaires who, in an outbreak at Constantinople, hoisted the flag over a brothel he frequented, the memory is perhaps too old to have reached men born much later than I, but for the twenty years of my first knowledge of European matters our representation abroad was a disgrace to America.

I landed in New York the day after the battle of Gettysburg, and for the first time in the history of our trouble I felt assured as to the end, for I perceived that the attempt at invasion by the Confederacy showed that the government of it felt its affairs to be in a desperate condition, and the determination on the part of the North was evidently unshaken. From that time I never felt any anxiety as to the final result. I found my brother at the head of the construction department of the revenue service, his friend Salmon P. Chase being Secretary of the Treasury. He was desirous to keep me at home to assist him, with which desire I was ready to conform, but the opposition of his wife was so bitter that he had to decide against my staying, and, taking my wife and boy, I returned to Rome. My brother was already attacked by the malady of which, two years later, he died.

Arriving in Rome, and resuming the direction of the consulate, I found to my dismay that General King had appointed as secretary of legation a local American banker, a "Copperhead," who had in the name of the government, but without authority, requested the Roman Ministry of Foreign Affairs to dispense with the visa on the passports of all American visitors, and Antonelli was, of course, too glad to be relieved of the embarrassment which had been often caused him by the regulation, which all the Southerners had asked to be relieved from. Thus I found that the principal resource of the consulate was gone. As the home government had given the strongest orders to protest against any such exception being made of American passports, I, of course, protested, but was informed that the rule had been taken at the request of my own government; and, though Antonelli knew perfectly that Hooker had no authority to enter into any negotiations with him on any subject, and that he had no official position, it suited him to accept the contrary, and my remonstrances to the minister, General King, had no effect. I then laid the matter before the Department of State at Washington, but, as General King was the close personal friend of Seward, who was quite indifferent to diplomatic scandals away from England, no attention was paid to my complaints, and I gave up the consulate to Brown, the consular agent at Civita Vecchia, to get what he could from it, and devoted myself entirely to painting, by which, with a little writing, I made enough to live in the simple manner which I was accustomed to.

Released from all obligations to remain at the consulate, I spent the most of my time in sketching on the Campagna. Of all the landscape I have ever seen, in the Alps, Sicily, Greece, the American forests and lakes, or semi-tropical Florida, nothing has impressed me as did the Roman Campagna in its then condition of decay and neglect. The beauty of line of its mountain framework is still there, and passages here and there are untouched, but the improvements of progress have intruded in so many points that, as a whole, the solemn and poetic aspect of those days is irretrievably lost. I used to sit out in the most lonely passages painting into the twilight until I could no longer distinguish my colors, and then tramp back to Rome at my fastest, to get in before the gates closed for the night. If it was not the rapture of art, it was the passion of poetic nature.

As fortune would have it, there was in Rome that winter Mr. George G. Fogg, the minister of the United States of America at Berne, a personal friend of Lincoln, and chairman of the Young Men's National Committee, which arranged the convention that nominated him. On Lincoln's election Fogg was offered his choice of the diplomatic appointments, and selected Berne, the most modest position he could take. He came to pass the Christmas holidays at Rome, and of course I laid my case before him. He in turn put it before his late colleagues in the House, and the committee on foreign affairs made a strong representation at the Department of State; and, when Seward refused to recall King, or take any measures to correct the injustice done me, they struck out from the consular and diplomatic appropriation bill the appropriation for the legation at Rome, which meant the abolition of the legation, and I was a little later transferred to Crete, a salaried post, where there was supposed to be nothing to do but make my quarterly report.

My commission must have been one of the very last Lincoln signed, for he was assassinated before it reached me. I was spending the evening at the quarters of one of my best Roman friends, Mr. John A. King (a cousin of, but not a sympathizer with, the general), when the news came of the murder of Lincoln and the attempt on Seward, and very vivid still is the recollection of the horror and grief we all felt. But we also felt that the President's work was done, and that his fame was set securely in history, beyond the chance of any political blunder to damage it. Could he ever have devised a better death in view of his future influence and honor? I learned from one of Lincoln's Illinois friends, whom I later saw in Rome, that the appointment in Crete was intended by the President as the recognition of the injustice with which Seward had treated my case. My experience of Seward's way of looking at public appointments and public interests, when crossed by his personal relations, certainly went to confirm the apprehensions of Mr. Fogg and his friends that Seward's personal following would stand between him and the best interests of the state. As Fogg used to put it, "He won't steal, himself, but he don't care how much his friends steal." But my misfortune brought about the abolition of what had always been a scandal and a job--the legation of the United States of America to the Pope.

www.bookjungle.com *email: sales@bookjungle.com fax: 630-214-0564 mail: Book Jungle PO Box 2226 Champaign, IL 61825*

The Codes Of Hammurabi And Moses
W. W. Davies

QTY

The discovery of the Hammurabi Code is one of the greatest achievements of archaeology, and is of paramount interest, not only to the student of the Bible, but also to all those interested in ancient history...

Religion **ISBN:** *1-59462-338-4* **Pages:**132
 MSRP $12.95

The Theory of Moral Sentiments
Adam Smith

QTY

This work from 1749. contains original theories of conscience amd moral judgment and it is the foundation for systemof morals.

Philosophy **ISBN:** *1-59462-777-0* **Pages:**536
 MSRP $19.95

Jessica's First Prayer
Hesba Stretton

QTY

In a screened and secluded corner of one of the many railway-bridges which span the streets of London there could be seen a few years ago, from five o'clock every morning until half past eight, a tidily set-out coffee-stall, consisting of a trestle and board, upon which stood two large tin cans, with a small fire of charcoal burning under each so as to keep the coffee boiling during the early hours of the morning when the work-people were thronging into the city on their way to their daily toil...

Childrens **ISBN:** *1-59462-373-2* **Pages:**84
 MSRP $9.95

My Life and Work
Henry Ford

QTY

Henry Ford revolutionized the world with his implementation of mass production for the Model T automobile. Gain valuable business insight into his life and work with his own auto-biography... "We have only started on our development of our country we have not as yet, with all our talk of wonderful progress, done more than scratch the surface. The progress has been wonderful enough but..."

Biographies/ **ISBN:** *1-59462-198-5* **Pages:**300
 MSRP $21.95

The Art of Cross-Examination
Francis Wellman

QTY

I presume it is the experience of every author, after his first book is published upon an important subject, to be almost overwhelmed with a wealth of ideas and illustrations which could readily have been included in his book, and which to his own mind, at least, seem to make a second edition inevitable. Such certainly was the case with me; and when the first edition had reached its sixth impression in five months, I rejoiced to learn that it seemed to my publishers that the book had met with a sufficiently favorable reception to justify a second and considerably enlarged edition. ..

Reference   ISBN: *1-59462-647-2*

Pages:412
MSRP $19.95

On the Duty of Civil Disobedience
Henry David Thoreau

QTY

Thoreau wrote his famous essay, On the Duty of Civil Disobedience, as a protest against an unjust but popular war and the immoral but popular institution of slave-owning. He did more than write—he declined to pay his taxes, and was hauled off to gaol in consequence. Who can say how much this refusal of his hastened the end of the war and of slavery?

Law   ISBN: *1-59462-747-9*

Pages:48
MSRP $7.45

Dream Psychology Psychoanalysis for Beginners
Sigmund Freud

QTY

Sigmund Freud, born Sigismund Schlomo Freud (May 6, 1856 - September 23, 1939), was a Jewish-Austrian neurologist and psychiatrist who co-founded the psychoanalytic school of psychology. Freud is best known for his theories of the unconscious mind, especially involving the mechanism of repression; his redefinition of sexual desire as mobile and directed towards a wide variety of objects; and his therapeutic techniques, especially his understanding of transference in the therapeutic relationship and the presumed value of dreams as sources of insight into unconscious desires.

Psychology   ISBN: *1-59462-905-6*

Pages:196
MSRP $15.45

The Miracle of Right Thought
Orison Swett Marden

QTY

Believe with all of your heart that you will do what you were made to do. When the mind has once formed the habit of holding cheerful, happy, prosperous pictures, it will not be easy to form the opposite habit. It does not matter how improbable or how far away this realization may see, or how dark the prospects may be, if we visualize them as best we can, as vividly as possible, hold tenaciously to them and vigorously struggle to attain them, they will gradually become actualized, realized in the life. But a desire, a longing without endeavor, a yearning abandoned or held indifferently will vanish without realization.

Self Help   ISBN: *1-59462-644-8*

Pages:360
MSRP $25.45

www.bookjungle.com *email: sales@bookjungle.com fax: 630-214-0564 mail: Book Jungle PO Box 2226 Champaign, IL 61825*

QTY

| | **The Rosicrucian Cosmo-Conception Mystic Christianity** *by* **Max Heindel** | ISBN: *1-59462-188-8* | **$38.95** |

The Rosicrucian Cosmo-conception is not dogmatic, neither does it appeal to any other authority than the reason of the student. It is: not controversial, but is: sent forth in the, hope that it may help to clear...   *New Age/Religion Pages 646*

Abandonment To Divine Providence *by* **Jean-Pierre de Caussade**   ISBN: *1-59462-228-0*   **$25.95**

"The Rev. Jean Pierre de Caussade was one of the most remarkable spiritual writers of the Society of Jesus in France in the 18th Century. His death took place at Toulouse in 1751. His works have gone through many editions and have been republished...   *Inspirational/Religion Pages 400*

Mental Chemistry *by* **Charles Haanel**   ISBN: *1-59462-192-6*   **$23.95**

Mental Chemistry allows the change of material conditions by combining and appropriately utilizing the power of the mind. Much like applied chemistry creates something new and unique out of careful combinations of chemicals the mastery of mental chemistry...   *New Age Pages 354*

The Letters of Robert Browning and Elizabeth Barret Barrett 1845-1846 vol II   ISBN: *1-59462-193-4*   **$35.95**

by **Robert Browning** and **Elizabeth Barrett**   *Biographies Pages 596*

Gleanings In Genesis (volume I) *by* **Arthur W. Pink**   ISBN: *1-59462-130-6*   **$27.45**

Appropriately has Genesis been termed "the seed plot of the Bible" for in it we have, in germ form, almost all of the great doctrines which are afterwards fully developed in the books of Scripture which follow...   *Religion/Inspirational Pages 420*

The Master Key *by* **L. W. de Laurence**   ISBN: *1-59462-001-6*   **$30.95**

In no branch of human knowledge has there been a more lively increase of the spirit of research during the past few years than in the study of Psychology, Concentration and Mental Discipline. The requests for authentic lessons in Thought Control, Mental Discipline and...   *New Age/Business Pages 422*

The Lesser Key Of Solomon Goetia *by* **L. W. de Laurence**   ISBN: *1-59462-092-X*   **$9.95**

This translation of the first book of the "Lernegton" which is now for the first time made accessible to students of Talismanic Magic was done, after careful collation and edition, from numerous Ancient Manuscripts in Hebrew, Latin, and French...   *New Age/Occult Pages 92*

Rubaiyat Of Omar Khayyam *by* **Edward Fitzgerald**   ISBN: *1-59462-332-5*   **$13.95**

Edward Fitzgerald, whom the world has already learned, in spite of his own efforts to remain within the shadow of anonymity, to look upon as one of the rarest poets of the century, was born at Bredfield, in Suffolk, on the 31st of March, 1809. He was the third son of John Purcell...   *Music Pages 172*

Ancient Law *by* **Henry Maine**   ISBN: *1-59462-128-4*   **$29.95**

The chief object of the following pages is to indicate some of the earliest ideas of mankind, as they are reflected in Ancient Law, and to point out the relation of those ideas to modern thought.   *Religiom/History Pages 452*

Far-Away Stories *by* **William J. Locke**   ISBN: *1-59462-129-2*   **$19.45**

"Good wine needs no bush, but a collection of mixed vintages does. And this book is just such a collection. Some of the stories I do not want to remain buried for ever in the museum files of dead magazine-numbers an author's not unpardonable vanity..."   *Fiction Pages 272*

Life of David Crockett *by* **David Crockett**   ISBN: *1-59462-250-7*   **$27.45**

"Colonel David Crockett was one of the most remarkable men of the times in which he lived. Born in humble life, but gifted with a strong will, an indomitable courage, and unremitting perseverance...   *Biographies/New Age Pages 424*

Lip-Reading *by* **Edward Nitchie**   ISBN: *1-59462-206-X*   **$25.95**

Edward B. Nitchie, founder of the New York School for the Hard of Hearing, now the Nitchie School of Lip-Reading, Inc, wrote "LIP-READING Principles and Practice". The development and perfecting of this meritorious work on lip-reading was an undertaking...   *How-to Pages 400*

A Handbook of Suggestive Therapeutics, Applied Hypnotism, Psychic Science   ISBN: *1-59462-214-0*   **$24.95**

by **Henry Munro**   *Health/New Age/Health/Self-help Pages 376*

A Doll's House: and Two Other Plays *by* **Henrik Ibsen**   ISBN: *1-59462-112-8*   **$19.95**

Henrik Ibsen created this classic when in revolutionary 1848 Rome. Introducing some striking concepts in playwriting for the realist genre, this play has been studied the world over.   *Fiction/Classics/Plays 308*

The Light of Asia *by* **sir Edwin Arnold**   ISBN: *1-59462-204-3*   **$13.95**

In this poetic masterpiece, Edwin Arnold describes the life and teachings of Buddha. The man who was to become known as Buddha to the world was born as Prince Gautama of India but he rejected the worldly riches and abandoned the reigns of power when...   *Religion/History/Biographies Pages 170*

The Complete Works of Guy de Maupassant *by* **Guy de Maupassant**   ISBN: *1-59462-157-8*   **$16.95**

"For days and days, nights and nights, I had dreamed of that first kiss which was to consecrate our engagement, and I knew not on what spot I should put my lips..."   *Fiction/Classics Pages 240*

The Art of Cross-Examination *by* **Francis L. Wellman**   ISBN: *1-59462-309-0*   **$26.95**

Written by a renowned trial lawyer, Wellman imparts his experience and uses case studies to explain how to use psychology to extract desired information through questioning.   *How-to/Science/Reference Pages 408*

Answered or Unanswered? *by* **Louisa Vaughan**   ISBN: *1-59462-248-5*   **$10.95**

Miracles of Faith in China   *Religion Pages 112*

The Edinburgh Lectures on Mental Science (1909) *by* **Thomas**   ISBN: *1-59462-008-3*   **$11.95**

This book contains the substance of a course of lectures recently given by the writer in the Queen Street Hall, Edinburgh. Its purpose is to indicate the Natural Principles governing the relation between Mental Action and Material Conditions...   *New Age/Psychology Pages 148*

Ayesha *by* **H. Rider Haggard**   ISBN: *1-59462-301-5*   **$24.95**

Verily and indeed it is the unexpected that happens! Probably if there was one person upon the earth from whom the Editor of this, and of a certain previous history, did not expect to hear again...   *Classics Pages 380*

Ayala's Angel *by* **Anthony Trollope**   ISBN: *1-59462-352-X*   **$29.95**

The two girls were both pretty, but Lucy who was twenty-one who supposed to be simple and comparatively unattractive, whereas Ayala was credited, as her Bombwhat romantic name might show, with poetic charm and a taste for romance. Ayala when her father died was nineteen...   *Fiction Pages 484*

The American Commonwealth *by* **James Bryce**   ISBN: *1-59462-286-8*   **$34.45**

An interpretation of American democratic political theory. It examines political mechanics and society from the perspective of Scotsman James Bryce   *Politics Pages 572*

Stories of the Pilgrims *by* **Margaret P. Pumphrey**   ISBN: *1-59462-116-0*   **$17.95**

This book explores pilgrims religious oppression in England as well as their escape to Holland and eventual crossing to America on the Mayflower, and their early days in New England...   *History Pages 268*

www.bookjungle.com *email: sales@bookjungle.com fax: 630-214-0564 mail: Book Jungle PO Box 2226 Champaign, IL 61825*

QTY

The Fasting Cure by *Sinclair Upton* ISBN: *1-59462-222-1* **$13.95**
In the Cosmopolitan Magazine for May, 1910, and in the Contemporary Review (London) for April, 1910, I published an article dealing with my experiences in fasting. I have written a great many magazine articles, but never one which attracted so much attention... New Age/Self Help/Health Pages 164

Hebrew Astrology by *Sepharial* ISBN: *1-59462-308-2* **$13.45**
In these days of advanced thinking it is a matter of common observation that we have left many of the old landmarks behind and that we are now pressing forward to greater heights and to a wider horizon than that which represented the mind-content of our progenitors... Astrology Pages 144

Thought Vibration or The Law of Attraction in the Thought World ISBN: *1-59462-127-6* **$12.95**
by *William Walker Atkinson* Psychology/Religion Pages 144

Optimism by *Helen Keller* ISBN: *1-59462-108-X* **$15.95**
Helen Keller was blind, deaf, and mute since 19 months old, yet famously learned how to overcome these handicaps, communicate with the world, and spread her lectures promoting optimism. An inspiring read for everyone... Biographies/Inspirational Pages 84

Sara Crewe by *Frances Burnett* ISBN: *1-59462-360-0* **$9.45**
In the first place, Miss Minchin lived in London. Her home was a large, dull, tall one, in a large, dull square, where all the houses were alike, and all the sparrows were alike, and where all the door-knockers made the same heavy sound... Childrens/Classic Pages 88

The Autobiography of Benjamin Franklin by *Benjamin Franklin* ISBN: *1-59462-135-7* **$24.95**
The Autobiography of Benjamin Franklin has probably been more extensively read than any other American historical work, and no other book of its kind has had such ups and downs of fortune. Franklin lived for many years in England, where he was agent... Biographies/History Pages 332

Name	
Email	
Telephone	
Address	
City, State ZIP	

☐ Credit Card ☐ Check / Money Order

Credit Card Number	
Expiration Date	
Signature	

Please Mail to: Book Jungle
   PO Box 2226
   Champaign, IL 61825
or Fax to: 630-214-0564

ORDERING INFORMATION

web: *www.bookjungle.com*
email: *sales@bookjungle.com*
fax: *630-214-0564*
mail: *Book Jungle PO Box 2226 Champaign, IL 61825*
or PayPal *to sales@bookjungle.com*

Please contact us for bulk discounts

DIRECT-ORDER TERMS

**20% Discount if You Order
Two or More Books**
Free Domestic Shipping!
Accepted: Master Card, Visa,
Discover, American Express

www.ingramcontent.com/pod-product-compliance
Lightning Source LLC
Chambersburg PA
CBHW080537170426
43195CB00016B/2589